Alternative Facts, Post-Truth and the Information War

The Reference Shelf
Volume 90 • Number 2
H.W. Wilson
A Division of EBSCO Information Services, Inc.

Published by
GREY HOUSE PUBLISHING
Amenia, New York
2018

The Reference Shelf

The books in this series contain reprints of articles, excerpts from books, addresses on current issues, and studies of social trends in the United States and other countries. There are six separately bound numbers in each volume, all of which are usually published in the same calendar year. Numbers one through five are each devoted to a single subject, providing background information and discussion from various points of view and concluding with an index and comprehensive bibliography that lists books, pamphlets, and articles on the subject. The final number of each volume is a collection of recent speeches. Books in the series may be purchased individually or on subscription.

Publisher's Cataloging-In-Publication Data
(Prepared by The Donohue Group, Inc.)

Names: Grey House Publishing, Inc., compiler.
Title: Alternative facts, post-truth and the information war / [compiled by] Grey House Publishing.
Other Titles: Reference shelf / H. W. Wilson, a division of EBSCO Information Services ; v. 90, no. 2.
Description: Amenia, NY : Grey House Publishing, [2018] | Includes bibliographical references and index.
Identifiers: ISBN 9781682178652 (v.90, no.2) | ISBN 9781682177471 (volume set)
Subjects: LCSH: Fake news--United States. | Journalism--Objectivity--United States. | Digital media--Moral and ethical aspects--United States. | Mass media and propaganda--United States. | Sensationalism in journalism--United States.
Classification: LCC PN4888.F35 A48 2018 | DDC 070.4/30973--dc23

Contents

4

Fake News and Your Health

5

Next Generation News Consumers

Preface

Dispatches From The Information War

Is the United States in the midst of an information war? Has the nation become more and more polarized? Is fake news everywhere? Is fake news threatening American democracy? The modern media environment has many critics, coming from every conceivable angle and across partisan lines. Some believe that fake news is radicalizing ideology, others believe that the mainstream media is fake news, and still others believe that the entire media problem is more of an illusion than a problem at all.

Sam And The Real News

Imagine a person, called Sam, who lives in a fictional society called the "Innies." The Innies live near, but separate from, another society known as the "Outies." Sam believes that his society has been becoming more and more dysfunctional, and, everywhere he looks, he sees evidence of this. Sam's perception of his world is being shaped by a number of factors.

1. The media environment has grown rapidly, from 10 to 10,000 possible sources, and Sam and his friends are increasingly getting their news from alternative sources. The variety of media is overwhelming so Sam counts on others in his social enviroment, as well as celebrities he likes, to help him find good news.

2. Sam and some others now like to exchange news "bits" through virtual social networks, which allow them to become part of the process, creating and commenting on other people's bits. The news Sam gets his is chosen by a magical computer based on what Sam tells the computer about himself.

3. Innie society has recently elected a new leader, Mr. Duck, and Sam likes Mr. Duck very much, seeing him as successful and famous. Mr. Duck suggests that most news is fake, created by corrupt politicians with agendas. Sam now listens to Mr. Duck directly, reading all of Mr. Duck's own news bits and paying attention to what kind of media Mr. Duck likes to use.

Sam, like all people, wants to be special, but Sam's need to be special is more acute than for some other people. He seeks out things that are different and gets a tattoo that says "I Am Special." Sam believes that Innie society is fundamentally better than Outie society because the Innies, too, are special group in an otherwise banal world. Being a proud Innie is one way that Sam feels special.

Sam also sees lots of groups within his society and he thinks that some of those groups are better than others. For instance, Sam believes that the group called the Innie-Outies are not "real" Innies because they have the wrong priorities and want

Innie society to be more like Outie society. Sam and his friends don't like the Innie-Outies and, what's more than that, neither does Mr. Duck, who says that the Innie-Outies have been damaging Innie society from within. Mr. Duck says that he and those who are with him are part of a resistance fighting back against the damage done to their society by the Outies and the Innie-Outies. Sam therefore sees himself as part of another special group, along with Mr. Duck, and his friends, and sees this group as those smart enough to see the truth of their society and what's best for their future.

Gradually, Sam begins to believe that his society is in the grips of an ideological war, and that the stakes are nothing less than his values, his morals, and perhaps his faith. Most people don't seem to believe this and, some people, instead think that Mr. Duck is the problem. Mr. Duck says this is because there is a conspiracy againt him and Sam begins to see himself as a victim of that same nefarious plot.

One day, Sam hears that a couple of Innie-Outies had been operating a child sex ring out of a restaurant. The mainstream media says there is no sex ring, but some of Sam's favorite news bits say that the sex ring is real and that the Innie-Outies and the mainstream media are conspiring to keep it secret. Mr. Duck doesn't say anything about it, but his statements about the Innie-Outies in the past suggest he thinks that they might be capable of something this horrendous. Sam gets a weapon and goes to the restaurant to save the children, but finds no children and is arrested. As Sam contemplates the time he will spend imprisoned for his actions, he may begin to question how he received and processed information, or the experience may deepen his convictions, with Sam seeing his imprisonment as part of the same conspiracy he set out to defeat.

The Post-Truth Truth

In this thought experiment, Sam is a victim and actor in the events that have unfolded in his life. The conspiracies that Sam sees in his world are in part the result of his deep-seated fear of cultural or political changes that he sees as a threat to his identity, and, in part, the result of Sam's need to bolster his own ego and sense of himself in his world. His internal and experiential predispositions and biases have left him vulnerable to manipulation and misinformation and his environment is clouded by those who would seek to use Sam and others like him for profit or power.

In reality, few Americans are as deeply affected by media manipulation as Sam. Research on the issue has resulted in conflicting results. For instance, a Dartmouth University study released in January of 2018 suggested that misleading or fake news stories had massive reach in the 2016 election, but little impact. Those who, like Sam, began gravitating almost exclusively towards propagandistic media, constituted only about 10 percent of news consumers according to the study.[1] However, this study does not explore how the continued proliferation of propaganda and ongoing attempt to delegitimize mainstream media is affecting consumers.

Historians note that what is today called "fake news," has always been part of the media environment. This has long been a tool for "issue entrepreneurs," who are individuals who use popular feeling about an issue to build support for another agenda. In the modern media environment, fake news is a for-profit industry in which individuals producing content can earn money by attracting advertisers to support their posts or articles. Politicians have also always used misinformation to promote their goals and, in fact, President John Adams and his Federalists were so concerned about fake political information in 1798 that they passed a law making it illegal to create fake or "scandalous" information about the president or the government itself.[2]

However, though misinformation and propaganda have always been part of the information environment, today, critics are seeing an increasingly powerful and insidious collection of intentional manipulators using misinformation to further their own agendas. The modern controversy is complicated by the fact that the Russian government pursued a peculiar information campaign with the seeming goal of destabilizing the U.S. government and promoting the political career of Donald Trump.[3] There are also foreign individuals flooding the United States with fake news stories for profit, using American interest to attract advertisers to their posts and websites. Some believe that these foreign actors, whether acting for fun, profit, or political gain, are a threat to American sovereignty, while others believe that these actors are little more than meddlers without any significant power to influence American politics or political discourse.

For some critics, Donald Trump's own behavior as both a candidate and then president constitutes one of the deepest and most impactful threats to the legitimacy of America's media. That Donald Trump frequently makes false claims is not really in question, despite the debate over the issue and Trump's denial, because many of the false statements made by the president are objectively disprovable. *Washington Post* fact-checker Glenn Kessler analyzed a 30-minute interview that Donald Trump gave in December of 2017 and found 24 false or misleading claims in that single interview.[4] The fact-checking organization Politifact found that 69 percent of all political claims made by Trump were false and the Washington Post found 1,950 false claims during 347 days of Trump's presidency.[5] A Quinnipiac Poll in 2018 found that only 34 percent of Americans viewed Trump as "honest," and Pew Research and other studies have found that public trust in the government is at the lowest levels ever measured.[6]

What isn't clear is why Trump frequently repeats false claims. Trump might be purposefully using misinformation for political gain, or Trump might be a victim of misinformation and has come to develop false beliefs himself. Trump's approach when questioned about the validity of his statements is to claim that the mainstream media is "fake news" and has engaged in a campaign to delegitimize his presidency.

Problems And Solutions

The dangers that some see in the evolution of America's media environment go beyond the election of Donald Trump or the various domestic and foreign actors creating propaganda and misleading information. The evolution of media, towards shorter news items, participatory rewards systems, and increasingly claustrophobic information environments, can have unintended effects on the brains of consumers.

Scientists have found evidence that this kind of media use limits the capability to form person-to-person relationships, increases the tendency for impulsive behavior, and can lead to problems with anger management.[7] Furthermore, the rapidity of information in modern media means that mistakes are amplified because there is insufficient time for consumers to effectively verify the statements they see or hear through the media.

Social media companies, and web search engines, use algorithms to determine who receives what kind of information, in the form of advertisements, suggested sites and connections, and sponsored content. Psychologists have also found that individuals tend to create social media networks consisting of like-minded individuals sharing certain ideological predilections. What this means is that the type of information a person receives can begin to become more and more homogenous, echoing the individuals beliefs instead of helping to shape them. As social media companies became the primary vector for "fake news," the social media "bubble" created by a person's interests, as determined and calculated by media company algorithms, also means that a person who demonstrates an interest in fake news, will probably receive more and more fake news in the future.

The plethora of problems seen by critics of the modern information environment are accompanied by a plethora of potential solutions. Some see governmental regulation as a key to countering misinformation. Such regulation might work in a variety of ways, regulating social media management, or requiring more transparency for all content carried through certain types of companies or Internet entities. Some see the problem as more about education, arguing that educational institutions and media outlets need to work together to increase media literacy, teaching consumers how to better evaluate various types of content and to use critical thinking when making decisions.

Messages And Meaning

The story of Sam and the Innies presented above symbolizes the potential experience of a consumer in America's modern media environment. The biases and psychological predispositions that influence Sam's reasoning are the same for all consumers, embracing answers to questions that confirm what he feels or believes, and reflecting, ultimately, what he wants to be true. Sam's biases influence the way he interacts with a cluttered, ephemeral information environment filled with both legitimate and illegitimate information. Sam's tendency to collect information and ideas that he likes and reject ones that he does not creates a closed environment in which Sam is surrounded by information that confirms, rather than challenges, his beliefs. Sam's president, Mr. Duck, frequently shares misleading or false information as well, and claims that legitimate news sources are producing fake information, and this provides an authoritative confirmation for some of the things that Sam believes.

Sam is fictional, but his story is not far-fetched. In 2016, a "fake news" story claiming that Hillary Clinton and some other Democrats were running a child-sex ring out of Comet Ping-Pong Pizza in Washington, D.C. went viral. The controversy, which came to be called "Pizzagate," resulted in North Carolina resident and legal gun-owner Edgar Welch bringing his AR-15 military rifle to Comet Ping-Pong Pizza to break up the sex ring himself. After his arrest, Welch expressed, in the courts and to reporters, his wish that he had been more careful in deciding whether or not to believe the story.

That a person could embrace a claim so apparently fantastic and easily disprovable, believing that a conspiracy like the one depicted in the story was at all believable, might seem incredible, but it occurred. After the sex-ring rumors died down, investigators looking into the entire Pizzagate issue found many frightening ripples emerging from the initial claim. For instance, in 2016 a journalist looking into the issue for Salon found that some social media users were using unrelated photos of children on the Internet and claiming that they had been victims of a Democrat-led abuse ring, while another claim implicated another pizzeria, with posts claiming that a vigilante investigation uncovered a menu offering child-sex acts. Tracing links to the original fake news items found that they were widely shared in Vietnam, the Czech Republic, Turkey, Cyprus, and through white supremacist and far-right conservative sites.[8]

Conservative critics of the mainstream media argue that there is a severe left-wing bias in the media that prevents conservative politicians and viewpoints from mainstream exposure. Complaints of media bias have been part of American conservative culture since the 1980s but intensified in the 2000s and 2010s. President Donald Trump has taken this claim to a new level by routinely calling mainstream media outlets like the *Washington Post* and *CNN* fake news. Progressives and liberals argue that the current state of media is largely the result of a lack of corporate regulations and to purposeful misinformation on the part of some political leaders and fake news creators. Therefore, both conservatives and progressives are unsatisfied with the state of media, but for different reasons.

Though evidence of fake news exists and publications and websites undoubtedly adhere to an editorial profile, the question that media analysts, critics, and activists are asking is whether the increasingly misleading news environment is a threat to the mental and intellectual health of more or perhaps all Americans? The answer to this is unclear because the evolution of the media environment is ongoing, and there is insufficient evidence to determine how modern media is changing behaviors and attitudes. Further, it is unclear whether or not Americans are, in general, dissatisfied with how these changes are occurring.

Ultimately, the evolution of media environment has always been a matter of manipulation and demand. Tabloids manipulate interest through outrageous claims and survive because they meet a demand. Newspapers survive because of the need for more substantive information, though interest in this type of expository exploration has lost some ground to non-traditional, user-generated, and algorithm-generated competitors. Companies and agents constantly work to manipulate demand towards their interest, in order to sell products, win elections, or accomplish goals, but this misinformation only works so long as those same agents provide consumers with the kind of media that they want. Consumers have an active role and can determine how news evolves through their choices and the feedback they provide to those providing and managing content. If users want accuracy, they can therefore demand it so long as they can recognize the difference between accurate and misleading information. Combating misinformation may take a variety of forms, therefore, but must also be represented in the demand of consumers, or such efforts are unlikely to make any serious difference.

Micah L. Issitt

Works Used

"2016 Presidential Campaign Hacking Fast Facts." *CNN.* CNN News. Feb 21, 2018. https://www.cnn.com/2016/12/26/us/2016-presidential-campaign-hacking-fast-facts/index.html. Accessed 26 Feb 2018.

Beckwith, Ryan Teague. "President Trump Made 1,950 Untrue Claims in 2017. That's Making His Job Harder." *Time.* Time Inc. Jan 2, 2018. http://time.com/5084420/donald-trump-lies-claims-fact-checks/. Accessed 26 Feb 2018.

Breiner, Andrew. "Pizzagate, explained: Everything you want to know about the Comet Ping Pong pizzeria conspiracy theory but are too afraid to search for on Reddit." *Salon.* Salon Media Group, Inc. Dec 10, 2016. https://www.salon.com/2016/12/10/pizzagate-explained-everything-you-want-to-know-about-the-comet-ping-pong-pizzeria-conspiracy-theory-but-are-too-afraid-to-search-for-on-reddit/. Accessed 26 Feb 2018.

Gentzkow, Matthew and Jesse M. Shapiro. "What Drives Media Slant? Evidence from U.S. Daily Newspapers. *Econometrica.* Vol 78, No 1. (Jan 2010), pg 35-71.

Guess, Andrew, Nyhan, Brenadan, and Jason Reifler. "Selective Exposure to Misinformation: Evidence from the consumption of fake news during the 2016 presidential campaign." *Dartmouth University.* http://www.dartmouth.edu/~nyhan/fake-news-2016.pdf. Accessed 24 Feb 2018.

Kessler, Glenn. "In a 30-minute interview, President Trump made 24 false or misleading claims." *The Washington Post.* Washington Post Co. Dec 29 2017. https://www.washingtonpost.com/news/fact-checker/wp/2017/12/29/in-a-30-minute-interview-president-trump-made-24-false-or-misleading-claims/?utm_term=.49df85cedb26. Accessed 26 Feb 2018.

Kessler, Glenn, Kelly, Meg, and Nicole Lewis. "President Trump has made 1,950 false or misleading claims over 347 days." *Washington Post.* Washington Post Co. Jan 2 ,2018. https://www.washingtonpost.com/news/fact-checker/wp/2018/01/02/president-trump-has-made-1949-false-or-misleading-claims-over-347-days/?utm_term=.6335c588aa87. Accessed 26 Feb 2018.

Puglisi, Riccardo and James M. Snyder Jr. "The Balanced US Press." *Journal of the European Economic Association.* Vol 13, Iss 2 (April 2015), pg 240-264.

Stepman, Jarrett. "The History of Fake News in the United States." *The Daily Signal.* The Heritage Foundation. Jan 1, 2018. http://dailysignal.com/2018/01/01/the-history-of-fake-news-in-the-united-states/. Accessed 26 Feb 2018.

Walton, Alice G. "6 Ways Social Media Affects Our Mental Health." *Forbes*. Forbes, inc. Jun 30, 2017. https://www.forbes.com/sites/alicegwalton/2017/06/30/a-run-down-of-social-medias-effects-on-our-mental-health/#70a1b4082e5a. Accessed 26 Feb 2018.

Notes

1. Guess, Nyhan, and Reifler, "Selective Exposure to Misinformation: Evidence from the consumption of fake news during the 2016 U.S. presidential campaign."
2. Stepman, "The History of Fake News in the United States."
3. "2016 Presidential Campaign Hacking Fast Facts," *CNN*.
4. Kessler, "In a 30-minute interview, President Trump made 24 false or Misleading claims."
5. Kessler, Kelly, Lewis, "President Trump has made 1,950 false or misleading claims over 347 days."
6. Beckwith, "President Trump Made 1,950 Untrue Claims in 2017. That's Making His Job Harder."
7. Walton, "6 Ways Social Media Affects Our Mental Health."
8. Breiner, "Pizzagate, explained: Everything you want to know about the Comet Ping Pong pizzeria conspiracy theory but are too afraid to search for on Reddit."

1
A Historical Perspective

by Michael E. Miller/The Washington Post via Getty Images

Kori and Danielle Hayes at a Pizzagate demonstration, outside the White House in Washington, DC on March 25, 2017.

Truth Is What You Fake of It

Is misinformation in the modern media environment unprecedented? Are politicians and political activists less truthful than in the past? While "fake news" and "post-truth" were buzzwords in 2017 and 2018, neither represents a new phenomenon in history. Historians have long known and been able to trace how issue entrepreneurs, opportunists, politicians, and ideological anarchists use misinformation for personal and political gain or entertainment.

Faking for Profit

Misinformation for profit is nothing new to the news industry. In 1835, British astronomer John Hershel used a newly invented telescope to view the moon. Across the Atlantic, the *New York Sun* carried stories about Hershel's discoveries alleging that the astronomer had found, among other things, giant bat-like people, blue-skinned goats, and temples made of sapphire. Stories like this were directly responsible for a massive surge in sales for the newspaper, which shot from 8,000 to more than 19,000 copies and, for a time, became the world's bestselling daily paper. Richard Adams Locke, then publisher of the paper, was directly responsible, purposefully producing fantastic stories to increase circulation and the strategy worked well. Curiosity about space and the potential for there to be life on other planets was widespread and news like this was front page material, but none of the true stories about the moon attracted nearly as much attention as the *Sun*'s fake coverage, which was later collected and sold in book form.[1]

Why did the *Sun* coverage of the moon sell better than London's the *Times*, previously the bestselling daily? In reality, the moon is a lifeless hunk of rock, fascinating and beautiful to some, but boring to others. Legitimate newspapers of the era presented readers with captivating depictions of an alien landscape, lifeless but nonetheless beautiful and serene, and this captivated audiences, but not nearly as much as the *Sun*'s more colorful coverage. The difference was that the *Sun* provided readers not with perplexing reality, but with something akin to what they hoped or fantasized might be true.

Fake news for profit predates the *Sun* debacle by centuries. Historians have found, for instance, that, after the dawn of the printing press in the 1600s, thousands of pamphlets and "newsbooks" containing entirely fabricated stories were sold throughout Europe. These publications were often purposefully inflammatory and provocative, making bold, outlandish claims, because such claims attracted more interest and thus generated more sales. This mattered little when publications were primarily one-offs, but the emerging legitimate media objected to this practice and it was the newspapers that first acted to ferret out illegitimate news. This happened because journalists perceived themselves as having a stake in their reputation and accuracy and so helped to expose the charlatanry of manipulators like Locke who misled the public for profit. The modern press evolved out of this movement, an internal drive for legitimacy that would make the press something more than entertainment, a service profiting from, but also operating in the public trust.

Faking for Power

In a 2016 article in *Politico* magazine, writer Jacob Soll explains how, in the 1400s, fake news gave rise to the spread of anti-Semitism in Italy. On Easter Sunday in 1475, after a young boy named Simonino had gone missing, a Franciscan preacher in Trento, Italy gave a series of sermons in which he claimed that the town's Jewish residents had kidnapped and killed the boy. Historians aren't entirely certain why the preacher, Bernardine of Feltre, was so violently opposed to Judaism, but his accusations, entirely without foundation or evidence, had devastating results. Stories of Jewish immorality spread from town to town via postings and written accounts from individuals claiming to have witnessed Jewish blood-drinking, child abuse, and other crimes firsthand. It was a concerted effort by the region's xenophobic and otherwise anti-Semitic population to dehumanize the Jewish population and the campaign worked. In Trento, the entire Jewish community was arrested and tortured with 15–17 burned at the stake after being convicted despite a complete lack of evidence.[2]

The fake news of the 1400s is an example of another popular and continuing strain of misinformation that has again come into vogue (or anti-vogue since most Americans state in polls that they disapprove of it) during and since the 2016 election cycle. Issue entrepreneurs use fake news of the type disseminated in the 1400s to gain political or social power and to motivate the public towards a certain goal or, more typically, against a perceived enemy. This is how much of the fake news identified from 2016–2018 was used, to connect political enemies or unfavorable ideologies with manufactured crimes and immoral behaviors/actions so as to motivate the public against those same enemies or ideologies.

There are many examples of this kind of misinformation in American history, and the proliferation of propagandistic claims intensifies around highly controversial issues. Creators of historic "fake news" have used misinformation to generate antipathy against immigrants in general, the Irish, Catholics, Asians, African Americans, and, more recently, Muslims. Though each campaign against a certain political, social, racial, ethnic, or religious group is unique there are common characteristics used by propagandists attempting to foment public conflict.

In 1906, a Bellingham, Washington newspaper, the *Puget Sound American*, used the term "Dusky Peril" to describe an influx of Sikhs arriving in the region to work in the lumber industry.[3] What's interesting in the coverage is that white residents in the community claimed that the Sikh residents had insulted and attacked white women in their community. This is a common tactic that generates hatred of a target group by suggesting that members of the group are so morally, ethically, and culturally deficient that they will attack the defenseless. By claiming that women are being attacked, the provocateur also has a better chance of engendering protective, defensive, and aggressive responses from male readers or viewers, and thus of encouraging violence. Similarly, "fake news" peddlers often hide their identity, or claim that the source of the information they present comes from an expert or an individual who would have little reason to lie about the claim in question. Coverage of the Sikh invasion led to a race riot in which the 200 Sikhs who had settled in Washington were violently beaten and driven from the town. Similarly, in a 2017 article in *Slate*, writer Mike Mariani discusses how "fake news" about Catholics abusing children in sex rings or attacking Protestant women, preceded the now infamous anti-Irish riots in Philadelphia in the 1830s.[4]

All-American Fakery

In 2017 and 2018, Donald Trump made numerous false claims about his political rivals and about contentious issues in American politics. This is a political tactic long employed in the United States and familiar even to the "founding fathers" of American society. For instance, historians have found that Benjamin Franklin produced fictional stories about the British paying Native Americans to scalp colonists in his effort to build support for the revolution. Similarly, in the lead up to the 1800 election, Federalists like John Adams and Alexander Hamilton spread a false rumor that Thomas Jefferson was secretly an atheist, an ideology widely feared and maligned in the 1800s in much the same way that some Americans in 2018 fear and believe misinformation about Islam and Muslims. In the 1800s, when the press was funded directly by politicians and lobbyists, the situation was very similar to the modern media environment.

Then, as now, the threat to American discourse was so acute the Thomas Jefferson felt misinformation was a threat to American discourse. In 1807, Jefferson wrote:

> "It is a melancholy truth, that a suppression of the press could not more completely [sic] depreive the nation of its benefits, than is done, by its abandoned prostitution to falsehood. Nothing can now be believed which is seen in a newspaper."[5]

Essentially Jefferson, in 1807, was making a similar claim to that made by Donald Trump in 2018, who frequently claims that most or all of the information presented by the "mainstream media" is "fake news." The situation perceived by the two presidents is similar, but the media environment in 1800 was fundamentally different from that of the twenty-first century. In Jefferson's era, the mainstream press was funded by lobbyists and interest groups and newspapers did not typically operate according to ethical guidelines. In Jefferson's era, alternative publications were the ones trying to provide legitimate information to counter the propaganda produced and paid for by politicians and issue entrepreneurs.

Over time, the mainstream press evolved so as to be more or less self-policing, with journalists encouraged and rewarded for calling out mistakes and misinformation presented by other journalists and journalists regularly punished for failing to correct their own mistakes. Over time, those who gravitated towards careers in the press did so not for profit, but out of a desire to contribute to informed public discourse and this meant that the newspapers and the journalists who wrote for them became more and more independent and increasingly served as an important check on the powers of the government, rather than a tool for governmental manipulation.

The mainstream press of the twenty-first century is nothing like the press that Jefferson so passionately condemned and, in fact, much of the content produced through the mainstream media would most likely have been quite appealing to a politician like Jefferson. In Jefferson's era, the mainstream press was more like the propaganda produced in the twenty-first century by the Russian government or white-nationalist Internet groups, proliferated through "fake news" sites and publications, or produced by pundits who are paid to shape public opinion rather than to inform the public. Today, misinformation is the "alternative" news, rather than the mainstream press and so Jefferson and Trump, though sharing the same message, were actually talking about opposite features of the media environment.

Under the Sun

There is a proverb in Ecclesiastes 1:9 that says:

> What has been will be again,

> What has been done with be done again;

> There is nothing new under the sun.[6]

Misinformation is profitable and effective as a tool for the political or ideological manipulation of public opinion and so, the use of misinformation is perennial and always a part of human societies. Critics might argue that those who intentionally use misinformation are guilty of some moral or ethical misdeed, but this is a matter of perspective. Those producing "fake news" for profit have their own proximate needs and concerns, which may outweigh any concern for how this activity affects others. Those who use misinformation for political or ideological purposes might believe that their cause is so righteous, or their enemies so insidiously evil and difficult to fight, that dishonesty is warranted by the need to mount an effective resistance.

Misinformation and propaganda appeals because it appears to confirm what people fear or what they want to believe. Those who purchased issues of the *Sun*, reading about man-bats and sapphire temples, might have wanted to believe that such an environment existed, or might have read about it because they feared what the existence of such a society might mean for them. In any case, the fantastic articles confirmed the feelings or ideas of those who gravitated towards them. The appeal of fantasy is also a fundamental part of the human psyche, enabling individuals to find, in fiction, what they fail to find in their lives, whether it be magical riches, youth, beauty, or ideological comfort and righteousness.

Micah L. Issitt

Works Used

"Ecclesiastes 1:9." *Biblehub*. Bible Hub. 2017. Web.

Friedman, Marcelle. "Why It Matters That House Hunters Is Fake." *Slate*. Slate Group. Jun 14, 2012. Web.

"Have We a Dusky Peril?" *SAADA*. South Asian American Digital Archive. 2017. Web.

Kirby, Emma Jane. "The City Getting Rich from Fake News." *BBC News*. BBC. Dec 5, 2016. Web.

Mariani, Mike. "Nativism, Violence, and the Origins of the Paranoid Style." *Slate*. Slate Group. Mar 22, 2017. Web.

Sandomir, Richard. "Albert Freedman, Producer of Rigged 1950s Quiz Show, Dies at 95." *The New York Times*. The New York Times, Co. Apr 22, 2017. Web.

Silverman, Craig. "How the Bizarre Conspiracy Theory behind 'Pizzagate' Was Spread." *Buzzfeed*. Buzzfeed. Dec 5, 2016. Web.

Soll, Jacob. "The Long and Brutal History of Fake News." *Politico*. Politico Magazine. Dec 18, 2016. Web.

Standage, Tom. "The True History of Fake News." *The Economist*. Economist 1843. June/July 2017. Web.

Umberti, David. "The Real History of Fake News." *CJR*. Columbia Journalism Review. Dec 15, 2016. Web. 26 Feb 2018.

Notes

1. Standage, "The True History of Fake News."
2. Soll, "The Long and Brutal History of Fake News."
3. "Have We a Dusky Peril?" *SAADA*.
4. Mariani, "Nativism, Violence, and the Origins of the Paranoid Style."
5. Umberti, "The Real History of Fake News."
6. "Ecclesiastes 1:9," *Biblehub*.

The Fake-News Fallacy

By Adrian Chen
The New Yorker, September 4, 2017

On the evening of October 30, 1938, a seventy-six-year-old millworker in Grover's Mill, New Jersey, named Bill Dock heard something terrifying on the radio. Aliens had landed just down the road, a newscaster announced, and were rampaging through the countryside. Dock grabbed his double-barrelled shotgun and went out into the night, prepared to face down the invaders. But, after investigating, as a newspaper later reported, he "didn't see anybody he thought needed shooting." In fact, he'd been duped by Orson Welles's radio adaptation of *The War of the Worlds*. Structured as a breaking-news report that detailed the invasion in real time, the broadcast adhered faithfully to the conventions of news radio, complete with elaborate sound effects and impersonations of government officials, with only a few brief warnings through the program that it was fiction.

The next day, newspapers were full of stories like Dock's. "Thirty men and women rushed into the West 123rd Street police station," ready to evacuate, according to the *Times*. Two people suffered heart attacks from shock, the *Washington Post* reported. One caller from Pittsburgh claimed that he had barely prevented his wife from taking her own life by swallowing poison. The panic was the biggest story for weeks; a photograph of Bill Dock and his shotgun, taken the next day, by a *Daily News* reporter, went "the 1930s equivalent of viral," A. Brad Schwartz writes in his recent history, *Broadcast Hysteria: Orson Welles's War of the Worlds and the Art of Fake News*.

This early fake-news panic lives on in legend, but Schwartz is the latest of a number of researchers to argue that it wasn't all it was cracked up to be. As Schwartz tells it, there was no mass hysteria, only small pockets of concern that quickly burned out. He casts doubt on whether Dock had even heard the broadcast. Schwartz argues that newspapers exaggerated the panic to better control the upstart medium of radio, which was becoming the dominant source of breaking news in the thirties. Newspapers wanted to show that radio was irresponsible and needed guidance from its older, more respectable siblings in the print media, such "guidance" mostly taking the form of lucrative licensing deals and increased ownership of local radio stations. Columnists and editorialists weighed in. Soon, the Columbia education professor and broadcaster Lyman Bryson declared that unrestrained radio was "one of the most dangerous elements in modern culture."

The argument turned on the role of the Federal Communications Commission, the regulators charged with insuring that the radio system served the "public interest, convenience and necessity." Unlike today's F.C.C., which is known mainly as a referee for media mergers, the F.C.C. of the thirties was deeply concerned with the particulars of what broadcasters put in listeners' ears—it had recently issued a reprimand after a racy Mae West sketch that so alarmed NBC it banned West from its stations. To some, the lesson of the panic was that the F.C.C. needed to take an even more active role to protect people from malicious tricksters like Welles. "Programs of that kind are an excellent indication of the inadequacy of our present control over a marvellous facility," the Iowa senator Clyde Herring, a Democrat, declared. He announced a bill that would require broadcasters to submit shows to the F.C.C. for review before airing. Yet Schwartz says that the people calling for a government crackdown were far outnumbered by those who warned against one. "Far from blaming Mr. Orson Welles, he ought to be given a Congressional medal and a national prize," the renowned columnist Dorothy Thompson wrote.

Thompson was concerned with a threat far greater than rogue thespians. Everywhere you looked in the thirties, authoritarian leaders were being swept to power with the help of radio. The Nazi Ministry for Public Enlightenment and Propaganda deployed a force called the Funkwarte, or Radio Guard, that went block by block to insure that citizens tuned in to Hitler's major broadcast speeches, as Tim Wu details in his new book, "The Attention Merchants." Meanwhile, homegrown radio demagogues like Father Charles Coughlin and the charismatic Huey Long made some people wonder about a radio-aided Fascist takeover in America. For Thompson, Welles had made an "admirable demonstration" about the power of radio. It showed the danger of handing control of the airwaves over to the state. "No political body must ever, under any circumstances, obtain a monopoly of radio," she wrote. "The greatest organizers of mass hysterias and the mass delusions today are states using the radio to excite terrors, incite hatreds, inflame masses."

Donald Trump's victory has been a demonstration, for many people, of how the Internet can be used to achieve those very ends. Trump used Twitter less as a communication device than as a weapon of information warfare, rallying his supporters and attacking opponents with hundred-and-forty-character barrages. "I wouldn't be here without Twitter," he declared on *Fox News* in March. Yet the Internet didn't just give him a megaphone. It also helped him peddle his lies through a profusion of unreliable media sources that undermined the old providers of established fact. Throughout the campaign, fake-news stories, conspiracy theories, and other forms of propaganda were reported to be flooding social networks. The stories were overwhelmingly pro-Trump, and the spread of whoppers like "Pope Francis Shocks World, Endorses Donald Trump for President"—hardly more believable than a Martian invasion—seemed to suggest that huge numbers of Trump supporters were being duped by online lies. This was not the first campaign to be marred by misinformation, of course. But the sheer outlandishness of the claims being made, and believed, suggested to many that the Internet had brought about a fundamental devaluing of the truth. Many pundits argued that the "hyper-democratizing" force of the Internet had helped usher in a "post-truth" world, where people based their opinions not on facts or reason but on passion and prejudice.

Yet, even among this information anarchy, there remains an authority of sorts. Facebook and Google now define the experience of the Internet for most people, and in many ways they play the role of regulators. In the weeks after the election, they faced enormous criticism for their failure to halt the spread of fake news and misinformation on their services. The problem was not simply that people had been able to spread lies but that the digital platforms were set up in ways that made them especially potent. The "share" button sends lies flying around the Web faster than fact checkers can debunk them. The supposedly neutral platforms use personalized algorithms to feed us information based on precise data models of our preferences, trapping us in "filter bubbles" that cripple critical thinking and increase polarization. The threat of fake news was compounded by this sense that the role of the press had been ceded to an arcane algorithmic system created by private companies that care only about the bottom line.

Not so very long ago, it was thought that the tension between commercial pressure and the public interest would be one of the many things made obsolete by the Internet. In the mid-aughts, during the height of the Web 2.0 boom, the pundit Henry Jenkins declared that the Internet was creating a "participatory culture" where the top-down hegemony of greedy media corporations would be replaced by a horizontal network of amateur "prosumers" engaged in a wonderfully democratic exchange of information in cyberspace—an epistemic agora that would allow the whole globe to come together on a level playing field. Google, Facebook, Twitter, and the rest attained their paradoxical gatekeeper status by positioning themselves as neutral platforms that unlocked the Internet's democratic potential by empowering users. It was on a private platform, Twitter, where pro-democracy protesters organized, and on another private platform, Google, where the knowledge of a million public libraries could be accessed for free. These companies would develop into what the tech guru Jeff Jarvis termed "radically public companies," which operate more like public utilities than like businesses.

But there has been a growing sense among mostly liberal-minded observers that the platforms' championing of openness is at odds with the public interest. The image of Arab Spring activists using Twitter to challenge repressive dictators has been replaced, in the public imagination, by that of ISIS propagandists luring vulnerable Western teen-agers to Syria via YouTube videos and Facebook chats. The openness that was said to bring about a democratic revolution instead seems to have torn a hole in the social fabric. Today, online misinformation, hate speech, and propaganda are seen as the front line of a reactionary populist upsurge threatening liberal democracy. Once held back by democratic institutions, the bad stuff is now sluicing through a digital breach with the help of irresponsible tech companies. Stanching the torrent of fake news has become a trial by which the digital giants can prove their commitment to democracy. The effort has reignited a debate over the role of mass communication that goes back to the early days of radio.

The debate around radio at the time of *The War of the Worlds* was informed by a similar fall from utopian hopes to dystopian fears. Although radio can seem like an unremarkable medium—audio wallpaper pasted over the most boring parts of your day—the historian David Goodman's book *Radio's Civic Ambition: American Broadcasting and Democracy in the 1930s* makes it clear that the birth of the technology brought about a communications revolution comparable to that of the Internet. For the first time, radio allowed a mass audience to experience the same thing simultaneously from the comfort of their homes. Early radio pioneers imagined that this unprecedented blurring of public and private space might become a sort of ethereal forum that would uplift the nation, from the urban slum dweller to the remote Montana rancher. John Dewey called radio "the most powerful instrument of social education the world has ever seen." Populist reformers demanded that radio be treated as a common carrier and give airtime to anyone who paid a fee. Were this to have come about, it would have been very much like the early online-bulletin-board systems where strangers could come together and leave a message for any passing online wanderer. Instead, in the regulatory struggles of the twenties and thirties, the commercial networks won out.

Corporate networks were supported by advertising, and what many progressives had envisaged as the ideal democratic forum began to seem more like Times Square, cluttered with ads for soap and coffee. Rather than elevating public opinion, advertisers pioneered techniques of manipulating it. Who else might be able to exploit such techniques? Many saw a link between the domestic on-air advertising boom and the rise of Fascist dictators like Hitler abroad. Tim Wu cites the leftist critic Max Lerner, who lamented that "the most damning blow the dictatorships have struck at democracy has been the compliment they have paid us in taking over and perfecting our prized techniques of persuasion and our underlying contempt for the credulity of the masses."

Amid such concerns, broadcasters were under intense pressure to show that they were not turning listeners into a zombified mass ripe for the Fascist picking. What they developed in response is, in Goodman's phrase, a "civic paradigm": radio would create active, rational, tolerant listeners—in other words, the ideal citizens of a democratic society. Classical-music-appreciation shows were developed with an eye toward uplift. Inspired by progressive educators, radio networks hosted "forum" programs, in which citizens from all walks of life were invited to discuss the matters of the day, with the aim of inspiring tolerance and political engagement. One such program, "America's Town Meeting of the Air," featured in its first episode a Communist, a Fascist, a Socialist, and a democrat.

Listening to the radio, then, would be a "civic practice" that could create a more democratic society by exposing people to diversity. But only if they listened correctly. There was great concern about distracted and gullible listeners being susceptible to propagandists. A group of progressive journalists and thinkers known as "propaganda critics" set about educating radio listeners. The Institute for Propaganda Analysis, co-founded by the social psychologist Clyde R. Miller, with funding from the department-store magnate Edward Filene, was at the forefront of the movement.

In newsletters, books, and lectures, the institute's members urged listeners to attend to their own biases while analyzing broadcast voices for signs of manipulation. Listening to the radio critically became the duty of every responsible citizen. Goodman, who is generally sympathetic to the proponents of the civic paradigm, is alert to the off notes here of snobbery and disdain: much of the progressive concern about listeners' abilities stemmed from the belief that Americans were, basically, dim-witted—an idea that gained currency after intelligence tests on soldiers during the First World War supposedly revealed discouraging news about the capacities of the average American. In the wake of *The War of the Worlds* panic, commentators didn't hesitate to rail against "idiotic" and "stupid" listeners. Welles and his crew, Dorothy Thompson declared, "have shown up the incredible stupidity, lack of nerve and ignorance of thousands."

Today, when we speak about people's relationship to the Internet, we tend to adopt the nonjudgmental language of computer science. Fake news was described as a "virus" spreading among users who have been "exposed" to online misinformation. The proposed solutions to the fake-news problem typically resemble antivirus programs: their aim is to identify and quarantine all the dangerous nonfacts throughout the Web before they can infect their prospective hosts. One venture capitalist, writing on the tech blog *Venture Beat*, imagined deploying artificial intelligence as a

> **This was not the first campaign to be marred by misinformation, of course. But the sheer outlandishness of the claims being made, and believed, suggested to many that the Internet had brought about a fundamental devaluing of the truth.**

"media cop," protecting users from malicious content. "Imagine a world where every article could be assessed based on its level of sound discourse," he wrote. The vision here was of the news consumers of the future turning the discourse setting on their browser up to eleven and soaking in pure fact. It's possible, though, that this approach comes with its own form of myopia. Neil Postman, writing a couple of decades ago, warned of a growing tendency to view people as computers, and a corresponding devaluation of the "singular human capacity to see things whole in all their psychic, emotional and moral dimensions." A person does not process information the way a computer does, flipping a switch of "true" or "false." One rarely cited *Pew* statistic shows that only four per cent of American Internet users trust social media "a lot," which suggests a greater resilience against online misinformation than overheated editorials might lead us to expect. Most people seem to understand that their social-media streams represent a heady mixture of gossip, political activism, news, and entertainment. You might see this as a problem, but turning to Big Data-driven algorithms to fix it will only further entrench our reliance on code to tell us what is important about the world—which is what led to the problem in the first place. Plus, it doesn't sound very fun.

The various efforts to fact-check and label and blacklist and sort all the world's information bring to mind a quote, which appears in David Goodman's book, from John Grierson, a documentary filmmaker: "Men don't live by bread alone, nor by fact alone." In the nineteen-forties, Grierson was on an F.C.C. panel that had been convened to determine how best to encourage a democratic radio, and he was frustrated by a draft report that reflected his fellow-panelists' obsession with filling the airwaves with rationality and fact. Grierson said, "Much of this entertainment is the folk stuff . . . of our technological time; the patterns of observation, of humor, of fancy, which make a technological society a human society."

In recent times, Donald Trump supporters are the ones who have most effectively applied Grierson's insight to the digital age. Young Trump enthusiasts turned Internet trolling into a potent political tool, deploying the "folk stuff" of the Web—memes, slang, the nihilistic humor of a certain subculture of Web-native gamer—to give a subversive, cyberpunk sheen to a movement that might otherwise look like a stale reactionary blend of white nationalism and anti-feminism. As crusaders against fake news push technology companies to "defend the truth," they face a backlash from a conservativemovement, retooled for the digital age, which sees claims for objectivity as a smoke screen for bias.

One sign of this development came last summer, in the scandal over Facebook's "Trending" sidebar, in which curators chose stories to feature on the user's home page. When the tech Web site Gizmodo reported the claim of an anonymous employee that the curators were systematically suppressing conservative news stories, the right-wing blogosphere exploded. Breitbart, the far-right torchbearer, uncovered the social-media accounts of some of the employees—liberal recent college graduates—that seemed to confirm the suspicion of pervasive anti-right bias. Eventually, Facebook fired the team and retooled the feature, calling in high-profile conservatives for a meeting with Mark Zuckerberg. Although Facebook denied that there was any systematic suppression of conservative views, the outcry was enough to reverse a tiny first step it had taken toward introducing human judgment into the algorithmic machine.

For conservatives, the rise of online gatekeepers may be a blessing in disguise. Throwing the charge of "liberal media bias" against powerful institutions has always provided an energizing force for the conservative movement, as the historian Nicole Hemmer shows in her new book, *Messengers of the Right*. Instead of focussing on ideas, Hemmer focusses on the galvanizing struggle over the means of distributing those ideas. The first modern conservatives were members of the America First movement, who found their isolationist views marginalized in the lead-up to the Second World War and vowed to fight back by forming the first conservative media outlets. A "vague claim of exclusion" sharpened into a "powerful and effective ideological arrow in the conservative quiver," Hemmer argues, through battles that conservative radio broadcasters had with the F.C.C. in the nineteen-fifties and sixties. Their main obstacle was the F.C.C.'s Fairness Doctrine, which sought to protect public discourse by requiring controversial opinions to be balanced by opposing viewpoints. Since attacks on the mid-century liberal consensus were inherently controversial, conservatives found themselves constantly in regulators' sights. In 1961, a watershed moment occurred with the leak of a memo from labor leaders to the Kennedy Administration which suggested using the Fairness Doctrine to suppress right-wing viewpoints. To many conservatives, the memo proved the existence of the vast conspiracy they had long suspected. A fund-raising letter for a prominent conservative radio show railed against the doctrine, calling it "the most dastardly collateral attack on freedom of speech in the history of the country." Thus was born the character of the persecuted truthteller standing up to a tyrannical government—a trope on which a billion-dollar conservative-media juggernaut has been built.

Today, Facebook and Google have taken the place of the F.C.C. in the conservative imagination. Conservative bloggers highlight the support that Jack Dorsey, the C.E.O. of Twitter, has expressed for Black Lives Matter, and the frequent visits that Google's Eric Schmidt made to the Obama White House. When Facebook announced that it was partnering with a group of fact checkers from the nonprofit Poynter Institute to flag false news stories, conservatives saw another effort to censor them under the guise of objectivity. Brent Bozell, who runs the conservative media-watchdog group Media Research Center, cited the fact that Poynter received funding from the liberal financier George Soros. "Just like George Soros and company underwrote the Fairness Doctrine several years ago," he said, "this is about going after conservative talk on the Internet and banning it by somehow projecting it as being false."

One lesson you get from Hemmer's research is that the conservative skepticism of gatekeepers is not without a historical basis. The Fairness Doctrine really was used by liberal groups to silence conservatives, typically by flooding stations with complaints and requests for airtime to respond. This created a chilling effect, with stations often choosing to avoid controversial material. The technical fixes implemented by Google and Facebook in the rush to fight fake news seem equally open to abuse, dependent, as they are, on user-generated reports.

Yet today, with a powerful, well-funded propaganda machine dedicated to publicizing any hint of liberal bias, conservatives aren't the ones who have the most to fear. As Facebook has become an increasingly important venue for activists documenting police abuse, many of them have complained that overzealous censors routinely block their posts. A recent report by the investigative nonprofit ProPublica shows how anti-racist activism can often fall afoul of Facebook rules against offensive material, while a post by the Louisiana representative Clay Higgins calling for the slaughter of "radicalized" Muslims was deemed acceptable. In 2016, a group of civil-rights activists wrote Facebook to demand that steps be taken to insure that the platform could be used by marginalized people and social movements organizing for change. There was no high-profile meeting with Zuckerberg, only a form letter outlining Facebook's moderation practices. The wishful story about how the Internet was creating a hyper-democratic "participatory culture" obscures the ways in which it is biased in favor of power.

The online tumult of the 2016 election fed into a growing suspicion of Silicon Valley's dominance over the public sphere. Across the political spectrum, people have become less trusting of the Big Tech companies that govern most online political expression. Calls for civic responsibility on the part of Silicon Valley companies have replaced the hope that technological innovation alone might bring about a democratic revolution. Despite the focus on algorithms, A.I., filter bubbles, and Big Data, these questions are political as much as technical. Regulation has become an increasingly popular notion; the Democratic senator Cory Booker has called for greater antitrust scrutiny of Google and Facebook, while Stephen Bannon reportedly wants to regulate Google and Facebook like public utilities. In the nineteen-thirties, such threats encouraged commercial broadcasters to adopt the civic paradigm. In that prewar era, advocates of democratic radio were united by a progressive vision of pluralism and rationality; today, the question of how to fashion a democratic social media is one more front in our highly divisive culture wars.

Still, Silicon Valley isn't taking any chances. In the wake of the recent, deadly white-supremacist rally in Charlottesville, Virginia, a slew of tech companies banned the neo-Nazi blog the *Daily Stormer*, essentially blacklisting it from the Web. Responding so directly to appeals to decency and justice that followed the tragedy, these companies positioned themselves less as neutral platforms than as custodians of the public interest.

Zuckerberg recently posted a fifty-seven-hundred-word manifesto announcing a new mission for Facebook that goes beyond the neutral-seeming mandate to "make the world more open and connected." Henceforth, Facebook would seek to "develop the social infrastructure to give people the power to build a global community that works for all of us." The manifesto was so heavy on themes of civic responsibility that many took it as a blueprint for a future political campaign. Speculation has only grown since Zuckerberg embarked on a fifty-state tour this summer to meet American Facebook users, posting photos of himself with livestock and unhealthy local delicacies. Those who think that Zuckerberg is preparing for a Presidential bid, however, should consider the emerging vectors of power in the digital era: for the man who runs Facebook, the White House might well look like a step down.

Print citations

CMS: Chen, Adrian. "The Fake-News Fallacy." In *The Reference Shelf: Alternative Facts, Post-Truth, and the Information War*, edited by Betsy Maury, 9-16. Ipswich, MA: H.W. Wilson, 2018.

MLA: Chen, Adrian. "The Fake-News Fallacy." In *The Reference Shelf: Alternative Facts, Post-Truth, and the Information War*. Ed. Betsy Maury. Ipswich: H.W. Wilson, 2018. 9-16. Print.

APA: Chen, A. (2018). The fake-news fallacy. In Betsy Maury (Ed.), *The reference shelf: Alternative facts, post-truth, and the information war* (pp. 9-16). Ipswich, MA: H.W. Wilson. (Original work published 2017)

The Evangelical Roots of Our Post-Truth Society

By Molly Worthen
The New York Times, April 13, 2017

The arrival of the "post-truth" political climate came as a shock to many Americans. But to the Christian writer Rachel Held Evans, charges of "fake news" are nothing new. "The deep distrust of the media, of scientific consensus—those were prevalent narratives growing up," she told me.

Although Ms. Evans, 35, no longer calls herself an evangelical, she attended Bryan College, an evangelical school in Dayton, Tenn. She was taught to distrust information coming from the scientific or media elite because these sources did not hold a "biblical worldview."

"It was presented as a cohesive worldview that you could maintain if you studied the Bible," she told me. "Part of that was that climate change isn't real, that evolution is a myth made up by scientists who hate God, and capitalism is God's ideal for society."

Conservative evangelicals are not the only ones who think that an authority trusted by the other side is probably lying. But they believe that their own authority—the inerrant Bible—is both supernatural and scientifically sound, and this conviction gives that natural human aversion to unwelcome facts a special power on the right. This religious tradition of fact denial long predates the rise of the culture wars, social media or President Trump, but it has provoked deep conflict among evangelicals themselves.

That innocuous phrase—"biblical worldview" or "Christian worldview"—is everywhere in the evangelical world. The radio show founded by Chuck Colson, "BreakPoint," helps listeners "get informed and equipped to live out the Christian worldview." Focus on the Family devotes a webpage to the implications of a worldview "based on the infallible Word of God." Betsy DeVos's supporters praised her as a "committed Christian living out a biblical worldview."

The phrase is not as straightforward as it seems. Ever since the scientific revolution, two compulsions have guided conservative Protestant intellectual life: the impulse to defend the Bible as a reliable scientific authority and the impulse to place the Bible beyond the claims of science entirely.

The first impulse blossomed into the doctrine of biblical inerrancy. Scripture became the irrefutable guide to everything from the meaning of fossils to the

> **They believe that their own authority—the inerrant Bible—is both supernatural and scientifically sound, and this conviction gives that natural human aversion to unwelcome facts a special power on the right.**

interpretation of archaeological findings in the Middle East, a "storehouse of facts," as the 19th-century theologian Charles Hodge put it.

The second impulse, the one that rejects scientists' standing to challenge the Bible, evolved by the early 20th century into a school of thought called presuppositionalism. The term is a mouthful, but the idea is simple: We all have presuppositions that frame our understanding of the world. Cornelius Van Til, a theologian who promoted this idea, rejected the premise that all humans have access to objective reality. "We really do not grant that you see any fact in any dimension of life truly," he wrote in a pamphlet aimed at non-Christians. If this sounds like a forerunner of modern cultural relativism, in a way it is—with the caveat that one worldview, the one based on faith in an inerrant Bible, does have a claim on universal truth, and everyone else is a myopic relativist.

Nowadays, ministries, schools and media outlets use the term "Christian worldview" to signal their orthodoxy. But its pervasiveness masks significant disagreement over what it means. Many evangelical colleges allow faculty and students to question inerrancy, creationism and the presumption that Jesus would have voted Republican.

Karl Giberson taught biology for many years at Eastern Nazarene College in Quincy, Mass., where freshmen take a course that covers "the Christian worldview" alongside topics like "racial and gender equity" and "cultural diversity." In the Church of the Nazarene, many leaders have been uneasy about the rationalist claims of biblical inerrancy, and Dr. Giberson openly taught the theory of evolution. "I was completely uncontroversial, for the most part," he told me. "The problems emerged when I began to publish, when I became a public spokesman for this point of view."

Nazarene pastors and church members—who absorbed the more fundamentalist worldview of mainstream evangelicalism—put pressure on the school. "The administrators were not upset that I was promoting evolution," he said. "But now they had a pastor telling the admissions department, 'we do not want you recruiting in our youth group.'" The controversy drove him to resign in 2011.

Dean Nelson, who runs the journalism program at Point Loma Nazarene University in San Diego, told me that he doesn't see "how you can teach 'Christian journalism' any more than you can teach 'Christian mathematics.'" But he acknowledged that "many of the students' parents were raised on Rush Limbaugh and Glenn Beck and distrust the mainstream news media. So it's a little bit of a dance with parents who are expecting us to perpetuate that distrust and raise up this tribe of 'Christian journalists.'"

The conservative Christian worldview is not just a posture of mistrust toward the secular world's "fake news." It is a network of institutions and experts versed in shadow versions of climate change science, biology and other fields, like Nathaniel Jeanson, a research biologist at the creationist ministry Answers in Genesis, in Petersburg, Ky.

Dr. Jeanson is as important an asset for the ministry as its life-size replica of Noah's Ark in Williamstown, Ky. He believes the earth was created in six days—and he has a Ph.D. in cell and developmental biology from Harvard.

Home-schooled until high school, Dr. Jeanson grew up going to "Worldview Weekend" Christian conferences. As an undergraduate at the University of Wisconsin, Parkside, he dutifully studied evolutionary biology during the day and read creationist literature at night.

This "reading double," as he calls it, equipped him to personify the contradictions that pervade this variety of Christian worldview. At Harvard Medical School, he chose a research topic that steered clear of evolution. "My research question is a present-tense question—how do blood cells function," he told me. "So perhaps it was easier to compartmentalize."

Dr. Jeanson rhapsodized about the integrity of the scientific method. Before graduate school, "I held this quack idea of cancer," he said. "But that idea got corrected. This is the way science works." Yet when his colleagues refuse to read his creationist papers and data sets, he takes their snub as proof that they can find no flaws in his research. "If people who devote their lives to it can't point anything out, then I think I may be on to something," he said.

Dr. Jeanson calls himself a "presuppositionalist evidentialist"—which we might define as someone who accepts evidence when it happens to affirm his nonnegotiable presuppositions. "When it comes to questions of absolute truth, those are things I've settled in my own mind and heart," he told me. "I couldn't call myself a Christian if I hadn't."

We all cling to our own unquestioned assumptions. But in the quest to advance knowledge and broker peaceful coexistence in a pluralistic world, the worldview based on biblical inerrancy gets tangled up in the contradiction between its claims on universalist science and insistence on an exclusive faith.

By contrast, the worldview that has propelled mainstream Western intellectual life and made modern civilization possible is a kind of pragmatism. It is an empirical outlook that continually—if imperfectly—revises its conclusions based on evidence available to everyone, regardless of their beliefs about the supernatural. This worldview clashes with the conservative evangelical war on facts, but it is not necessarily incompatible with Christian faith.

In fact, evangelical colleges themselves may be the best hope for change. Members of traditions historically suspicious of a pseudoscientific view of the Bible, like the Nazarenes, should revive that skepticism. Mr. Nelson encourages his students to be skeptics rather than cynics. "The skeptic looks at something and says, 'I wonder,'" he said. "The cynic says, 'I know,' and then stops thinking."

He pointed out that "cynicism and tribalism are very closely related. You protect your tribe, your way of life and thinking, and you try to annihilate anything that might call that into question." Cynicism and tribalism are among the gravest human temptations. They are all the more dangerous when they pose as wisdom and righteousness.

Print Citations

CMS: Worthen, Molly. "The Evangelical Roots of Our Post-Truth Society." In *The Reference Shelf: Alternative Facts, Post-Truth, and the Information War*, edited by Betsy Maury, 17-20. Ipswich, MA: H.W. Wilson, 2018.

MLA: Worthen, Molly. "The Evangelical Roots of Our Post-Truth Society." *The Reference Shelf: Alternative Facts, Post-Truth, and the Information War*. Ed. Betsy Maury. Ipswich: H.W. Wilson, 2018. 17-20. Print.

APA: Worthen, M. (2018). The evangelical roots of our post-truth society. In Betsy Maury (Ed.), *The reference shelf: Alternative facts, post-truth, and the information war* (pp. 17-20). Ipswich, MA: H.W. Wilson. (Original work published 2017)

Do Social Media Threaten Democracy?

The Economist, November 4, 2017

In 1962 a British political scientist, Bernard Crick, published *In Defence of Politics*. He argued that the art of political horse-trading, far from being shabby, lets people of different beliefs live together in a peaceful, thriving society. In a liberal democracy, nobody gets exactly what he wants, but everyone broadly has the freedom to lead the life he chooses. However, without decent information, civility and conciliation, societies resolve their differences by resorting to coercion.

How Crick would have been dismayed by the falsehood and partisanship on display in this week's Senate committee hearings in Washington. Not long ago social media held out the promise of a more enlightened politics, as accurate information and effortless communication helped good people drive out corruption, bigotry and lies. Yet Facebook acknowledged that before and after last year's American election, between January 2015 and August this year, 146m users may have seen Russian misinformation on its platform. Google's YouTube admitted to 1,108 Russian-linked videos and Twitter to 36,746 accounts. Far from bringing enlightenment, social media have been spreading poison.

Russia's trouble-making is only the start. From South Africa to Spain, politics is getting uglier. Part of the reason is that, by spreading untruth and outrage, corroding voters' judgment and aggravating partisanship, social media erode the conditions for the horse-trading that Crick thought fosters liberty.

A Shorter Attention Spa...Oh, Look at That!

The use of social media does not cause division so much as amplify it. The financial crisis of 2007-08 stoked popular anger at a wealthy elite that had left everyone else behind. The culture wars have split voters by identity rather than class. Nor are social media alone in their power to polarise—just look at cable TV and talk radio. But, whereas *Fox News* is familiar, social-media platforms are new and still poorly understood. And, because of how they work, they wield extraordinary influence.

They make their money by putting photos, personal posts, news stories and ads in front of you. Because they can measure how you react, they know just how to get under your skin. They collect data about you in order to have algorithms to determine what will catch your eye, in an "attention economy" that keeps users scrolling, clicking and sharing—again and again and again. Anyone setting out to shape opinion can produce dozens of ads, analyse them and see which is hardest to resist. The result is compelling: one study found that users in rich countries touch their phones 2,600 times a day.

It would be wonderful if such a system helped wisdom and truth rise to the surface. But, whatever Keats said, truth is not beauty so much as it is hard work—especially when you disagree with it. Everyone who has scrolled through Facebook knows how, instead of imparting wisdom, the system dishes out compulsive stuff that tends to reinforce people's biases.

This aggravates the politics of contempt that took hold, in the United States at least, in the 1990s. Because different sides see different facts, they share no empirical basis for reaching a compromise. Because each side hears time and again that the other lot are good for nothing but lying, bad faith and slander, the system has even less room for empathy. Because people are sucked into a maelstrom of pettiness, scandal and outrage, they lose sight of what matters for the society they share.

> Breaking up social-media giants might make sense in antitrust terms, but it would not help with political speech—indeed, by multiplying the number of platforms, it could make the industry harder to manage.

This tends to discredit the compromises and subtleties of liberal democracy, and to boost the politicians who feed off conspiracy and nativism. Consider the probes into Russia's election hack by Congress and the special prosecutor, Robert Mueller, who has just issued his first indictments. After Russia attacked America, Americans ended up attacking each other. Because the framers of the constitution wanted to hold back tyrants and mobs, social media aggravate Washington gridlock. In Hungary and Poland, without such constraints, they help sustain an illiberal, winner-takes-all style of democracy. In Myanmar, where Facebook is the main source of news for many, it has deepened the hatred of the Rohingya, victims of ethnic cleansing.

Social Media, Social Responsibility

What is to be done? People will adapt, as they always do. A survey this week found that only 37% of Americans trust what they get from social media, half the share that trust printed newspapers and magazines. Yet in the time it takes to adapt, bad governments with bad politics could do a lot of harm.

Society has created devices, such as libel, and ownership laws, to rein in old media. Some are calling for social-media companies, like publishers, to be similarly accountable for what appears on their platforms; to be more transparent; and to be treated as monopolies that need breaking up. All these ideas have merit, but they come with trade-offs. When Facebook farms out items to independent outfits for fact-checking, the evidence that it moderates behaviour is mixed.

Moreover, politics is not like other kinds of speech; it is dangerous to ask a handful of big firms to deem what is healthy for society. Congress wants transparency about who pays for political ads, but a lot of malign influence comes through people carelessly sharing barely credible news posts. Breaking up social-media giants might make sense in antitrust terms, but it would not help with political speech—indeed, by multiplying the number of platforms, it could make the industry harder to manage.

There are other remedies. The social-media companies should adjust their sites to make clearer if a post comes from a friend or a trusted source. They could accompany the sharing of posts with reminders of the harm from misinformation. Bots are often used to amplify political messages. Twitter could disallow the worst—or mark them as such. Most powerfully, they could adapt their algorithms to put clickbait lower down the feed. Because these changes cut against a business-model designed to monopolise attention, they may well have to be imposed by law or by a regulator.

Social media are being abused. But, with a will, society can harness them and revive that early dream of enlightenment. The stakes for liberal democracy could hardly be higher.

Print citations

CMS: "Do Social Media Threaten Democracy?" In *The Reference Shelf: Alternative Facts, Post-Truth, and the Information War*, edited by Betsy Maury, 21-23. Ipswich, MA: H.W. Wilson, 2018.

MLA: "Do Social Media Threaten Democracy?" *The Reference Shelf: Alternative Facts, Post-Truth, and the Information War*. Ed. Betsy Maury. Ipswich: H.W. Wilson, 2018. 21-23. Print.

APA: The Economist. (2018). Do social media threaten democracy? In Betsy Maury (Ed.), *The reference shelf: Alternative facts, post-truth, and the information war* (pp. 21-23). Ipswich, MA: H.W. Wilson. (Original work published 2017)

Language: The Most Disruptive Technology

by Charles Hill

Hoover Institution, October 12, 2017

This essay is an excerpt of a larger paper the author delivered at a conference of the Hoover Institution, "Governing in a Time of Technological Change."

Language is arguably the most fundamental human tool. At certain points in history, when other technologies have enhanced or damaged the use of language, major changes in world order have resulted. We are witnessing such a phenomenon now.

At present, a "language revolution" is under way, propelled by an eruption of electronic communication technologies that, while enhancing productivity, are also creating social and political chaos. The e-revolution in communication is now challenging, even threatening, the conduct of responsible governance. Thanks to digital technologies, marginal sociopaths are being empowered to organize and act collectively as never before; dictatorial regimes are perfecting powerful tools to monitor and suppress entire populations; and instantaneous popular judgments on political issues are beginning to overwhelm representative government as designed by the Founders to avoid the chaos-producing "direct" democracy of pre-modern societies.

The e-revolution in language is the next great "Revolution" in human history. Through it, any person anywhere in the world can instantly and constantly communicate with every other person. At the same time, technology has taken command of language to both serve technology and distort linguistic standards; one need only look at the average self-published book, blog post, or tweet for evidence. This process disrupts and corrodes the foundations of the modern era and shows no sign of being able to positively reconstruct from what it is tearing down.

In three significant cases, the modern approach is now being undermined by the disruptive powers of twenty-first-century language technology.

Empowering Sociopaths

Freud's *Civilization and its Discontents,* revealed that the benefits of civilized order and progress require the relegation of powerfully disruptive behaviors and desires to "the unconscious" mind. While many assume that societies primarily shape individuals, "Freud thought that it was the other way around," according to Louis Menand, "that society is just a macro form of the individual, and takes its imprint

From "Governing in a Time of Technological Change." A talk given at the Hoover Institution October 12, 2017. Reprinted with permission.

from individual psychology." Most today would agree that human and societal development is a two-way street, dependent on one another.

Today's social media distorts this relationship. Instant communication by way of platforms such as Twitter, make it possible for individuals to immediately express the slightest emotionally disruptive and damaging reaction to events or ideas to a worldwide audience. Opinions and private outbursts once perceived as self-harmful blunders, resolved by improving one's repressive subconscious mechanisms, are now instantly exposed to multitudes in permanent form. Civilization depends upon the time and ability to contain such eruptions; the "discontents" created by acts of self-control are the price of civil society. Were every discontent expressed, the public sphere would collapse as "all communication, all the time," instantly, produces a surrounding effect. As the astute columnist Peggy Noonan wrote, we are agitating and exciting "the unstable" sector of the population, a sector that increasingly grows larger, a Pandora's Box of once subconscious partisan venom breaking open as no one becomes able to suppress the slightest discontent.

Enlarging Dictatorial Powers

As the individual is "liberated" by the ability to promulgate unconstrained feelings in every direction, the governing regimes of the world are gaining new powers of surveillance, intrusion, and control over their populations. The 2011 "Arab Spring" uprisings were considered at first to be made possible by the new language-spreading technologies in every young person's hand; it was widely agreed, at the time, that such tools of expression would be beyond the abilities of dictators to control. Such an assumption was foolhardy; the Arab Spring was crushed in a few short months as the old powers—colonels, hereditary monarchs, strong-armed clans with puppet "parliaments"—regained control even as they were assaulted by even more ideologically autocratic radicals claiming religious dominion.

The major one-party authoritarian regimes, too, notably Russia and the People's Republic of China, are perfecting their own domination of the new languages of disruption: techniques of interception, cooperation, blockage, elimination, falsification, and more. This reality sharply reverses earlier assumptions that major multinational corporations would be replacing states as the most potent international entities. Recent steps by the People's Republic of China to assert "cyber-sovereignty" bear this out. When Apple had no choice but to accept the PRC's ban on "apps" that could bypass the regime's "Great Firewall of China," the power of the autocratic state over the private corporate entity was made clear to all.

This trend has begun to give authoritarian regimes unprecedented powers to suppress freedom of speech and to indoctrinate entire populations in twenty-first-century versions of Orwellian "Newspeak" such as China's propaganda that communism and capitalism are one and the same.

Disdaining the American Design: From Moderate Republic to Direct Democracy

Another recent phenomenon is the deterioration of respect traditionally given to "the deliberative process." This process, once deemed essential to the civil discourse of a polity, values balance and consensus over strident factionalism. Individuals and associations engaged in the political process were allowed the space, time, and confidentiality to examine and debate a range of options, unexposed to outside criticism, before reaching their decision and putting it before the public, and the opposing party's view. The new language technologies, combined with crowbar-like legal methods, have made the deliberative process nearly extinct. With every individual, insider or outsider, now in effect in possession of a recording, filming, broadcasting, and publicizing piece of handheld equipment, any and all varieties of thoughtful expression are so vulnerable to premature exposure that periods for careful deliberation prior to acts of decision have become rare. Equally troubling, even when such occasions are held, open discourse on policy is increasingly subject to political or legal risk.

Democracy itself, in the unique form designed by the Founders and described in Tocqueville's *Democracy in America*, is being disrupted by the new techniques of instantaneous language. To the ancient world, democracy was a tempting ideal, but understood to be dangerous, a producer of chaos that called forth a tyrant to restore order. Thucydides's Athens provided the classic case in point: swift, direct (thumbs up or down), with no patience for deliberation, and unable to prevent the deterioration of its language until "words lost their meaning." The result, as Alexander Hamilton wrote in *Federalist Papers* Number 6, was "that famous and fatal war, distinguished in the Grecian annals by the name of the Peloponnesian war; which, after various vicissitudes, intermissions, and renewals, terminated in the ruin of the Athenian commonwealth."

The result was the Founders' design for a republic that would be utterly unique: buffered against the dangers of mass decisions swiftly taken; checked and balanced, with separated powers and layered sovereignty; all within a concept of genius, *Federalist* Number 10, that would enable democracy to function effectively on a continental scale, the world's first, and still only, such example. The United States was, and still is, as Professor Samuel Huntington recognized, a "pre-modern" polity in a modern world. If the modern era is ending, the United States should be better suited to manage such change than any other nation.

But not if the safeguards that make America an exceptional democracy are forfeited, lost without awareness of how or why. Yet, the   e-revolution can do this. The array of techniques that turn language into instantaneous power of opinion, all in the touch of a screen or a handful of words, threatens to override the protections instituted when the republic was born.

The electronic revolution is a *language* revolution. Each of the revolutions of the modern age—French, Russian, Chinese—has brought ruination. The world is now afflicted by an Islamist revolution, begun after the collapse of the Ottoman Empire and Caliphate in the years after World War I. It produced the Islamic Republic of Iran in 1979, has been carried on by al-Qaeda and the Islamic State, and is violently opposed to every element of the established modern international state system. Like all modern revolutions, it promulgates a concocted language as a weapon of power.

> **Today's social media distorts this relationship. Instant communication by way of platforms such as Twitter, make it possible for individuals to immediately express the slightest emotionally disruptive and damaging reaction to events or ideas to a worldwide audience.**

Only the American Revolution understood that language, like any tool or technology, must be used with care. The Founders understood that decisions made *now*, by those with power *now*, thinking only about *now*, guarantee disaster.

Understanding the inextricable centrality of language to democracy begins with the way democracy in America was designed to overcome the flaws of ancient democracy. Athens in the Periclean Age was archetypically democratic: recognized as potentially the best form of governance, but also as dangerously prone to collapse. As portrayed in Thucydides's *Peloponnesian War*, Pericles spoke proudly of Athenian democracy as swift to act by the *direct* decisions of the *demos*, the people, and unencumbered by institutions that would delay such actions. But language broke down under political, military, and societal pressures; the undeliberated decision to send a naval expedition to Sicily failed because the values of patience and foresight, the proper allocation of resources, and mature deliberation lost meaning.

The Founders of the United States knew the story of Athens in the Peloponnesian War well. They were determined that America would become a free republic, not a direct democracy. It would be a government by representatives, with dispersed sovereignty, three equal branches of government, and a variety of "checks and balances."

Other political thinkers would add vitally important concepts to democracy in the modern world to overcome the problems faced in antiquity.

Kant, staying rigorously within the Enlightenment's requirement to employ "reason" alone without dependence upon outside foundational authorities, such as religion, argued his way step-by-step to demonstrate that the core of political success was *transparency* because the purpose of a state was justice, and that could only be had when the people were sovereign and could demand that their government's actions could be open to examination and approval. Transparency could only truly exist in a republic, and a republic's added advantage would be that a free people would be disinclined to go to war or would hasten to end a war if war could not be avoided.

Hegel, as noted earlier, added the centrality of history, specifically "the history of the *consciousness* of freedom." In other words, history had a direction, a progression, propelled by freedom.

Tocqueville supplemented this view, seeing democracy as a force of history observable across the past several hundred years. But he knew that only if "democracy in America" is conducted wisely can democracy continue its modern trajectory.

Two concerns were paramount. First, democracy's powerful pressure is for ever-greater equality. Equality is essential, but liberty must be maintained as well so that equality does not eradicate freedom in the drive to make all outcomes equal. Second, there is, Tocqueville observed, a distinctively American democratic logic chain: religion informs mores, which inform laws, which ensures liberty, and liberty protects religion. America is unique, Tocqueville said (we could also say "exceptional"), in that only in America are religion and liberty compatible; elsewhere, religion tends to suppress liberty, and liberty tends to resent and resist the demands of religion. But in America, religion sees liberty as the protector of its observances, and liberty sees religion as the cradle of its birth (as when the New England Puritan congregation was easily transposed into the town meeting.)

The e-revolution in communication is doing damage to this Tocquevillian narrative of American exceptionalism by making every issue "presentist" as a matter of struggles for power in current politics. If "history" appears in this battle for supremacy in current events, it is ignorantly distorted in the service of scoring power points here and now.

Print Citations

CMS: Hill, Charles. "Language: The Most Disruptive Technology." In *The Reference Shelf: Alternative Facts, Post-Truth, and the Information War*, edited by Betsy Maury, 24-28. Ipswich, MA: H.W. Wilson, 2018.

MLA: Hill, Charles. "Language: The Most Disruptive Technology." *The Reference Shelf: Alternative Facts, Post-Truth, and the Information War*. Ed. Betsy Maury. Ipswich: H.W. Wilson, 2018. 24-28. Print.

APA: Hill, C. (2017) Language: The Most Disruptive Technology. In Betsy Maury (Ed.), *The reference shelf: Alternative facts, post-truth, and the information war* (pp. 24-28). Ipswich, MA: H.W. Wilson. (Original work published 2017)

2

Bad Actors in the Information War

U.S. Deputy Attorney General Rod Rosenstein announces the indictment of 13 Russian nationals and 3 Russian organizations for meddling in the 2016 U.S. presidential election February 16, 2018 at the Justice Department in Washington, DC. The indictments are the first charges brought by special counsel Robert Mueller while investigating interference in the election.

Offenders in the Information War

Who is responsible for the state of the modern media environment? Are foreign actors manipulating American consumers? Are unscrupulous political propagandists clouding the reality of political debates? Many different individuals and groups have been identified as contributors to the "fake news" and media legitimacy debate, some within the United States and some participating in the creation and distribution of fake news from abroad. Opinions differ as to whether one or more of these actors have had a major impact or whether the entire controversy has been exaggerated by the critics who most acutely perceive a threat.

Foreign Influence

The revelation that the government of Russia attempted to influence the outcome of the 2016 election and to support the presidency of Donald Trump has become the most well-known and controversial example of foreign participation in the media legitimacy debate. A 2018 article from *Time* magazine featured an interview with St. Petersburg, Russia resident Vitaly Bespalov, who was hired to be a professional "Internet troll." The term "troll" has developed to refer to a person who posts intentionally inflammatory comments to incite emotional reactions from others. Sometimes trolls troll for fun or amusement, while, in some situations trolls can be used to achieve a political goal.

Professional troll Bespalov told *Time* that his job was to create fake accounts on social media and then to use those accounts to post comments delivered to him by his superiors. This then became part of a state-run effort to influence the outcome of US elections. Investigators at the Federal Bureau of Investigation (FBI) believe that Russian trolls are not only targeting the United States but were using information warfare to influence politics in many different nations. For instance, Bespalov was instructed to depict Barack Obama as unintelligent, while Angela Merkel of Germany was supposed to be depicted as fascist.[1]

The overall goal is not entirely understood, but it is generally believed that Russians equated the election of Donald Trump as a destabilizing factor, broadening partisan divides so as to render the nation less effective and influential on the global stage. However, it is not well known how effective or influential the Russian campaign was. Some believe that the impact was significant, while others argue that Russian actors were merely imitating content already created by other Americans and thus added little to the misinformation already generated within the nation.[2]

Russia's use of misinformation as a tool for cyberwarfare is only one of several sources of foreign fake news affecting America's political discourse. Researchers in 2017 found a host of teenage and young adult entrepreneurs in Veles, Macedonia who developed an industry manufacturing fake articles to attract American social media users. As the sites and posts these young Macedonians create attract views, sometimes millions of them, advertisers become interested and the Macedonian content creators profit through ad revenues based on the number of hits, shares, likes, and views that their fake stories receive. The town of Veles, with a population of 55,000, hosted 100 pro-Trump websites disseminating fake news to American consumers containing claims such as a popular meme that Hillary Clinton was going to be indicted on criminal charges or that the pope supports Trump, when in fact the pope has criticized Trump's behavior as president.[3]

The Presidential Angle

Donald Trump is one of the most important actors in the fake news controversy within the United States. In part this is because President Trump has adopted a political strategy of claiming any media that is critical of him or his administration is "fake news." To provide one of many examples, in February Trump met with leaders of several US-based companies doing business overseas. Trump then announced that his meetings resulted in the companies in question deciding to bring more jobs back to the United States. Numerous media outlets reported that the jobs returning to the United States were not the result of Trump's meetings. Trump reacted to this by claiming that the mainstream media was lying about his role.

On February 3, Trump tweeted: "Totally biased @NBCNews went out of its way to say that the big announcement from Ford, G.M., Lockheed & others that jobs are coming back...to the U.S., but had nothing to do with TRUMP, is more FAKE NEWS. Ask top CEO's of those companies for real facts. Came back because of me!"

News outlets then did as Trump suggested and asked the "top CEO's" of those companies what impact Trump had on the return of jobs to the United States. The decision to reinvest in the United States, according to those executives, had been developing for several years and was not a result of Trump's election.

When *Fox News* commentator Neil Cavuto asked Ford CEO Mark Fields, "Would you have done this [the moves announced] if Donald Trump were not elected president?" Fields answered "Yes, absolutely." Similarly, General Motors CEO Mary Barra agreed that Trump's influence was not the key factor, and told reporters that, in the auto industry, "Decisions of products that we are launching right now were made, two, three, four years ago. Over the last two years, we've invested $11 billion in the United States."[4]

In another example, on November 27, 2016, Trump tweeted: "in addition to winning the Electoral College in a landslide, I won the popular vote if you deduct the millions of people who voted illegally."

In response, election officials around the country responsible for identifying and preventing voting fraud issued reports on illegal voting in the 2016 elections. It is important to note, that the nation's election officials represent the Republican and Democratic parties. Some are conservative, others are liberal, and some have mixed ideological views. Across the nation, these officials objected to Trump's claim, asserting that there was no evidence to suggest widespread voter fraud. For instance, the state of Tennessee identified 40 suspicious but not definitively fraudulent ballots out of 4.3 million, while Georgia found 25 possible instances of voting fraud out of 4.1 million votes.[5]

Trump's claim that at least 3 million illegal votes were cast in the election, by illegal immigrants, is an example of a demonstrably false claim. For this claim to be true, one would have to believe that hundreds of individuals representing all of America's political parties, some of whom are supporters of Trump himself, are involved in a conspiracy to cover up the fraud the president claims occurred. Trump did not retract the claim or suggest that he might've been in error and refused to answer requests for him to validate his claims with a source. Reporters were only able to find one possible source for the false claim, an Internet post purportedly from an individual who witnessed millions of illegal migrants voting in California.

Internal Dissent

Those creating fake news within the United States are also motivated by profit and power, either earning revenues by attracting consumers or trying to promote a political view by using misinformation to call attention to what they see as a real issue. Like the fake news industry in Macedonia, American companies like Disinfomedia purposefully create fake stories as a way to earn a profit through social media advertising revenues. Being that US citizens who work as fake news creators live within the nation, these architects are better able to read the local political environment and so many of the claims that they post and publish speak to more specific political debates. Disinfomedia's products are aimed primarily at the far-right and conservative readers. Another domestic fake news company, National Report, was discontinued in 2014 but was well known for an often shared story claiming that President Barack Obama used federal government funding to keep a Muslim museum open during the federal government shutdown in 2013.

Psychological researchers exploring his issue explain that the ability to reason is influenced by emotion and individuals who have highly charged emotional reactions to certain issues are less able to reason effectively with regard to claims associated with those beliefs. Every ideological group is therefore predisposed to be more susceptible to mistaken beliefs or false claims regarding issues in which they perceive a personal, and emotional stake.[6] This does not explain, however, why so much of the misinformation in the modern environment is directed at right-wing consumers. A study from Oxford University published in 2018 found that individuals identifying as "Trump supporters," were responsible for producing or sharing 95 percent of fake news items that appeared on Twitter. On Facebook, 91 percent of fake news stories were also associated with far-right consumers and producers.[7] The right-wing campaign against the legitimacy of the mainstream media may hold the key to understanding the current conservative predisposition.

A study at Fairleigh Dickinson University found that news readers and consumers who list National Public Radio as their chief source of information were able to answer specific questions about current events better than those listing any other source. Persons who listed *Fox News* as their primary source performed the worst of all respondents in terms of being able to answer questions about current events.[8] This study was criticized for methodology, though no subsequent research disproved the study's findings. A 2015 study by conservative economist Bruce Bartlett published in 2015 found similar results, that Fox News, the mainstay of conservative media, created a highly-skewed and unrealistic view of key issues.[9]

Before Donald Trump, perceptions of left-wing bias in mainstream media led to a movement against mainstream news sources among some factions of the conservative population. This seems to have intensified through networks like Fox News that repeatedly promote the idea that there is an information war against the conservative ideology. Donald Trump has since taken this to the next level, suggesting that any mainstream media outlet that criticizes his performance or presidency, should be seen by his supporters as "fake news." It is therefore possible that the long-term conservative attack on the legitimacy of mainstream media has left conservative consumers with few trusted sources for legitimate information. Further, the suggestion that mainstream news is fake suggests a conspiratorial dimension to the news environment that might predispose those who embrace this view to seek out nontraditional sources and so leave them vulnerable to manipulation through individuals using fake news for profit or political gain.

Micah L. Issitt

Works Used

Bartlett, Bruce. "How Fox News Changed American Media and Political Dynamics." *SSRN*. Elsevier. June 4, 2015. Web. 23 Feb 2018.

Beaujon, Andrew. "Survey: NPR's Listeners Best-Informed, Fox Viewers Worst-Informed." *Poynter*. The Poynter Institute. May 23, 2012. Web. 23 Feb 2018.

Carroll, Aaron E. "Not Up for Debate: The Science Behind Vaccination." *The New York Times*. The New York Times, Co. Sep 17, 2015. Web. 23 Feb 2018.

Douthat, Ross. "The Trolling of the American Mind." *The New York Times*. The New York Times, Co. Feb 21, 2018. Web. 23 Feb 2018.

Farley, "Trump: Jobs Returning 'Because of Me'." *Factcheck*. Annenberg Public Policy Center. The Wire. Jan 21, 2017. Web. 23 Feb 2018.

Maheshwari, Sapna. "10 Times Trump Spread Fake News." *The New York Times*. The New York Times Co. Jan 18, 2017. Web. 23 Feb 2018.

Mooney, Chris. "What Is Motivated Reasoning? How Does It Work? Dan Kahan Answers." *Discover Magazine*. The Intersection. May 5, 2011. Web. 23 Feb 2018.

Narayanan, Vidya, et al. "Polarization, Partisanship and Junk News Consumption over Social Media in the US." *Comprop Data Memo*. Oxford University. February 6, 2018. Web. 23 Feb 2018.

Shuster, Simon and Sandra Ifraimova. "A Former Russian Troll Explains How to Spread Fake News." *Time*. Time, Inc. Feb 21, 2018. Web. 23 Feb 2018.

Subramanian, Samanth. "Inside the Macedonian Fake-News Complex." *Wired*. Condé Nast. Feb 15, 2017. Web. 23 Feb 2018.

Wines, Michael. "All This Talk of Voter Fraud? Across U.S., Officials Found Next to None." *The New York Times*. The New York Times, Co. Dec 18, 2016. Web. 23 Feb 2018.

Notes

1. Shuster and Ifraimova, "A Former Russian Troll Explains How to Spread Fake News."
2. Douthat, "The Trolling of the American Mind."
3. Subramanian, Samanth. "Inside the Macedonian Fake-News Complex."
4. Farley, " Trump: Jobs Returning 'Because of Me'."
5. Wines, "All This Talk of Voter Fraud? Across U.S., Officials Found Next to None."
6. Mooney, "What Is Motivated Reasoning? How Does It Work? Dan Kahan Answers."
7. Narayanan, et al., "Polarization, Partisanship and Junk News Consumption over Social Media in the US."
8. Beaujon, "Survey: NPR's Listeneners Best-Informed, Fox Viewers Worst-Informed."
9. Bartlett, "How Fox News Changed American Media and Political Dynamics."

The New Information Warfare

By Murtaza Hussain

The Intercept, November 25, 2017

Decades before smartphones, the internet, and social media, philosopher Marshall McLuhan, who worked on media theory, predicted a future world war fought using information. While World War I and World War II were waged using armies and mobilized economies, "World War III [will be] a guerrilla information war with no division between military and civilian participation," McLuhan said, a prophecy included in his 1970 book of reflections, *Culture Is Our Business*.

McLuhan's prediction may have felt outlandish in his own era, but it seems very close to our present-day reality. Decades ago, the barriers to entry for broadcasting and publishing were so high that only established institutions could meaningfully engage in news dissemination. But over the past 10 to 15 years, ordinary individuals have been radically empowered with the ability to record, publish, and broadcast information to millions around the world, at minimal cost.

The revolutionary impact of this new information environment—where any individual or network of individuals can create their own mini-CNN—is transforming our societies. The loss of gatekeeping authority held by legacy media institutions has opened up opportunities for long-suppressed groups to have their narratives heard: Palestinians, African-American activists, feminists, environmentalists, and dissident groups working in authoritarian societies can all find ways, not always without some trouble, to be heard.

This new media landscape, though, also created a world susceptible to unprecedented levels of propaganda, conspiracy, and disinformation. The epistemological chaos created by the global explosion of "news," some of it of questionable veracity, has already led to serious disruptions in both politics and daily life. But there is another area of life that might be most seriously impacted by the changing information landscape: armed conflict.

Propaganda and information warfare was once the purview of nation-states, militaries, and intelligence services. Today, even ordinary people have become important players in these campaigns. Battles over narratives and information have become an integral part of modern war and politics; the role played by bloggers, activists, and "citizen journalists" in shaping narratives has proven vital.

The examples are rapidly piling up in the second decade of the 21st century. Citizen journalists and accidental activists helped change the course of history during uprisings in Egypt, Bahrain, Tunisia, Syria, and Libya—as well as during Israel's

2014 war against Palestinians in the occupied Gaza Strip. Very quickly, people who were once considered to be victims of war and great-power politics have become empowered as political actors. During Israel's 2014 bombardment of Gaza and the 2016 Russian aerial bombardment of the rebel-held Syrian city of Aleppo, young women and children came to international attention for their updates from war zones, helping wage battles to shape global public opinion.

Distinct from traditional information operations waged by states, the narratives of ordinary people and activists benefit from a greater sense of personal authenticity and emotional connection. This currency has always been difficult for institutions to capture, but comes naturally to individuals and activists. Social media's ability to bypass traditional media gatekeepers also blew apart the biggest barriers to marginalized voices being heard: political and corporate control over publishing.

"Powerful institutions still exist and remain very powerful, but there is another currency that has emerged because of social media and the internet, which you might call authenticity or emotional appeal," says Matt Sienkiewicz, an assistant professor of communication and international studies at Boston College and the author of *The Other Air Force: U.S. Efforts to Reshape Middle Eastern Media Since 9/11*.

"Everyone focuses on the producers of media in shaping public opinion, but it's really at the distribution level of information where the bottleneck has traditionally been," adds Sienkiewicz. "This is what social media has fundamentally changed. There is a lot of focus on the ugly side, with respect to viral conspiracies and misinformation—but there is also reason to be optimistic, because many stories that would've been ignored before are now being heard."

The emergence of online citizen journalism has also, however, increasingly blurred the distinction between participants and non-participants in conflict, as well as activists and journalists. For those lacking decent media education, discerning truth from falsehood is becoming an increasingly Sisyphean task.

Picking through the pieces of the past few years, a few writers have begun to examine the ways that social media is shaping our understanding and experience of modern conflict and politics. *War in 140 Characters*, by the journalist and author David Patrikarakos, and *Digital World War*, by Haroon Ullah, an author and former U.S. State Department official, both represent early attempts to understand the gravity of our current information crisis.

With the lines of armed conflicts' central distinctions already being blurred—between peacetime and war, combatant and civilian—social media has the potential to draw the entire world into a gray zone where the lines between participants and non-participants in conflict are unclear. Whereas the last World War was a clearly defined clash of nation-states with uniformed armies, our new era of tech-driven information warfare holds the potential to become so amorphous and all-encompassing that it could seep into every aspect of society, transforming the experience of both politics and war in the process.

The 2014 war between Israel and Palestinian factions in the Gaza Strip was perhaps the first war in which social media was successfully employed as a radical levelling force by the weaker party. In previous wars between Israel and the Palestinians, the Israeli government's ability to manage access to the battlefield allowed it to help shape the narra-

> **Propaganda and information warfare was once the purview of nation-states, militaries, and intelligence services. Today, even ordinary people have become important players in these campaigns.**

tive of the war, portraying it the way that it preferred—as a fight against terrorism. But with the proliferation of smartphones and social media accounts in Gaza over the past several years, this conflict wound up being viewed very differently by a variety of observers.

As bombs rained down on Gaza neighborhoods, following a pattern that included the killing and maiming of many ordinary people, Palestinians rushed to social media to share their own narrative of the war. Young men and women living in the Strip shared photos of apparent atrocities committed against civilians, alongside often emotional updates about their own experiences trying to survive the Israeli military onslaught. In previous conflicts, most of these voices would never have been heard. Broadcast directly onto the global public spheres of Twitter and Facebook, however, accounts of Palestinian suffering and resistance became impossible for the world to ignore.

Writing in Middle East Eye on social media's role in the conflict, Yousef al-Helou reflected:

> Even when the power was out, citizen journalists managed to post pictures of dead bodies, destroyed neighborhoods and injured people to the outside world. Photography has always been a powerful force, but the Gaza conflict was one of the first wars to be photographed mainly by amateurs and social media platforms, allowing those images to spread far and wide at the click of a button, helping the people of Gaza win hearts and minds, and subsequently causing unprecedented outrage against Israel. In demonstrations around the world, such photos were enlarged and carried by demonstrators, demanding that their respective governments take action to halt Israel's onslaught.

As the public outcry over the war grew, even establishment media outlets in the U.S. were forced to take note of the Palestinian experience of the conflict. In response to the growing public relations disaster caused by images of dead Gazan civilians, Israeli Prime Minister Benjamin Netanyahu accused the Hamas government in the territory of using "telegenically dead Palestinians for their cause"—a statement that did little to quell rising international outrage over the civilian deaths.

In military terms, there was no real parity between the two sides. By the time the conflict ended, more than 2,100 Palestinians had been killed, compared with just 66 Israelis. The physical infrastructure of the besieged territory suffered devastating damage, with Israeli attacks crippling water and power sources to Gaza residents. Despite their advantage in brute strength, the lopsided death toll, and destruction of only one party's territory, it's not clear that the Israelis won the conflict. In the battle over the narrative of the war—vitally important in a conflict whose power dynamics are strongly impacted by outside actors—the Palestinians managed to win significant traction for their cause.

Instead of another case of the Israeli military attacking an amorphous group of Islamist terrorists, a counternarrative of the conflict spread globally. In this version of events, Israel was not a democratic state waging a war of self-defense against terrorists, but a U.S.-backed military behemoth pummeling the people of an impoverished territory. The death toll seemingly proved to the world that disproportionate force was being inflicted on a weak and isolated territory.

"During Protective Edge"—the name the Israeli military gave to the campaign—"the people who suffered most were Palestinians, under siege from Israel's superior military force," Patrikarakos writes in his book. "This is the democratization of the wartime narrative in action, and it benefitted only one side: the Palestinians."

During the war, no one was more emblematic of the changing power dynamics than Farah Baker, a 16-year-old Palestinian girl who came to international attention for her social media updates about life in Gaza. Baker was not tied to any political group, and her perspective on the war was a personal one. Yet her social media presence catapulted her to global attention and told the Palestinian story to the world in a way that resonated emotionally. It also empowered Baker as a political actor, something that she had never expected and that could never have occurred in any previous conflict.

Normally, a young teenage girl living under aerial bombardment would have been considered a bystander, at best, or a victim, at worst. But thanks to her Twitter feed, where she shared both her fears as well as her attempts to maintain a normal life amid the war, Farah became an important part of the Palestinian effort to sway global opinion on the conflict.

"At only sixteen, Farah understood, even if only instinctively, the importance of social media in wartime, especially to a perpetual underdog like the Palestinians," Patrikarakos wrote. "She understood the power that it gave to a single individual and to networks of individuals, power that previously would have been impossible."

In Gaza, like in Syria and Ukraine, there have been instances of alleged faked suffering and atrocity spread for propaganda purposes. Here, too, social media has changed the way the conflict is perceived. Through social media's ability to give accounts from multiple separate sources on the ground, verify information, and share evidence, outside observers can better evaluate the credibility of reports from the ground.

During the Gaza conflict, the Israeli Defense Forces attempted to rebut the onslaught of Palestinian citizen journalism with their own information war, disseminating infographics and videos intended to show the Israeli side of the story. Ultimately, the Israelis were at a disadvantage. The personal authenticity of Gaza's tech-savvy young people resonated more naturally with observing audiences than the official statements and flashy messaging released by Israeli military officials, messages that were indelibly stamped with the alienating face of a bureaucracy.

The impact of this disparity was notable. In a column in *Foreign Policy* following the war, titled *On Israel's Defeat in Gaza*, international relations scholar David Roth-kopf reflected on the global impact of the scenes of mayhem that had ensued in Gaza, including images of young children being killed on a beach by Israeli military forces. "There is no Iron Dome" —a sophisticated and expensive Israeli missile de-fense system— "that can undo the images of suffering and destruction burned into our memories or justify away the damage to Israel's legitimacy that comes from such wanton slaughter," Rothkopf wrote.

While Barack Obama's presidential administration stood by Israel during the conflict, calling for restraint from both sides, two years later, as he prepared to leave office, the U.S. took the significant step of distancing itself from Israel at the United Nations by allowing an anti-settlement resolution to pass—a rare instance of the U.S. acceding to public censure of Israeli actions. While far from a sea-change in America's stance on the conflict, the move reflected growing dissatisfaction with Israeli actions in the United States, which, though not shared by the Trump admin-istration, continue to be echoed by high-ranking former officials.

In her own small way, with her tweets and updates during the war, Farah Baker had played a role in shifting the narrative and forcing the world to grapple with the Palestinian narrative of the conflict.

"I don't have the ability to carry a weapon and I would never kill anyone, so my only weapon was to broadcast the truth and to let people know what was happening here," Baker told Patrikarakos in an interview at her Gaza home. "I was more effec-tive than I ever imagined, because of the amount of followers I got and because so many people told me I had changed their minds [about the war] and opened their eyes."

During the initial upsurge of enthusiasm about the 2011 Arab Spring revolu-tions, observers noted how effectively social media had been used as an organiz-ing tool by young activists. While it would be overstating the case to attribute the revolutions themselves to social media (as some of the more breathless analyses did at the time), the impact that online social networks, cellphones, and new satellite television stations had on mobilizing and informing people in these societies was undeniable. The idea of young people using social media to topple dictatorships played into the narrative of "tech-utopianism," still in vogue at the time, stimulating the idea that future political changes might be organized from below through the liberating power of the internet.

The grim years that followed the initial uprisings have mostly dispelled this nar-rative. While liberal activists were adept at organizing online, so were political Is-lamists and jihadi groups. These groups were better funded, better organized, and already had experience operating clandestinely—using the latest technologies for propaganda, recruitment, and networking. Over time, it would be Islamist groups like the Muslim Brotherhood, as well as jihadis, that moved into the vanguard of the revolutions, pushing aside the liberal activists who had initially captured the world's imagination.

"Digital World War" is an analysis of how opposition movements, and Islamists in particular, have used social media as a tool of waging war against established governments. Haroon Ullah is a former State Department official and expert on Pakistan's Jamaat-e-Islami movement. Unlike Patrikarakos's book, *Digital World War* is a staid academic analysis of how social media and other new technologies are altering the dynamics between central governments and opposition movements, both Islamist and liberal. But Ullah's work also addresses the crux of how social media is upending the traditional power dynamics governing war and politics.

Perhaps the most destabilizing aspect of new technologies is the way that they have potentially supercharged the speed of political change. Youth-led revolutions in Egypt and Tunisia began and ended within a matter of weeks, toppling governments that had been in place for decades. Although both countries had suffered from long-standing structural problems, the sparks for both uprisings were lit over individual outrages—corruption and police brutality—that were spread and rapidly popularized over social media. Though many bystanders later joined the protests for other reasons, the speed and scale with which people initially organized would have been impossible in an era before cellphones and the internet.

The very speed of these movements, however, made it hard to build a sustainable order out of the collapse of the old regimes. While it was true that online mobilization played a role in toppling both Egyptian strongman Hosni Mubarak and Tunisian dictator Zine El Abidine Ben Ali, it also allowed little time for real leaders to emerge or for political platforms to be agreed upon. While the people who went into the streets were united in their indignation over injustice and their opposition to the old order, they had very different ideas about the future of their countries. When the regimes collapsed, the only parties established enough to take advantage were those aligned with the long-suppressed Muslim Brotherhood.

"It was not a matter of Islam being some defining feature of Tunisian identity—despite the Islamists claims," Ullah writes, regarding the Tunisian revolution and the subsequent election of the liberal Islamist party Ennahda, "Rather, the victory was the natural outcome of the inevitable schism between the nature of the revolution and the readiness of the Islamists for power."

Social media is not the first information technology that has had helped galvanize revolutionary change. Radio, telegraph, and even the printing press all helped precipitate major socio-political transformations in the past, the latter famously helping enable the Christian Reformation.

More recently, the groundwork for the 1979 Iranian Revolution was laid with the help of a relatively new technology: Popular speeches by the revolution's leader, Ayatollah Ruhollah Khomeini, were recorded and copied onto cassette tapes, which were then rapidly replicated and distributed. Unlike social media movements that can close the cycle between outrage and protest to a matter of days, however, it took Khomeini years of painstaking media work to help build mass support for an opposition movement in Iran. By the time the that Iranians finally went into the streets against the Shah—motivated by many different ideological currents—Khomeini was a well-known and popular spiritual leader within the opposition. When the monarchy fell, he was well-placed to marginalize his ideological rivals and consolidate clerical power over the country.

The difference between Iran's uprising and the leaderless revolutions of today is vast and points to one of the major pitfalls of internet activism. Online organizing and propaganda can be legitimately useful for destabilizing regimes, especially rigidly authoritarian ones that need to strictly control the flow of information. But because of the speed with which it can precipitate change, it is less useful for building up the networks and organizations needed to fill the gap created when old governments actually fall.

"When there is no single leader to focus a political movement—Khomeini, Mandela, Lenin —there may be more and faster revolutions than previously, but there are fewer revolutionary outcomes and scenarios," Ullah writes. "So when a dictatorship—by definition and decree the sole and strongest institution in a country—is deposed by insurrections like the Arab Spring, what comes into the place of the power vacuum is not dictated by those who have created it."

In a 2007 paper titled "Of Networks and Nations," John Arquilla, an expert of new patterns of warfare at the Naval Postgraduate School, argued that loosely knit sets of global and regional networks, enabled by the internet, had begun to challenge the authority of nation-states in the same way that nation-states had challenged the authority of empires a century earlier.

In recent years, transnational militant groups, civil society activists, and hackers have all been able to inflict defeats on lumbering state adversaries, in part by leveraging the speed of connectivity and communication afforded by the internet. "The networks came to push, to prod, and to confront. They came to solve the supranational problems of injustice, inequity and environmental degradation that a nation-based capitalist system could never, in their view, deal with adequately," wrote Arquilla. "In short, the networks came to change things, and they came not in peace but with swords."

The 21st century has seen the rise of "gray-zone conflicts," where armed force, politics, and media increasingly blur together, such as the 2014 war between Israel and the Palestinians. Gray-zone conflicts are seldom interstate wars but are more likely to be civil uprisings, conflicts between states and militant groups, and domestic insurgences. As scholars David Barno and Nora Bensahel have written, these conflicts "involve some aggression or use of force, but in many ways their defining characteristic is ambiguity—about the ultimate objectives, the participants, whether international treaties and norms have been violated, and the role that military forces should play in response."

It is within this ambiguous environment that information warfare waged online by activist groups and individuals is playing a critical, at times even definitive role. As the dominance over information flows held by nation-states evaporates, their ability to control the trajectory of conflicts by managing international opinion and maintaining domestic authority is eroding as well.

The threat of this change, as well as the political impact of viral misinformation, has led to calls from some corners for greater regulation and involvement by tech companies in putting curbs on online speech. Although improved media education for the general public is likely necessary, any nostalgia for an earlier era when information was controlled by a few hegemonic media institutions is wildly misplaced.

"If we allow the problems that exist with social media and new technologies to be used as a pretext to roll things back, it would be the ultimate crime," says Sienkiewicz. "The old media environment in which billions of people had little access to getting their stories told—in which entire classes of people were effectively deemed by media institutions as not worth reporting on – is not something that we should want to return to. We should address the problems that exist with new media, not try to turn back the clock and deem this all a failed experiment."

For better or worse, thanks to social media and smartphones, a version of the "guerilla world war" predicted by Marshall McLuhan—a war over information drawing in states, militaries, activists, and ordinary people in equal measure—has come into existence. The consequences are likely to transform politics, conflict, and daily life for generations to come. McLuhan himself suggested that surviving in this new world would be possible only through a conscious embrace of change, rather than a retreat into reactionary policies.

"The new technological environments generate the most pain among those least prepared to alter their old value structures," he said, in a 1969 interview with *Playboy* Magazine. "When an individual or social group feels that its whole identity is jeopardized by social or psychic change, its natural reaction is to lash out in defensive fury."

"But for all their lamentations, the revolution has already taken place."

Print citations

CMS: Hussain, Murtaza. "The New Information Warfare." In *The Reference Shelf: Alternative Facts, Post-Truth, and the Information War*, edited by Betsy Maury, 37-44. Ipswich, MA: H.W. Wilson, 2018.

MLA: Hussain, Murtaza. "The New Information Warfare." *The Reference Shelf: Alternative Facts, Post-Truth, and the Information War*. Ed. Betsy Maury. Ipswich: H.W. Wilson, 2018. 37-44. Print.

APA: Murtaza, H. (2018). "The new information warfare." In Betsy Maury (Ed.), *The reference shelf: Alternative facts, post-truth, and the information war* (pp. 37-44). Ipswich, MA: H.W. Wilson. (Original work published 2017)

Why Is Finland Able to Fend Off Putin's Information War?

By Reid Standish
Foreign Policy, March 1, 2017

With elections coming up this year in France, Germany, the Netherlands, the Czech Republic, and perhaps Italy, European intelligence services across the Continent have been sounding the alarm about Russian attempts to influence the outcome though targeted disinformation and propaganda, as they appeared to do in the U.S. presidential election.

That brand of information war can range from pushing fake news stories and conspiracy theories to fanning the flames of existing problems—all serving to undermine public confidence in governments and institutions. Elsewhere in the Baltics and former Soviet Union, Russian-linked disinformation has worked to stoke panic and force local governments into knee-jerk, counterproductive responses that have boosted Kremlin goals across the region.

But in the face of this mounting pressure, one of Russia's neighbors has emerged unusually resistant to the wider information war waged by Moscow across Europe: Finland.

Like other countries along the Baltic Sea or in Eastern Europe, Finland has seen a notable increase in fake news stories and propaganda targeted against it that can be linked back to Russia since Moscow's annexation of Crimea in 2014. These attacks have sought to undermine the government and often coincided with military shows of force along the Russian border.

But unlike its neighbors, Helsinki reckons it has the tools to effectively resist any information attack from its eastern neighbor. Finnish officials believe their country's strong public education system, long history of balancing Russia, and a comprehensive government strategy allow it to deflect coordinated propaganda and disinformation.

"The best way to respond is less by correcting the information, and more about having your own positive narrative and sticking to it," Jed Willard, director of the Franklin Delano Roosevelt Center for Global Engagement at Harvard, told Foreign Policy. Willard, who is currently working for the Swedish government, was hired by Finnish officials to help them develop a public diplomacy program to understand and identify why false information goes viral and how to counter propaganda.

That initiative started at the top. In October 2015, Finnish President Sauli

Niinisto took the first step, when he acknowledged that information warfare is real for Finland, and said that it was the duty of every citizen to combat it. In January 2016, the prime minister's office enrolled 100 officials in a program across several levels of the Finnish government to identify and understand the spread of disinformation based on Willard's advice.

Lots of governments in the West don't have the same kind of narrative to respond with as does Helsinki.

A homogeneous country of 5.4 million people, Finland routinely ranks at the top of the Organisation for Economic Co-operation and Development's quality of life metrics and, in addition to strong social welfare programs, the country's education system is the best in the world, according to the World Economic Forum.

Willard says this combination of widespread critical thinking skills among the Finnish population and a coherent government response makes a strong defense against concerted outside efforts to skew reality and undermine faith in institutions.

"This stuff is real. It is as real as war," said Willard. "But the Finns very quickly realized this and got out in front of the problem."

René Nyberg, a former Finnish ambassador to Moscow, says Finland has a couple of key advantages when it comes to parrying Russian disinformation. Helsinki is painfully well-versed in dealing with Russia, as it has had to do through war and annexation, and most recently the decades-long staring match of the Cold War. That left Finland with a sober understanding of the Kremlin's real motives. Plus, it helps that Finland is not Russia's main target when it comes to undermining European unity.

"The real intensity is Germany … Merkel is the main course," Nyberg told FP. "We're just a side dish."

The case of the false "Lisa story" in Germany from January 2016 is often cited as a textbook example of Moscow's modern information capabilities. Russian-language media reported allegations that a 13-yearold Russian-German girl had been raped by migrants in Berlin before local authorities had time to verify the information; those Russian reports were then picked up by mainstream news media in Germany and elsewhere. When the story was finally de-

> **Finnish officials believe their country's strong public education system, long history of balancing Russia, and a comprehensive government strategy allow it to deflect coordinated propaganda and disinformation.**

bunked, subsequent accusations of a cover-up by Berlin were reported by Channel One, Russia's prime state TV station, and were even hinted at by Russian Foreign Minister Sergei Lavrov, who said the incident "was hushed up for a long time for some reason" during a press conference. The spread of the false story also prompted protests across the country by anti-immigrant groups and Russian Germans.

Experts say it's nearly impossible to track the extent to which these pro-Russian positions are directly shaped by the Kremlin. Indeed, to be most effective, Moscow does not invent issues out of whole cloth, they say. Instead, disinformation attacks seek to inflame existing tensions by putting out viral web stories that would then be republished by local news outlets and on social media to distort political debates about wedge issues like the European Union, immigration, and NATO.

Weaponizing information has a long history in Russia, and the Kremlin ran an extensive operation to subvert the West in Soviet times. In an age of social media where news can quickly spread around the globe, Russia deployed its arsenal of trolls, propaganda, and false information to a new level that has allowed Moscow to perfect its techniques over the last decade. These techniques have even become enshrined in official Kremlin doctrine.

But responding to such tactics can often backfire and risks replicating the Kremlin-backed narrative. Estonia, Latvia, and Lithuania—as well as other former Soviet countries like Ukraine and Georgia—have been less successful in pushing back against Russian disinformation.

Pro-Russian media, including the state-owned Channel One, already reach huge numbers of homes across the former Soviet Union. In the Baltic states, which have large Russian-speaking minorities, attempts to restrict or ban Russian broadcasters, websites, or journalists have often polarized relations with the local Russian community and given more material for Kremlin-backed propaganda and disinformation. In Ukraine and Georgia, Russian propaganda often amplifies and distorts the very real problem of state corruption, seeking to destroy confidence in pro-Western political parties.

In contrast, Finland, which ranks as the world's third-least corrupt country according to Transparency International, and which has only a tiny Russian-speaking population, has fewer obvious targets to be exploited. In March 2016, the Finnish-language bureau for *Sputnik*, the state-funded Russian media outlet, closed after it failed to attract enough readers.

"Nothing has been very harmful for the public so far," Markku Mantila, director general for government communications at the Finnish prime minister's office, told FP. "Finns are well-educated and because of that, we are very resilient to such attempts."

But Finland does have one thing that drives the Kremlin to distraction: an 830-mile border with Russia. Fears over NATO's eastward expansion—including, potentially, to Finland—are behind much of Russia's aggressive posture toward the West.

Finnish officials claim to have documented 20 disinformation campaigns against their country that have come directly from the Kremlin. Those attempts tend to focus on a narrow but sensitive topic: Helsinki's carefully balanced relations with Moscow.

After two wars with Russia in two years in the 1940s, Finland during the Cold War followed a carefully crafted policy of neutrality, allowing it to balance integration with Europe while maintaining good relations with the Soviet giant next door.

The country refrained from joining NATO and often bowed to Moscow's wishes to preserve its independence, a stance that some Western detractors condemned as too accommodating to the Soviets. Cold Warriors even dubbed it, derisively, "Finlandization."

Following the collapse of the Soviet Union in 1991, Helsinki quickly distanced itself from its Cold War legacy, but the country's policymakers still walk a tightrope with Russia.

Public opinion on NATO membership is strongly divided, making Finland an important target for Russia as it seeks to influence the public discourse of its neighbors and sow divisions in Europe.

Russian disinformation campaigns have spun a narrative of the Finnish government discriminating against ethnic Russians. In February, reports of dual Russian-Finnish citizens being rejected from military and foreign service jobs became a talking point in pro-Kremlin media in Russia. A measure discussed in Finnish parliament to prevent Russian citizens from owning land near military sites also rallied the pro-Kremlin propaganda machine. A similar line of attack, which has involved doctored photos, saw Kremlin outlets accuse Finnish authorities of child abduction in disputes arising over child welfare and custody battles for Finnish-Russian marriages. The accusations, which Finnish officials deny, first materialized in 2012, but continue to flare up—giving Russian lawmakers more opportunity to make inflammatory statements about their neighbor.

"It's not just about Finland's relationship with Russia," Saara Jantunen, the author of *Info-War*, a book about Russian disinformation in Finland, told FP. "It's about showing what kind of rhetoric in Finnish society and the media is acceptable."

One noticeable aspect of the Kremlin's approach in other parts of Europe is to support anti-establishment forces, which often parrot pro-Russian positions. A similar dynamic is at play in the case of Jessikka Aro, an investigative journalist for the social media division of Finland's state broadcaster, Yle Kioski.

In 2014, Aro followed up on reports of a Russian "troll factory" in St. Petersburg that was seeking to influence public opinion in the West about Kremlin maneuvers abroad. After she published her initial investigation, which documented how pro-Russian voices were attempted to shape the public discourse on Ukraine, her name appeared on Russian nationalist websites where she was derided as a Western intelligence agent, bombarded with anonymous abusive messages on social media, and labeled a drug dealer.

The man who became the main voice targeting Aro was Johan Backman. An outspoken supporter of the Kremlin who is fluent in Russian, Backman—a Finn—was responsible for the bulk of the derisive commentary that appeared about Aro. Backman serves as the representative in Northern Europe for the Russian Institute for Strategic Studies, a state-funded research group known for its Kremlin connections during the Cold War and currently led by a Soviet-era intelligence officer. Backman has defended his commentary as free speech.

MV-lehti—a Finnish-language news site hosted abroad that is known for its right-wing, anti-immigrant, and anti-EU views—also produced some of the false information about Aro. Ilja Janitskin, the news site's founder and head who lives in Spain, told the *New York Times* in 2016 that he had no connections to Moscow. Still, both men are currently being investigated by Finnish police for harassment and hate speech for targeting Aro.

Finnish authorities have been trying to extradite Janitskin from Spain, but he is currently on the run.

Adding another layer to the case, the Helsinki police department announced in October 2016 that an employee from Yle, the Finnish broadcaster for whom Aro works, is suspected of providing the information that was later used to defame her. The case is awaiting a date in court.

Aro told FP that she became a target because her reporting brought into question Helsinki's traditionally measured line with Moscow.

"NATO is at the core of everything," Aro said. "The goal of these campaigns is to discredit the voices in Finland that are critical of Russia."

Print citations

CMS: Standish, Reid. "Why Is Finland Able to Fend Off Putin's Information War?" In *The Reference Shelf: Alternative Facts, Post-Truth, and the Information War*, edited by Betsy Maury, 45-49. Ipswich, MA: H.W. Wilson, 2018.

MLA: Standish, Reid. "Why Is Finland Able to Fend Off Putin's Information War?" *The Reference Shelf: Alternative Facts, Post-Truth, and the Information War*. Ed. Betsy Maury. Ipswich: H.W. Wilson, 2018. 45-49. Print.

APA: Standish, R. (2018). Why is Finland able to fend off Putin's information war? In Betsy Maury (Ed.), *The reference shelf: Alternative facts, post-truth, and the information war* (pp. 45-49). Ipswich, MA: H.W. Wilson. (Original work published 2017)

We Tracked Down a Fake-News Creator in the Suburbs: Here's What We Learned

By Laura Sydell
NPR, November 23, 2016

A lot of fake and misleading news stories were shared across social media during the election. One that got a lot of traffic had this headline: "FBI Agent Suspected In Hillary Email Leaks Found Dead In Apparent Murder-Suicide." The story is completely false, but it was shared on Facebook over half a million times.

We wondered who was behind that story and why it was written. It appeared on a site that had the look and feel of a local newspaper. *Denverguardian.com* even had the local weather. But it had only one news story—the fake one.

We tried to look up who owned it and hit a wall. The site was registered anonymously. So we brought in some professional help.

By day, John Jansen is head of engineering at Master-McNeil Inc., a tech company in Berkeley, Calif. In the interest of real news he helped us track down the owner of *Denverguardian.com*.

Jansen started by looking at the site's history. "Commonly that's called scraping or crawling websites," he says.

Jansen is kind of like an archaeologist. He says that nothing you do on the Web disappears—it just gets buried—like a fossil. But if you do some digging you'll find those fossils and learn a lot of history.

The "Denver Guardian" was built and designed using a pretty common platform—WordPress. It's used by bloggers and people who want to create their own websites. Jansen found that the first entry ever for the site was done by someone with the handle LetTexasSecede.

"That was sort of the thread that started to unravel everything," Jansen says. "I was able to track that through to a bunch of other sites which are where that handle is also present."

The sites include *NationalReport.net*, *USAToday.com.co*, *WashingtonPost.com.co*. All the addresses linked to a single rented server inside Amazon Web Services. That meant they were all very likely owned by the same company. Jansen found an email address on one of those sites and was able to link that address to a name: Jestin Coler.

Online, Coler was listed as the founder and CEO of a company called Disinfomedia. Coler's LinkedIn profile said he once sold magazine subscriptions, worked as a database administrator and as a freelance writer for among others, *International Yachtsman* magazine. And, using his name, we found a home address.

On a warm, sunny afternoon I set out with a producer for a suburb of Los Angeles. Coler lived in a middle-class neighborhood of pastel-colored one-story beach bungalows. His home had an unwatered lawn—probably the result of California's ongoing drought. There was a black minivan in the driveway and a large prominent American flag.

We rang the front doorbell and a man answered, his face obscured by a heavy mesh steel screen. I asked for Jestin Coler. The man indicated that's who he was. But when I asked about Disinfomedia, he said, "I don't know what to tell you guys. Have a good day."

We left Coler our contact information thinking he wasn't likely to talk. But a couple of hours later he had a change of heart. He sent us an email and we set up an interview.

Coler is a soft-spoken 40-year-old with a wife and two kids. He says he got into fake news around 2013 to highlight the extremism of the white nationalist alt-right.

"The whole idea from the start was to build a site that could kind of infiltrate the echo chambers of the alt-right, publish blatantly or fictional stories and then be able to publicly denounce those stories and point out the fact that they were fiction," Coler says.

He was amazed at how quickly fake news could spread and how easily people believe it. He wrote one fake story for *NationalReport.net* about how customers in Colorado marijuana shops were using food stamps to buy pot.

"What that turned into was a state representative in the House in Colorado proposing actual legislation to prevent people from using their food stamps to buy marijuana based on something that had just never happened," Coler says.

During the run-up to the presidential election, fake news really took off. "It was just anybody with a blog can get on there and find a big, huge Facebook group of kind of rabid Trump supporters just waiting to eat up this red meat that they're about to get served," Coler says. "It caused an explosion in the number of sites. I mean, my gosh, the number of just fake accounts on Facebook exploded during the Trump election."

Coler says his writers have tried to write fake news for liberals—but they just never take the bait.

Coler's company, Disinfomedia, owns many faux news sites—he won't say how many. But he says his is one of the biggest fake-news businesses out there, which makes him a sort of godfather of the industry.

At any given time, Coler says, he has between 20 and 25 writers. And it was one of them who wrote the story in the "Denver Guardian" that an FBI agent who leaked Clinton emails was killed. Coler says that over 10 days the site got 1.6 million views. He says stories like this work because they fit into existing right-wing conspiracy theories.

"The people wanted to hear this," he says. "So all it took was to write that story. Everything about it was fictional: the town, the people, the sheriff, the FBI guy. And then ... our social media guys kind of go out and do a little dropping it throughout Trump groups and Trump forums and boy it spread like wildfire."

And as the stories spread, Coler makes money from the ads on his websites. He wouldn't give exact figures, but he says stories about other fake-news proprietors making between $10,000 and $30,000 a month apply to him. Coler fits into a pattern of other faux news sites that make good money, especially by targeting Trump supporters.

However, Coler insists this is not about money. It's about showing how easily fake news spreads. And fake news spread wide and far before the election. When I pointed out to Coler that the money gave him a lot of incentive to keep doing it regardless of the impact, he admitted that was "correct."

Coler says he has tried to shine a light on the problem of fake news. He has spoken to the media about it. But those organizations didn't know who he actually was. He gave them a fake name: Allen Montgomery.

Coler, a registered Democrat, says he has no regrets about his fake news empire. He doesn't think fake news swayed the election.

"There are many factors as to why Trump won that don't involve fake news," he says. "As much as I like Hillary, she was a poor candidate. She brought in a lot of baggage."

Coler doesn't think fake news is going away. One of his sites—*NationalReport. net*—was flagged as fake news under a new Google policy, and Google stopped running ads on it. But Coler had other options.

"There are literally hundreds of ad networks," he says. "Early last week, my inbox was just filled every day with people because they knew that Google was cracking down—hundreds of people wanting to work with my sites."

Coler says he has been talking it over with his wife and may be getting out of the fake-news racket. But, he says, dozens, maybe hundreds of entrepreneurs will be ready to take his place. And he thinks it will only get harder to tell their websites from real news sites. They know now that fake news sells and they will only be in it for the money.

Below are highlights of NPR's interview with Coler.

Interview Highlights

Tell me a little about why you started Disinfomedia?

Late 2012, early 2013 I was spending a lot of time researching what is now being referred to as the alt-right. I identified a problem with the news that they were spreading and created Disinfomedia as a response to that. The whole idea from the start was to build a site that could infiltrate the echo chambers of the alt-right, publish blatantly false or fictional stories and then be able to publicly denounce those stories and point out the fact that they were fiction.

What got you engaged in this?

My educational background is in political science. I've always enjoyed the ideas of propaganda and misinformation. Then I coupled that with an interest in what makes things go viral. So that led me to finding those groups and ultimately to finding contributors. But it was just something I had an interest in that I wanted to pursue.

When did you notice that fake news does best with Trump supporters?

Well, this isn't just a Trump-supporter problem. This is a right-wing issue. Sarah Palin's famous blasting of the lamestream media is kind of record and testament to the rise of these kinds of people. The post-fact era is what I would refer to it as. This isn't something that started with Trump. This is something that's been in the works for a while. His whole campaign was this thing of discrediting mainstream media sources, which is one of those dog whistles to his supporters. When we were coming up with headlines it's always kind of about the red meat. Trump really got into the red meat. He knew who his base was. He knew how to feed them a constant diet of this red meat.

> Coler's company, Disinfomedia, owns many faux news sites—he won't say how many. But he says his is one of the biggest fake-news businesses out there, which makes him a sort of godfather of the industry.

We've tried to do similar things to liberals. It just has never worked, it never takes off. You'll get debunked within the first two comments and then the whole thing just kind of fizzles out.

How many domains do you own and run?

Well, I would say there's somewhere around 25 domains that I am currently managing. *National Report* has been my bread and butter, where I've spent most of my time. I have people who work with me and for me in developing and maintaining the other sites and social media kind of stuff. [Coler later said not all his sites are fake news.] So I, for the most part, focus on *National Report*, and a lot of the other stuff is run by other folks on the team.

So, you're the publisher of an empire.

Well I wouldn't go so far as to call it an empire but, yes, it's several sites [chuckle].

How many people do you have writing for you?

It comes and goes, and as for actual employed writers, again these guys sort of make their own money through ad code. So I don't say, 'Hey, you have to write 10 stories this week' and this and that. Really, we have a more free-form idea where people, when their creativity strikes them then they can write something. And if they're in a slump then they just go dormant for a while. With that said, at any given time there's probably 20, 25 contributors all over the country. ...

Talk about the "Denver Guardian."

Well, it's kind of a side project. We have some people working on next steps in the fake-news industry, and that came from that whole discussion. We had purchased several domain names that sounded legitimate. ... More local news sort of stories. The idea was to make the sites look as legit as possible so the home page is going to be local news and local forecast, local sports, some obituaries and things of that nature, and then the actual fake news stories were going to be buried off the home page.

We've tried lots of things in the past. The dot-com-dot-co domains were something I toyed in for a while. Those I quickly got away from because you don't get away long with borrowing someone's copyright or trademark. That was something that worked very well from a fake-news perspective. People were fooled into the domain name, but that wasn't so much what we were after. So again, the next step was to go after more city-type sites. And the "Denver Guardian" was one of those sites.

You're talking about the future of this (fake-news business) which looks more insidious because it's more real?

That's the way that it's going to be. Not just from where I am. I mean, this is probably going to be my last run in the fake-news biz, but I can promise you that it's not going to go away. It's even going to grow bigger and it's going to be harder to identify as it kind of evolves through these steps. ...

Do you know who wrote the actual FBI Clinton story?

I do know who wrote the story, but only through an anonymous pen name. Privacy is something that we take very seriously in our writers group. The actual reasonings behind that story ... it's one of hundreds that have been written about mysterious deaths of Clinton associates or political foes. This one kind of took off more than others, I believe, just because of the nature of the story. The people wanted to hear this. So all it took was to write that story. Everything about it was fictional. The town, the people, the sheriff, the FBI guy. Then, we had our social media guys kind of go out and do a little dropping it throughout Trump groups and Trump forums and boy it spread like wildfire.

Why hide your identity?

This isn't the safest business to be in, to be honest. Just the number of death threats I've received. I have a beautiful family, a beautiful life.

Some of these people that we ... bait is probably the right word—are often— let's call them the deplorables, right? They're not the safest crowd. Some of them I would consider domestic terrorists. So they're just not people that I want to be knocking on my door.

It seems like National Report ***is getting spoofier.***

If you went to *National Report* today, it's specifically satire. "Chris Christie nominated to Supreme Food Court." "Sarah Palin Banning Muslims from Entering Bristol

Palin." They're a little bit more offensive than some people care for their satire. I mean fat-shaming and slut-shaming isn't something that is normally met with applause. But again, it's a lot more fun in nature.

Do you make serious money?

It depends on what you would call serious money. I think I do pretty well.

Can you say how well?

I would rather not. There have been some people who have been reported on recently. The folks in Long Beach that were doing just all right stuff. They were reporting $10,000 to $30,000 a month; I think that's probably a relative ballpark.

So you're doing as well as those?

Yes.

You're making money through the ads?

Yes.

Who do you work with?

We have several advertisers. Google was one, although they shut down my account last week. We've replaced them with other advertisers.

Can I ask who?

There are literally hundreds of ad networks. Literally hundreds. Last week my inbox was just filled everyday with people, because they knew that Google was cracking down—hundreds of people wanting to work with my sites. I kind of applaud Google for their steps, although I think what they're doing is kind of random. They don't really have a process in place for identifying these things. I happen to know a very successful site that, as of today, of this morning is still serving Google ads. So it seems to be a kind of arbitrary step that they're taking either based on, I don't know if it was my reputation within the industry or specifically the "Denver Guardian" site that angered them, or I don't know what it is, but back to your question, there's hundreds of people that will work with me.

What can be done about fake news?

Some of this has to fall on the readers themselves. The consumers of content have to be better at identifying this stuff. We have a whole nation of media-illiterate people. Really, there needs to be something done.

Do you consider yourself an entrepreneur?

Sure.

Are you one of the biggest in the fake-news biz?

If you look at someone who has specifically sometimes peddled in fictional news then I think that I would probably be considered one of the larger sites.

As a liberal, do you have any regrets?

I don't. Again, this is something that I've been crying about for a while. But outside of that, there are many factors as to why Trump won that don't involve fake news, right? As much as I like Hillary, she was a poor candidate. She brought in a lot of baggage.

You don't feel responsible.

I do not.

Do you think you would have kept doing it if it wasn't so lucrative?

Really, the financial part of it isn't the only motivator for me. I do enjoy making a mess of the people that share the content that comes out of our site. It's not just the financial incentive for me. I still enjoy the game I guess.

Would you do this all over again?

Well, I guess it came to a head here and we're talking about it. It'll be interesting to see what happens moving forward. If I had to, if I knew specifically the "Denver Guardian" situation, that would have been handled differently. But everything else, as far as the work I've done with *National Report*, I'm very proud of, and I'm going to continue doing it.

Print citations

CMS: Sydell, Laura. "We Tracked Down a Fake-News Creator in the Suburbs: Here's What We Learned." In *The Reference Shelf: Alternative Facts, Post-Truth, and the Information War*, edited by Betsy Maury, 50-56. Ipswich, MA: H.W. Wilson, 2018.

MLA: Sydell, Laura. "We Tracked Down a Fake-News Creator in the Suburbs: Here's What We Learned." *The Reference Shelf: Alternative Facts, Post-Truth, and the Information War*. Ed. Betsy Maury. Ipswich: H.W. Wilson, 2018. 50-56. Print.

APA: Sydell, L. (2018). We tracked down a fake-news creator in the suburbs: Here's what we learned. In Betsy Maury (Ed.), *The reference shelf: Alternative facts, post-truth, and the information war* (pp. 50-56). Ipswich, MA: H.W. Wilson. (Original work published 2016)

Tone-Deaf: How Facebook Misread America's Mood on Russia

By Deepa Seetharaman, Robert McMillan and Georgia Wells
The Wall Street Journal, March 2, 2018

Weeks after Facebook, Inc. disclosed it had been exploited by Russia-backed propagandists, the company was still underestimating its problems, with users and advertisers and, crucially, Washington.

At an October off-the-record conference of tech-industry elites in Hawaii, Facebook's head of advertising, Rob Goldman, defended Facebook's response and argued the Russians bought ads to exploit social divisions, not primarily to sway the 2016 U.S. presidential election, say people who heard his remarks. It struck some attendees as tone-deaf. "There was not a lot of contrition there," said one attendee.

Last month, Mr. Goldman made a similar argument publicly, following an indictment by special counsel Robert Mueller of Russians allegedly involved in the influence campaign. On Twitter, he criticized the media, touted Facebook's steps to address Russian manipulation and suggested there were "easy" solutions to the problem that included a better-educated population. He said influencing the election wasn't the "main goal" of the Russian ads, which some in Washington interpreted as contradicting the indictment.

Facebook users, advertisers and Democrats in Washington slammed the tweets as a sign the company's leaders still hadn't reckoned with its role in the Russian campaign. Facebook said Mr. Goldman was stating his own views. He later apologized to colleagues for the controversy.

It isn't clear whether the Russian activity on Facebook made a difference in the election, a position some Facebook executives still privately maintain, and no evidence has emerged that it tipped the result to President Donald Trump. What is clear, however, is that the social-media giant's months-long obliviousness to deepening public concern about its social impact has worsened a backlash against it and other Silicon Valley giants.

That misjudgment appears particularly to have fueled new tension between Facebook and Democrats, who had long been close to the company. "Facebook was very slow to recognize the scope of the problem," Virginia Democratic Senator Mark Warner said in an email to *The Wall Street Journal* on Wednesday. "I think they have taken some important steps, but they still have a lot more work to do to eliminate opportunities for manipulation of their services."

Facebook, which generated $40 billion in annual revenue from its ability to narrowly target advertisers' messages to receptive audiences, failed repeatedly to grasp what message its own actions were sending, especially in Washington. Last fall, it expected accolades for proactively disclosing information about the Russian ad buys—but instead faced complaints it wasn't sharing enough. Facebook responded with more data, but each disclosure fueled more questions about what else it knew but hadn't revealed.

First alert

Facebook's executive team was alerted to the potential Russian manipulation efforts in a December 9, 2016, memo from the company's security team, say people familiar with the memo. But the company waited nine months before publicly saying that Russian manipulation had occurred.

That disclosure was followed by a cascade of further disclosures as public anger grew, with Facebook acknowledging in an October congressional hearing that the Russian efforts had reached 126 million people.

"They were in denial about the size of the problem and in denial about the effect it was having," says Clint Watts, a former Federal Bureau of Investigation counterterrorism agent now at the Foreign Policy Research Institute, a Philadelphia-based think tank. Mr. Watts added that Facebook has done more to address the Russian issue than other tech companies, but has borne the brunt of public criticism.

Asked to comment for this article, Facebook's vice president of global policy, Joel Kaplan, in a written statement said: "The issue of Russian election interference on our platform is something we continued to learn more about as we conducted our own internal reviews and provided information to law enforcement officials and legislators to inform their own inquiries."

"At each stage of the process, we have worked to share as much information as possible with the appropriate authorities and with the public," he said.

Chief Executive Mark Zuckerberg has said he is "dead serious" about stopping foreign manipulation of Facebook. In January, he devoted 2018 to "fixing" a litany of problems facing the company and has said publicly he was willing to forfeit some short-term profitability to do so. Facebook has shared the Russian ads, account names and other data with Mr. Mueller's team as well as with Congress.

Russia has denied trying to influence the election. A Russian Embassy spokesman in Washington referred inquiries to comments by Russia's foreign minister stating that the Mueller indictment lacked evidence. A spokesman for Mr. Mueller declined to comment and referred to a Justice Department news release saying it had received "exceptional cooperation" from Facebook.

Facebook executives say they were caught off-guard by the Russian activity. Many of them privately argue Facebook has been unfairly singled out because it has been more forthcoming with information than Alphabet Inc.'s Google and Twitter Inc., both of which were misused by the Russians, according to the Mueller indictment.

"It's a combination of the company coming to terms with the responsibility that comes with the power we have and then us realizing that there are a lot of people in the me-

> **'Personally I think the idea that fake news on Facebook...influenced the election in any way is a pretty crazy idea.'**
> **—CEO Mark Zuckerberg, November 2016**

dia who want to blame us for everything," says one Facebook employee.

The controversy over Russian manipulation has contributed to the biggest image crisis in Facebook's 14-year history. Since the 2016 election, it has been lambasted for allowing objectionable content, including violent live videos and fabricated news articles, to proliferate on its service.

Mr. Zuckerberg has sought to shape Facebook's mission as transcending sales and profit. He said when the company went public in 2012 that it was "built to make the world more open and connected," a goal he enhanced in February 2017 to include building global "social infrastructure" to fight problems such as disease.

By the time of that statement, Russia's alleged efforts to use Facebook and other social-media platforms to undermine U.S. democracy were well under way, according to the Mueller indictment. A pro-Kremlin group, the Internet Research Agency, or IRA, started around July 2013 and later began its social-media offensive to interfere in the 2016 U.S. presidential race and "spread distrust towards the candidates and the political system in general," the indictment says.

In that era, Facebook's security efforts were focused on hackers, spam and other more-traditional threats, say people familiar with the company's efforts.

That started to change after the election. Facebook's security team sent a memo in December 2016 to Mr. Zuckerberg, Chief Operating Officer Sheryl Sandberg and other senior officials outlining how Russian-backed actors tried to leak stolen information from the Democratic Party on Facebook, people familiar with the memo say. The memo warned that there could be other Russian activity on the platform that hadn't yet been detected.

The next month, the U.S. intelligence community said in a declassified report that the IRA interfered with the election. At that point, Facebook got more serious about weeding out Russian influence, say people familiar with Facebook's response.

Over the next several months, Facebook built special tools to gather more evidence of Russian manipulation. The security team, led by Chief Security Officer Alex Stamos, began drafting a report detailing the extent of what they knew about the various "information operations" on the platform, some of the people say.

There was internal tension over how much to reveal. Facebook's security team was pushing to mention Russia's role in the report, the Journal reported in October. Policy and legal officials, resisted, saying it was risky for a private company to call out a foreign state and Facebook needed to be sure, say people familiar with the episode.

On April 27, Facebook had released a 13-page report about information operations on its platform that didn't mention Russia. By June, Facebook had found pages it suspected were set up by Russians to spread misinformation and play different sides of divisive political issues to fuel disputes—but Facebook didn't publicly disclose the discovery—people familiar with the company's Russia probe say.

Facebook's lack of public disclosure was angering lawmakers. In late May, Senator Warner and his staff flew to Facebook's Menlo Park, Calif., headquarters and repeatedly asked executives if Russian actors bought ads on the platform, a Warner aide says. Facebook said it hadn't found evidence, say people familiar with the response, but the meeting prompted a deeper probe into the ad system.

A Facebook spokesman told the *Journal* on July 14 the company had no evidence of Russian entities buying ads on its platform related to the presidential election.

By late July, Facebook researchers were confident the IRA had bought Facebook ads. The company found ads used to try to attract new "likes" for

> '**After the election, I made a comment that I thought the idea misinformation on Facebook changed the outcome of the election was a crazy idea. Calling that crazy was dismissive and I regret it.'**
> **—Mr. Zuckerberg, September 2017**

divisive Facebook groups that appeared to be backed by the IRA, a person familiar with the efforts says. Researchers linked the ads back to a group of 400 accounts, not all of which bought ads, this person says.

The reluctance to speak openly about Russia in part reflected Facebook's concerns about hurting its public image, say some people familiar with the company's response at the time. In early 2017, an internal metric closely watched by Facebook as a measure of user sentiment—the "good for the world" metric—slipped slightly, says a person familiar with the figures.

Reluctance to speak

The reticence also reflected a limited view in Facebook about the extent of its responsibilities, several current and former executives say. Facebook still viewed itself as a young company fighting for survival and united under Mr. Zuckerberg's mission to connect the world, they say.

"You're so focused on building good stuff," says Mike Hoefflinger, a former Facebook executive who published a book about Facebook's corporate culture in 2017, "you're not sitting there thinking, if we get lucky enough to build this thing and get two and a quarter billion people to use it, then this other bad stuff could happen."

Indeed, while the security team worked to uncover Russian accounts through 2017, Facebook assigned a small team to boost user growth in Russia and other markets, says a person familiar with the team. The team considered developing Russia-specific products such as a music service, although it didn't launch it, the person says.

Facebook ran into snags in Washington. Over the summer, it contacted Mr. Mueller's team about the ads and fake accounts. To complicate matters, the Mueller probe had legal powers that went beyond those available to Congress and had issued a gag order preventing Facebook from talking about its work with Mr. Mueller in much detail, say people familiar with the matter. So while Facebook was able to hand over complete data on the Russian ads to the special counsel, it wasn't able to seek public credit for that.

Also, its lawyers initially felt unable to provide the same level of information to Congress because of their interpretation of the company's privacy policies, these people say.

On Sept. 6, when Facebook disclosed that the IRA accounts bought $100,000 in ads, lawmakers were angered when it wouldn't show them the full library of ads.

The blowback startled Facebook. Employees expected more credit for disclosing the information.

Facebook lawyers examined the company's policies, eventually finding a loophole that allowed them to share more information.

On September 21, Mr. Zuckerberg's first day back from paternity leave, he broadcast live from Facebook and outlined nine changes it would make to prevent foreign meddling, including handing the IRA ads to Congress.

In October, Mr. Goldman, the Facebook ad chief, flew to Hawaii for the conference. During an impromptu discussion, he defended Facebook's handling of the Russia crisis and said it was taking aggressive steps to shore up its ad systems, say people familiar with his remarks. He argued that the Russian ads were primarily intended to sow division, the people say.

Many attendees pushed back. Someone asked Mr. Goldman about the fact that the Russians bought ads in rubles, drawing laughter from the crowd. "I wouldn't say there were jeers," one attendee says, "but there were eye rolls."

Some Facebook executives agree with Mr. Goldman's view that Russian Facebook ads weren't primarily intended to shape the election, say people familiar with the sentiments.

The feeling that Facebook was being singled out solidified after its top lawyer fielded the bulk of the questioning during the congressional hearings on October 31 and November 1.

Within Facebook, Mr. Goldman's February 16 tweets didn't initially cause much commotion, say people inside the company, until Mr. Trump retweeted one, triggering fury from Trump opponents and creating another political mess for Facebook.

Facebook's communications team spent the Presidents Day long weekend debating a public response to the furor that would respect Mr. Mueller's probe without drawing Mr. Trump's ire, say people familiar with the debate. Employees asked in internal forums if Mr. Goldman's views reflected Facebook's latest position on the Russia probe, another person says, adding, "people kind of freaked out internally."

After Facebook distanced itself from Mr. Goldman's tweets, Mr. Zuckerberg did the same the following week during a companywide question-and-answer session, people familiar with his comments say.

Print Citations

CMS: Seetharaman, Deepa, Robert McMillan and Georgia Wells. "Tone-Deaf:How Facebook Misread America's Mood on Russia." In *The Reference Shelf: Alternative Facts, Post-Truth, and the Information War*, edited by Betsy Maury, 57-62. Ipswich, MA: H.W. Wilson, 2018.

MLA: Seetharaman, Deepa, Robert McMillan and Georgia Wells. "Tone-Deaf:How Facebook Misread America's Mood on Russia." *The Reference Shelf: Alternative Facts, Post-Truth, and the Information War*. Ed. Betsy Maury. Ipswich: H.W. Wilson, 2018. 57-62. Print.

APA: Seetharaman, D., McMillan, R. and Wells, G. (2018). Tone-Deaf: How Facebook Misread America's Mood on Russia. In Betsy Maury (Ed.), *The reference shelf: Alternative facts, post-truth, and the information war* (pp. 57-62). Ipswich, MA: H.W. Wilson. (Original work published 2016)

3
Media vs. The Algorithm

Richard Salgado, director of law enforcement and information security with Google Inc., from right, Sean Edgett, acting general counsel with Twitter, Inc., and Colin Stretch, general counsel with Facebook, Inc., listen during a Senate Judiciary Crime and Terrorism Subcommittee hearing in Washington, D.C., U.S., on Tuesday, Oct. 31, 2017 Congress is putting Facebook, Twitter and Google under a public microscope about Russia's use of their networks to meddle in the 2016 election, a day after Special Counsel Robert Mueller's criminal investigation disclosed its first indictments and guilty plea.

The Interest Equation

Should media cover President Trump's personal tweets? Should social media companies filter news media based on what their users seem to want? One of the central issues in the information debate of 2018 concerns how news is generated and whether or not the current actors in the media market are creating a problem.

Algorithm Ethics

An algorithm is a computer code or set of codes used to carry out a certain set of instructions. An algorithm can therefore be thought of as an action plan for a computer. Once a task is given to the computer, the algorithm determines what steps are taken and in what order. The algorithms used by social media companies determine what appears in a person's news feed and this is seen by critics as a factor in the state of the modern media environment. The algorithms used by social media companies create aggregate maps of a person's interests based on their behavior online. By tracking where individuals go on the Internet, the types of media that a person engages with, and tapping into "trends" for people who are lumped together in certain categories, social media companies present news and suggestions to users based on these algorithmic categorizations.

The use of algorithms has generated numerous controversies. For one thing, consumer data is the currency of the social media environment, generating advertising revenues by collecting and selling information about consumers as well as compiling profiles of consumers that can then be used to offer advertisers a way to target people who are more likely to be interested in their products. The wealth of information available on the Internet is thus filtered through a set of corporate considerations determining what information a person receives based on his or her history of engagement and susceptibility to marketing. Privacy is one aspect of the controversy over algorithms, with consumers increasingly forced to choose between convenience and engagement in new media and their right to privacy and ability to resist corporate manipulation.

In the news environment, algorithms are used to calculate what information to present to users. On one hand, this means that algorithms give information, but, in reality, the primary function of news and media algorithms is necessarily to restrict information flow. This is because the volumes of possible information is far greater than would be useful for a system meant to deliver media of interest to a consumer. Algorithms like this function both in search engine rankings and in calculating the kind of information that appears in a person's news feed, or in the "suggestions" given to individuals about products or services. Because algorithms shape a person's information environment, the use of such algorithms raises other ethical issues and these news and information algorithms were identified as a major factor in the spread of "fake news," propaganda, and misinformation in the 2016 election.

Another controversial aspect of the increasing use of algorithms is the fact that consumers have not been provided with sufficient information to develop informed opinions about how this process works. The algorithms used by Twitter and Facebook are trade secrets and both companies refuse to release information about how these algorithms work on the basis that doing so would limit their ability to compete in the market. However, without information, consumers using social media are participating in a system about which they understand little and so cannot judge the ethical or moral implications of their online behaviors, preferences, and the methods used by companies to influence their thoughts and behaviors.[1]

Privacy and Legitimacy

A 2016 *Pew Research* report found that 74 percent of Americans believe it is "very important" to be able to control who can get information about them, and 91 percent of Americans believe that consumers have lost control of how personal data is collected and used by companies.[2] Public opinion might therefore be seen as support for stronger regulation over the collection and use of private information and yet, this has not occurred because businesses spend billions in political lobbying to resist such regulation and justify this by arguing that free market competition is a more effective control on the behavior of companies than governmental rules or regulations.

In a 2014 poll of tech and privacy experts by *Pew Research* the authors found expert-consensus on three factors collectively influencing the modern social media culture and industry: The inherent laziness of consumers who choose convenience over protecting their data or evaluating their media activities, the inherent exploitation of the free-market system in which companies function to maximize profit and not to produce products that are better for consumers in terms of protecting consumer interests, and the domination of America's political environment by the influential pro-business lobby.[3]

Concentrating specifically on the effect of algorithms on the news environment, critics are concerned that algorithmic influence increases the tendency for consumers to become trapped in "echo chambers" or "social media bubbles" wherein, more and more, the information they see comes from a limited number of sources reinforcing, rather than challenging their views. A conservative person who regularly visits conservative media sites will thus see more and more conservative media sites in his or her newsfeed and in recommendations for future consumption. This makes sense for advertisers, who want to deliver their products to consumers most likely to support their products, but also creates the impression of consensus.

For instance, there is a small group of individuals sometimes called "birthers," who put forth the theory that former President Barack Obama was secretly a Muslim. There is no legitimate evidence to support this theory, and plenty of evidence to refute it, but the conspiratorial idea nevertheless remained popular. In 2011, Trump said in a radio interview speaking about Obama's allegedly mysterious birth certificate, "Now, somebody told me—and I have no idea if this is bad for him or not, but perhaps it would be—that where it says 'religion,' it might have said 'Muslim'."[4]

So, though not willing to give a full-throated endorsement, Trump clearly also liked the theory that Obama was secretly Muslim. Imagine a person who does a fair amount of Internet research on this issue, coupled with reading other right-wing publications and blogs. The social media algorithm will start to suggest similar stories and ideas and, before long, the person is seeing so many news items, Tweets, and posts connecting Obama with Islam that it begins to appear that is part of a legitimate consensus view. By following and amplifying the user's habits as representations of his or her tastes, the algorithm can give the illusory sense of validity, such that even a completely false idea can be imbued with a sense of relevance and import far greater than it deserves in the broader marketplace of ideas.

In January 2018, a Pew Research report found that residents of 38 countries surveyed overwhelmingly agreed that they wanted unbiased coverage of political issues. In the United States, a full 78 percent of consumers say they want accurate and unbiased news coverage.[5] Polls like these show that the public, in general, wishes to avoid illegitimate and politically biased news and yet, for those who receive news through algorithmic delivery, the corporate model makes it more likely that they will receive biased news and misinformation. Algorithms are corporate tools that maximize advertising efforts but are also designed to give users a personalized experience. As the system currently exists, accessing these features, apps, and games is linked to accepting privacy policies that give partial ownership of all data to the companies marketing and selling that data. Thus, consumers are left with a puzzling conundrum, where the best way to minimize manipulation and to avoid corporate invasions of privacy requires opting out of the modern frontier of technology and the many conveniences that the use of this technology represents.

Ultimately, critics are now asking an important question, are social media companies and Internet search engines entertainment or news agencies? Increasingly, social media companies are functioning as news agencies, determining, through often obscure methods, what kind of news a person consumes and yet, by claiming that their services are for entertainment purposes, and that they are simply a forum for free speech, these companies claim they are not bound by journalistic ethics. Some critics are now suggesting that social media and Internet companies need to make a choice, to either remove themselves from the news environment entirely, or to embrace that they have an ethical role and take steps to ensure that the information presented through their services is clearly defined for readers.

Media Culpability

Other critics of the current media environment have argued that traditional news sources are increasingly following in the wake of social media, investing in covering minor news items rather than impactful issues. For instance, a 2017 study of the 2016 election coverage found that 1-in-6 studies about Donald Trump referenced or examined one of Trump's tweets and that 85 percent of stories covering a Trump tweet focused on personality and leadership, rather than substantive political issues or policies.[6]

A 2016 study released by the Shorenstein Center at Harvard University claimed that the media failed the public in the 2016 election by focusing on sensationalism and negativity, which had a corrosive effect on the public perception of the media. Overwhelmingly negative coverage of Trump was thus increasingly seen as partisan, though many of the criticisms of Trump were legitimate beyond partisan preference. Critics thus allege that, had the media focused on covering issues, on debates about the benefits of various policies, a more realistic view of the contest might have been created. Further the negative tone of news stories about key issues, including immigration, Muslims, healthcare, and the economy contributed to an overall negative impression of these issues, which appeared to validate Trump's rhetoric during the election.

For instance, the Shorenstein report found that 84 percent of press coverage on immigration was negative in tone, which echoed Trump's assertion that immigration is one of America's biggest problems.[7] This negative coverage contrasts with views of immigration as a whole, with Americans in 2017–2018 demonstrating that a majority of Americans believe immigrants are good for the country, that immigration rates do not need to be reduced, and that America should strive to embody its role as a haven for immigrants. Furthermore, studies indicated that, for most Americans, immigration wasn't a leading concern.[8] Thus, media coverage validated the tone and tenor of Trump's claims, creating negative coverage that presented a negative impression, even as, in general, the public does not view the issue negatively.

Writing in the *Harvard Business Review*, Bharat N. Anand believes that the problems with American media are the result of demand and changing desires among media consumers. Anand believes that three factors—connectivity through social media, an outdated marketing model for traditional media, and the changing preferences of consumers—limited the impact of legitimate news media and amplified the impact of "fake news" and social media "bubbles" during the election. Consumers tend to ignore ideas contrary to their beliefs and so, even if the media made an effort to provide accurate coverage, those choosing to believe an idea not supported by data would likely continue to do so. Anand thus argues that media cannot address the problems with the information environment unless they can encourage consumers to view legitimacy and accuracy as a key consumer preference.[9]

Ways Forward

Ultimately, transparency and accountability are essential for public welfare. Currently, the anti-regulation lobby has made it possible for social media companies to keep their policies and processes opaque and obscure. Protecting the trade secrets of businesses is part of the American free market approach, and the mythos of America's free market holds that competition between those corporate entities benefits consumers. This only holds true when consumers have sufficient information. From a purely economic perspective, the free market cannot benefit consumers unless the consumers are able to make choices between a company and its competitors. Without information, therefore, consumers make choices without understanding what those choices mean in the broader sphere. Unless this changes with regard to social and new media, consumers will likely continue to embrace convenience even as they regret the loss of privacy and the potential for corporate and political manipulation resulting from those choices.

Micah L. Issitt

Works Used

Anand, Bharat N. "The U.S. Media's Problems Are Much Bigger Than Fake News and Filter Bubbles." *Harvard Business Review*. Jan 5, 2017. Web. 26 Feb 2018.

Edwards-Levy, Ariel. "Most Americans Think Legal Immigrants Are Good For The Country." *Huffington Post*. Aug 10, 2017. Web. 26 Feb 2018.

"Ethics of Algorithms." *CIHR*. Centre For Internet and Human Rights. Frankfurt University. Web. 26 Feb 2018.

Ghonim and Rashbass, "It's Time to End the Secrecy and Opacity of Social Media." *The Washington Post*. The Washington Post Co. Oct 31, 2017. Web. 26 Feb 2018.

Grieco, Elizabeth and Jeffrey Gottfried. "In Trump's First 100 Days, News Stories Citing His Tweets Were More Likely to Be Negative." *Pew Research*. Pew Research Center. Oct 18, 2017. Web. 26 Feb 2018.

Johnson, Jenna and Abigail Hauslohner. "'I Think Islam Hates Us': A Timeline of Trump's Comments about Islam and Muslims." *The Washington Post*. The Washington Post Co. May 20, 2017. Web. 26 Feb 2018.

Mitchell, Amy, Simmons, Katie, Matsa, Katerina Eva, and Laura Silver. "Publics Globally Want Unbiased News Coverage, but are Divided on Whether Their News Media Delivers." *Pew Research*. Pew Research Center. Jan 11 2018. Web. 26 Feb 2018.

Patterson, Thomas E. "News Coverage of the 2016 General Election: How the Press Failed the Voters." *Shorenstein Center*. Harvard Kennedy School. Dec 7, 2016. Web. 26 Feb 2018.

Rainie, Lee. "The State of Privacy in Post-Snowden America." *Pew Research*. Facttank. Sep 21, 2016. Web. 26 Feb 2018.

Rainie, Lee and Janna Anderson. "The Future of Privacy." *Pew Research*. Pew Research Center Internet & Technology. Dec 18 2014. Web. 26 Feb 2018.

Notes

1. "Ethics of Algorithms," *CIHR*.
2. Rainie, "The State of Privacy in Post-Snowden America."
3. Rainie and Anderson, "The Future of Privacy."
4. Johnson and Hauslohner, "'I Think Islam Hates Us': A Timeline of Trump's Comments about Islam and Muslims."
5. Mitchell, et al., "Publics Globally Want Unbiased News Coverage, but Are Divided on Whether Their News Media Delivers."

6. Grieco and Gottfried, "In Trump's First 100 Days, News Stories Citing His Tweets Were More Likely to Be Negative."
7. Patterson, "News Coverage of the 2016 General Election: How the Press Failed the Voters."
8. Edwards-Levy, "Most Americans Think Legal Immigrants Are Good for the Country."
9. Anand, Bharat N. "The U.S. Media's Problems Are Much Bigger Than Fake News and Filter Bubbles."

Facebook and Twitter Are Being Used to Manipulate Public Opinion—Report

By Alex Hern
The Guardian, June 19, 2017

Propaganda on social media is being used to manipulate public opinion around the world, a new set of studies from the University of Oxford has revealed.

From Russia, where around 45% of highly active Twitter accounts are bots, to Taiwan, where a campaign against President Tsai Ing-wen involved thousands of heavily co-ordinated—but not fully automated—accounts sharing Chinese mainland propaganda, the studies show that social media is an international battleground for dirty politics.

The reports, part of the Oxford Internet Institute's Computational Propaganda Research Project, cover nine nations also including Brazil, Canada, China, Germany, Poland, Ukraine, and the the United States. They found "the lies, the junk, the misinformation" of traditional propaganda is widespread online and "supported by Facebook or Twitter's algorithms" according to Philip Howard, Professor of Internet Studies at Oxford.

At their simpler end, techniques used include automated accounts to like, share and post on the social networks. Such accounts can serve to game algorithms to push content on to curated social feeds. They can drown out real, reasoned debate between humans in favour of a social network populated by argument and soundbites and they can simply make online measures of support, such as the number of likes, look larger—crucial in creating the illusion of popularity.

The researchers found that in the US this took the form of what Samuel Woolley, the project's director of research, calls "manufacturing consensus" —creating the illusion of popularity so that a political candidate can have viability where they might not have had it before.

The US report says: "The illusion of online support for a candidate can spur actual support through a bandwagon effect. Trump made Twitter centre stage in this election, and voters paid attention."

While the report finds some evidence of institutional support for the use of bots, even if only in an "experimental" fashion by party campaign managers, Woolley emphasises that it's just as powerful coming from individuals. "Bots massively multiply the ability of one person to attempt to manipulate people," he says. "Picture your annoying friend on Facebook, who's always picking political fights. If they had an army of 5,000 bots, that would be a lot worse, right?"

Russian propaganda on social media is well known in the west for its external-facing arm, including allegations of state involvement in the US and French presidential elections. But the nation's social media is also heavily infiltrated with digital propaganda domestically according to the report on that country.

It shows that Russia first developed its digital propaganda expertise for dealing with internal threats to stability and drowning out dissent to Putin's regime while providing the same illusion of overwhelming consensus that was used in the US election years later. "Political competition in Putin's Russia created the demand for online propaganda tools," the report's author, Sergey Sanovich, writes, "and … market competition was allowed to to efficiently meet this demand and create tools that were later deployed in foreign operations".

> In Germany, fear of online destabilisation outpaced the actual arrival of automated political attacks and has led to the proposal and implementation of world-leading laws requiring social networks to take responsibility for what gets posted on their sites.

Woolley adds: "Russia is the case to look to see how a particularly powerful authoritarian regime uses social media to control people."

If Russia is the progenitor of many of the techniques seen worldwide, then Ukraine is the example of how the conflict might progress. There, says Woolley, "we're seeing how computational propaganda will be in five years, because the country is a testing ground for current Russian tactics." As a result, however, civil society organisations dedicated to tackling the problem are similarly advanced.

The report on the country's efforts to tackle Russian misinformation highlights the StopFake project, a collaborative effort to tackle fake stories "produced mainly by the Russian media." It also mentions a Chrome extension that allowed automatic blocking of thousands of Russian websites, and even a straightforward ban from the government aimed at certain Russian social networks, including VKontakte and Yandex, as part of the country's sanctions against Russia.

Facebook and Twitter Must Act

The reports suggested an apparent disinterest from the social media firms in how their networks were being used. Facebook, for instance, leaves most of its anti-propaganda work to external organisations such as *Snopes* and the *Associated Press*, who operate semi-autonomous fact-checking teams aimed at marking viral news stories as true or false while Twitter's anti-bot systems are effective at fighting commercial activity on the site, but seem less able or willing to take down automated accounts engaging in political activity.

The researchers are presenting their findings to a group of "senior" representatives from the technology industry in Palo Alto. They say that the social networks need to do more, and fast.

"For the most part, they leave it to the user community to police themselves, and flag accounts," Howard says. He points out while social networks tend to comply only with the minimum legal requirements, occasionally they'll be ahead of public opinion—as happened when the company decided to ban adverts for payday loans. "Of all the public policy issues, I don't know why they landed on that one. They clearly can have an impact, and between violent extremism and payday loans there's a span of issues."

The researchers did find one country to be significantly different to the others. In Germany, fear of online destabilisation outpaced the actual arrival of automated political attacks and has led to the proposal and implementation of world-leading laws requiring social networks to take responsibility for what gets posted on their sites.

"Germany leads the way as a cautionary authority over computational propaganda, seeking to prevent online manipulation of opinion rather than addressing already present issues," the report says, although it adds that "many of those measures lack legitimacy and suitable enforcement, and some are disproportionate responses considering their implications for freedom of expression".

Print citations

CMS: Hern, Alex. "Facebook and Twitter Are Being Used to Manipulate Public Opinion—Report." In *The Reference Shelf: Alternative Facts, Post-Truth, and the Information War*, edited by Betsy Maury, 71-73. Ipswich, MA: H.W. Wilson, 2018.

MLA: Hern, Alex. "Facebook and Twitter Are Being Used to Manipulate Public Opinion—Report." *The Reference Shelf: Alternative Facts, Post-Truth, and the Information War*. Ed. Betsy Maury. Ipswich: H.W. Wilson, 2018. 71-73. Print.

APA: Hern, A. (2018). Facebook and Twitter are being used to manipulate public opinion—report. In Betsy Maury (Ed.), *The reference shelf: Alternative facts, post-truth, and the information war* (pp. 71-73). Ipswich, MA: H.W. Wilson. (Original work published 2017)

How Facebook, Google and Twitter "Embeds" Helped Trump in 2016

By Nancy Scola
Politico, October 26, 2017

Facebook, Twitter and Google played a far deeper role in Donald Trump's presidential campaign than has previously been disclosed, with company employees taking on the kind of political strategizing that campaigns typically entrust to their own staff or paid consultants, according to a new study released Thursday.

The peer-reviewed paper, based on more than a dozen interviews with both tech company staffers who worked inside several 2016 presidential campaigns and campaign officials, sheds new light on Silicon Valley's assistance to Trump before his surprise win last November.

While the companies call it standard practice to work hand-in-hand with high-spending advertisers like political campaigns, the new research details how the staffers assigned to the 2016 candidates frequently acted more like political operatives, doing things like suggesting methods to target difficult-to-reach voters online, helping to tee up responses to likely lines of attack during debates, and scanning candidate calendars to recommend ad pushes around upcoming speeches.

Such support was critical for the Trump campaign, which didn't invest heavily in its own digital operations during the primary season and made extensive use of Facebook, Twitter and Google "embeds" for the general election, says the study, conducted by communications professors from the University of North Carolina at Chapel Hill and the University of Utah.

The companies offered such services, without charge, to all the 2016 candidates, according to the study, which details extensive tech company involvement at every stage of the race. But Hillary Clinton's campaign declined to embed the companies' employees in her operations, instead opting to develop its own digital apparatus and call in the tech firms to help execute elements of its strategy.

"Facebook, Twitter, and Google [went] beyond promoting their services and facilitating digital advertising buys," the paper concludes, adding that their efforts extended to "actively shaping campaign communications through their close collaboration with political staffers."

"The extent to which they were helping candidates online was a surprise to us," said co-author Daniel Kreiss, from UNC Chapel Hill. He called the assistance "a form of subsidy from technology firms to political candidates."

The study was published Thursday in the journal *Political Communication*.

Kreiss and the University of Utah's Shannon McGregor interviewed tech company liaisons to the Trump and Clinton operations as well as officials from a range of campaigns, including those of former Gov. Jeb Bush and Sens. Bernie Sanders, Ted Cruz and Marco Rubio.

The researchers' findings add to the many questions surrounding the part that the country's biggest tech companies played in the 2016 election. Facebook, Google and Twitter already face heavy criticism for allowing the spread of disinformation, "fake news" and divisive advertising during the campaign—much of which targeted Clinton. All three companies are set to testify at congressional hearings beginning next week on Russian use of their platforms to interfere with the election.

The idea that the tech companies were so deeply enmeshed in the efforts to elect Trump in particular could also complicate the companies' reputations as political actors. Facebook CEO Mark Zuckerberg is among those in liberal-leaning Silicon Valley who have roundly condemned Trump's actions as president on topics like LGBT issues and immigration.

As Trump emerged as the likely Republican nominee, staffers from each of the three companies set up shop in a strip-mall office rented by the Trump campaign in San Antonio, Texas, home to the campaign's lead digital strategist, Brad Parscale, the study reports. It attributes that information to Nu Wexler, a Twitter communications official at the time, who is explicit about the value of the arrangement for Trump.

"One, they found that they were getting solid advice, and two, it's cheaper. It's free labor," Wexler said in the study.

While the paper does not detail the specific tasks Facebook carried out for Trump, it describes the sort of work the company did generally for 2016 candidates, including coordinating so-called dark posts that would appear only to selected users and identifying the kinds of photos that perform best on Facebook-owned Instagram. Twitter, meanwhile, would help candidates analyze the performances of their tweet-based fundraising pushes to recommend what moves the campaigns should make next. Google kept tabs on candidates' travels to recommend geographically targeted advertisements.

Digital experts interviewed by the researchers concluded that the tech company employees, who would work in San Antonio for days at a time, helped Trump close his staffing gap with Clinton.

The White House referred questions to the Trump campaign, and Parscale did not respond to requests for comment. Parscale said in an Oct. 8 episode of *60 Minutes* that he actively solicited the companies' support, saying that he told them: "I wanna know everything you would tell Hillary's campaign plus some. And I want your people here to teach me how to use it."

A source close to the Clinton campaign rejected the notion that her team failed to take advantage of a valuable resource, arguing that her operation was in regular contact with the tech companies to tap their expertise. The source, who would only speak anonymously because of the sensitivity around attributing causes of Clinton's defeat, said there would have been no advantage to having tech company employees sitting at desks at Clinton's Brooklyn headquarters.

One unnamed tech company staffer is quoted in the study as saying, "Clinton viewed us as vendors rather than consultants."

Asked about the arrangement with Trump, the tech companies were quick to point out that they make their services available to all political players regardless of party.

"Facebook offers identical levels of support to candidates and campaigns across the political spectrum, whether by Facebook's politics and government or ad sales teams," a spokesperson for the social network said in a statement.

That sentiment was echoed by Twitter, which said it offered help to both the Clinton and Trump campaigns, and by Google, which stressed that it is up to each candidate to determine how extensively to work with the company.

> **Facebook, Google and Twitter already face heavy criticism for allowing the spread of disinformation, "fake news" and divisive advertising during the campaign—much of which targeted Clinton.**

During the primary season, Google made available to each candidate an eight-hour session with the company's creative teams, but only Kentucky Republican Sen. Rand Paul's campaign took them up on it, according to the study.

But at least one tech veteran said he can see how it would raise alarms that the bulk of Silicon Valley's hands-on campaign support went to Trump rather than to Clinton.

"It can be confusing from the outside looking in when it appears one campaign or another is getting more support," Adam Sharp, a former Twitter executive who led the company's elections team from 2010 to 2016, said in an interview. But while the companies strive to be balanced, they cannot inform voters "when a candidate doesn't heed the help," he said.

An intimate relationship between tech companies and candidates has considerable upside for both. The campaign gets high-quality advice and advance notice on cutting-edge products. The company gets national exposure for its products and builds relationships with politicians who might be in a position to regulate it once they get to Washington.

Silicon Valley had additional considerations during the 2016 campaign. The big tech companies were eager to fight the perception they were unfair to conservatives—and few in the liberal-leaning industry expected Trump to win, with or without their assistance.

Kreiss and McGregor recount one interview in which a pair of Facebook reps struggled to come up with a shorthand way of describing the support they provide candidates. Katie Harbath, head of Facebook's elections team, suggested "customer service plus." Ali-Jae Henke, who as an account executive at Google worked with

Republican campaigns, including Trump's, described the role as "serving in an advisory capacity."

The history of the tech companies' campaign outreach dates back to the 2008 presidential contest. That year, Randi Zuckerberg, sister of Facebook's CEO, traveled to both the Democratic and Republican conventions to pitch the political utility of the then-4-year-old social network. Around that same time, the company began offering congressional offices one-on-one guidance on how to use Facebook.

The outreach didn't always work at first. "I was, like, begging people to meet with us," Randi Zuckerberg said of the GOP's 2008 convention. But as political spending on Facebook's ad products and elected leaders' dependence on the platform skyrocketed over the years, so too did the company's close work with politicians.

One constant in the dynamic: The companies break down their political outreach teams along party lines. Facebook's point of contact to Clinton's 2016 White House run, Crystal Patterson, was a veteran of Democratic politics, and Henke—Google's liaison to the Trump operation and other 2016 Republican bids—was once the director of operations for the Western Republican Leadership Conference.

That partisan matching is needed, company representatives say, to allow all involved to speak freely when providing advice. Caroline McCain, social media manager for Rubio's White House bid, is quoted in the paper saying that when tech company staffers have a similar political background as the campaign they're assigned to, it raises the campaign's comfort level in working with them.

"When you realize, 'Oh yeah, the person I'm working with at Google, they actually worked on Romney back in 2012,' like, 'Oh, okay, they actually might have our best interest at heart,'" McCain said. After the campaign, McCain took a position at Facebook.

Kreiss, the paper's co-author, said the symbiotic relationship between Silicon Valley and political campaigns demands further examination.

"It raises the larger question of what should be the transparency around this, given that it's taking place in the context of a democratic election," he said.

Print citations

CMS: Scola, Nancy. "How Facebook, Google and Twitter 'Embeds' Helped Trump in 2016." In *The Reference Shelf: Alternative Facts, Post-Truth, and the Information War*, edited by Betsy Maury, 74-77. Ipswich, MA: H.W. Wilson, 2018.

MLA: Scola, Nancy. "How Facebook, Google and Twitter 'Embeds' Helped Trump in 2016." *The Reference Shelf: Alternative Facts, Post-Truth, and the Information War*. Ed. Betsy Maury. Ipswich: H.W. Wilson, 2018. 74-77. Print.

APA: Scola, N. (2018). How Facebook, Google and Twitter "embeds" helped Trump in 2016. In Betsy Maury (Ed.), *The reference shelf: Alternative facts, post-truth, and the information war* (pp. 74-77). Ipswich, MA: H.W. Wilson. (Original work published 2017)

Don't Blame the Election on Fake News: Blame It on the Media

By Duncan J. Watts and David M. Rothschild
Columbia Journalism Review, December 5, 2017

Since the 2016 presidential election, an increasingly familiar narrative has emerged concerning the unexpected victory of Donald Trump. Fake news, much of it produced by Russian sources, was amplified on social networks such as Facebook and Twitter, generating millions of views among a segment of the electorate eager to hear stories about Hillary Clinton's untrustworthiness, unlikeability, and possibly even criminality. "Alt-right" news sites like *Breitbart* and *The Daily Caller* supplemented the outright manufactured information with highly slanted and misleading coverage of their own. The continuing fragmentation of the media and the increasing ability of Americans to self-select into like-minded "filter bubbles" exacerbated both phenomena, generating a toxic brew of political polarization and skepticism toward traditional sources of authority.

Alarmed by these threats to their legitimacy, and energized by the election of a president hostile to their very existence, the mainstream media has vigorously shouldered the mantle of truth-tellers. *The Washington Post* changed its motto to "Democracy Dies in Darkness" one month into the Trump presidency, and the *New York Times* launched a major ad campaign reflecting the nuanced and multifaceted nature of truth during the Oscars broadcast in February. Headline writers now explicitly spell out falsehoods rather than leaving it to the ensuing text. And journalists are quick to call out false equivalence, as when President Trump compared Antifa protesters to Nazis and heavily armed white supremacists following the violence in Charlottesville.

At the same time, journalists have stepped up their already vigorous critiques of technology companies—Facebook in particular, but also Google and Twitter—highlighting the potential ways in which algorithms and social sharing have merged to spread misinformation. Many of the mainstream media's worst fears were reinforced by a widely cited *BuzzFeed* article reporting that the 20 most-shared fake news articles on Facebook during the final three months of the campaign outperformed the 20 most-shared "real news" articles published over the same period. Numerous stories have reported on the manipulation of Facebook's ad system by Russian-affiliated groups. Lawmakers such as Senator Mark Warner, a Democrat from Virginia, have been prominently profiled on account of their outspoken criticism of the tech industry, and even Facebook's own employees have reportedly expressed anxiety over their company's role in the election.

We agree that fake news and misinformation are real problems that deserve serious attention. We also agree that social media and other online technologies have contributed to deep-seated problems in democratic discourse such as increasing polarization and erosion of support for traditional sources of authority. Nonetheless, we believe that the volume of reporting around fake news, and the role of tech companies in disseminating those falsehoods, is both disproportionate to its likely influence in the outcome of the election and diverts attention from the culpability of the mainstream media itself.

To begin with, the breathlessly repeated numbers on fake news are not as large as they have been made to seem when compared to the volume of information to which online users are exposed. For example, a *New York Times* story reported that Facebook identified more than 3,000 ads purchased by fake accounts traced to Russian sources, which generated over $100,000 in advertising revenue. But Facebook's advertising revenue in the fourth quarter of 2016 was $8.8 billion, or $96 million per day. All together, the fake ads accounted for roughly 0.1 percent of Facebook's *daily* advertising revenue.

> **We also agree that social media and other online technologies have contributed to deep-seated problems in democratic discourse such as increasing polarization and erosion of support for traditional sources of authority.**

The 2016 *BuzzFeed* report that received so much attention claimed that the top 20 fake news stories on Facebook "generated 8,711,000 shares, reactions, and comments" between August 1 and Election Day. Again, this sounds like a large number until it's put into perspective: Facebook had well over 1.5 billion active monthly users in 2016. If each user took only a single action per day on average (likely an underestimate), then throughout those 100 days prior to the election, the 20 stories in *BuzzFeed*'s study would have accounted for only 0.006 percent of user actions.

Even recent claims that the "real" numbers were much higher than initially reported do not change the basic imbalance. For example, an October 3 *New York Times* story reported that "Russian agents...disseminated inflammatory posts that reached 126 million users on Facebook, published more than 131,000 messages on Twitter and uploaded over 1,000 videos to Google's YouTube service." Big numbers indeed, but several paragraphs later the authors concede that over the same period Facebook users were exposed to 11 trillion posts—roughly 87,000 for every fake exposure—while on Twitter the Russian-linked election tweets represented less than 0.75 percent of all election-related tweets. On YouTube, meanwhile, the total number of views of fake Russian videos was around 309,000—compared to the five billion YouTube videos that are watched every day.

In addition, given what is known about the impact of online information on opinions, even the high-end estimates of fake news penetration would be unlikely to have had a meaningful impact on voter behavior. For example, a recent study by two economists, Hunt Allcott and Matthew Gentzkow, estimates that "the average US adult read and remembered on the order of one or perhaps several fake news articles during the election period, with higher exposure to pro-Trump articles than pro-Clinton articles." In turn, they estimate that "if one fake news article were about as persuasive as one TV campaign ad, the fake news in our database would have changed vote shares by an amount on the order of hundredths of a percentage point." As the authors acknowledge, fake news stories could have been more influential than this back-of-the-envelope calculation suggests for a number of reasons (e.g., they only considered a subset of all such stories; the fake stories may have been concentrated on specific segments of the population, who in turn could have had a disproportionate impact on the election outcome; fake news stories could have exerted more influence over readers' opinions than campaign ads). Nevertheless, their influence would have had to be much larger—roughly 30 times as large—to account for Trump's margin of victory in the key states on which the election outcome depended.

Finally, the sheer outrageousness of the most popular fake stories—Pope Francis endorsing Trump; Democrats planning to impose Islamic law in Florida; Trump supporters chanting "We hate Muslims, we hate blacks;" and so on—made them especially unlikely to have altered voters' pre-existing opinions of the candidates. Notwithstanding polls that show almost 50 percent of Trump supporters believed rumors that Hillary Clinton was running a pedophilia sex ring out of a Washington, DC pizzeria, such stories were most likely consumed by readers who already agreed with their overall sentiment and shared them either to signal their "tribal allegiance" or simply for entertainment value, not because they had been persuaded by the stories themselves.

As troubling as the spread of fake news on social media may be, it was unlikely to have had much impact either on the election outcome or on the more general state of politics in 2016. A potentially more serious threat is what a team of Harvard and MIT researchers refer to as "a network of mutually reinforcing hyper-partisan sites that revive what Richard Hofstadter called 'the paranoid style in American politics,' combining decontextualized truths, repeated falsehoods, and leaps of logic to create a fundamentally misleading view of the world." Unlike the fake news numbers highlighted in much of the post-election coverage, engagement with sites like *Breitbart News*, *InfoWars*, and *The Daily Caller* are substantial—especially in the realm of social media.

Nevertheless, a longer and more detailed report by the same researchers shows that by any reasonable metric—including Facebook or Twitter shares, but also referrals from other media sites, number of published stories, etc.—the media ecosystem remains dominated by conventional (and mostly left-of-center) sources such as *the Washington Post, the New York Times, HuffPost,* CNN, and *Politico*.

Given the attention these very same news outlets have lavished, post-election, on fake news shared via social media, it may come as a surprise that they themselves dominated social media traffic. While it may have been the case that the

20 most-shared fake news stories narrowly outperformed the 20 most-shared "real news" stories, the overall volume of stories produced by major newsrooms vastly outnumbers fake news. According to the same report, "*The Washington Post* produced more than 50,000 stories over the 18-month period, while *the New York Times*, CNN, and *Huffington Post* each published more than 30,000 stories." Presumably not all of these stories were about the election, but each such story was also likely reported by many news outlets simultaneously. A rough estimate of thousands of election-related stories published by the mainstream media is therefore not unreasonable.

What did all these stories talk about? The research team investigated this question, counting sentences that appeared in mainstream media sources and classifying each as detailing one of several Clinton- or Trump-related issues. In particular, they classified each sentence as describing either a scandal (e.g., Clinton's emails, Trump's taxes) or a policy issue (Clinton and jobs, Trump and immigration). They found roughly four times as many Clinton-related sentences that described scandals as opposed to policies, whereas Trump-related sentences were one-and-a-half times as likely to be about policy as scandal. Given the sheer number of scandals in which Trump was implicated—sexual assault; the Trump Foundation; Trump University; redlining in his real-estate developments; insulting a Gold Star family; numerous instances of racist, misogynist, and otherwise offensive speech—it is striking that the media devoted more attention to his policies than to his personal failings. Even more striking, the various Clinton-related email scandals—her use of a private email server while secretary of state, as well as the DNC and John Podesta hacks—accounted for more sentences than all of Trump's scandals combined (65,000 vs. 40,000) and more than twice as many as were devoted to all of her policy positions.

To reiterate, these 65,000 sentences were written not by Russian hackers, but overwhelmingly by professional journalists employed at mainstream news organizations, such as *the New York Times, the Washington Post*, and *the Wall Street Journal*. To the extent that voters mistrusted Hillary Clinton, or considered her conduct as secretary of state to have been negligent or even potentially criminal, or were generally unaware of what her policies contained or how they may have differed from Donald Trump's, these numbers suggest their views were influenced more by mainstream news sources than by fake news.

To shed more light on this possibility, we conducted an in-depth analysis of a single media source, the *New York Times*. We chose the *Times* for two reasons: First, because its broad reach both among policy elites and ordinary citizens means that the *Times* has singular influence on public debates; and second, because its reputation for serious journalism implies that if the *Times* did not inform its readers of the issues, then it is unlikely such information was widely available anywhere.

We gathered two datasets that captured the *Times*'s coverage of the final stage of the 2016 presidential election. The first dataset comprised all articles that appeared on the front page of the printed newspaper (399 total) over the last 69 days of the campaign, beginning on September 1 and ending on November 8 (Election Day).

The second comprised all of the 13,481 articles published online by the *Times* over the same period. In both datasets, we first identified all articles that were relevant to the election campaign. We then further categorized each of these articles as belonging to one of three categories: *Campaign Miscellaneous*, *Personal/Scandal*, and *Policy*. Within *Personal/Scandal* we then further classified the article as focused on Clinton or Trump, and within *Policy* classified it as one of the following: *Policy no details*, *Policy Clinton details*, *Policy Trump details*, and *Policy both details* (more details on our methodology can be found below):

Campaign Miscellaneous articles focused on the "horse race" elements of the campaign, such as the overall likelihood of victory of the candidates, details of intra-party conflicts, or the mobilization of specific demographic groups. For example, an October 12 story with the headline "Republican Split Over Trump Puts States into Play," which described how Clinton's campaign was taking advantage of Trump's battle with the Republican Party. This article was manifestly about the campaign, but treated it mostly as a contest in which a dramatic twist had just taken place. It contained little information that would have helped potential voters understand the candidates' policy positions and hence their respective agendas as president.

Personal/Scandal articles focused on the controversial actions and/or statements of the candidates either during the election itself or prior to it, as well as on the fallout generated by those controversies. An example of the former would be an October 8 article "Tape Reveals Trump Boast About Groping Women," which discussed the infamous *Access Hollywood* An example of the latter would be an October 29 article, "New Emails Jolt Clinton Campaign in Race's Last Days," which discussed the impact of the reopening of a FBI investigation into Clinton's private email server on the campaign. In addition, we classified each *Personal/Scandal* article as being primarily about Clinton (e.g., emails, Benghazi, the Clinton Foundation) or Trump (e.g., sexual harassment, Trump University, Trump Foundation, etc.).

Policy articles mentioned policy issues such as healthcare, immigration, taxation, abortion, or education. Articles coded as *Policy No Details* mentioned policy issues as impacting the campaign, but did not describe the actual policies of the candidates. For example, an October 26 article, "Growing Costs of Health Law Pose a Late Test" described Donald Trump attacking Hillary Clinton over health premium increases, but did not mention the policy proposals of the two candidates, nor did it note that due to subsidies the hikes would not affect the actual price paid by 86 percent of people in marketplaces. *Policy Clinton Details* or *Policy Trump Details* counted articles that mentioned specifics of the Clinton or Trump platforms respectively but not both, while *Policy Both Details* compared the specifics of the two candidates' platforms. For example, an October 3 article, "Next President Likely To Shape Health Law Fate," noted that Clinton had endorsed "a new government-sponsored health plan, the so-called public option, to give consumers an additional choice." It also noted that "Donald J. Trump and Republicans in Congress would go in the direction of less government, reducing federal regulation and requirements so insurance would cost less and no-frills options could proliferate. Mr. Trump would, for example, encourage greater use of health savings accounts, allow insurance policies to be purchased across state lines and let people take tax deductions for insurance premium payments."

Of the 150 front-page articles that discussed the campaign in some way, we classified slightly over half (80) as *Campaign Miscellaneous*. Slightly over a third (54) were *Personal/Scandal*, with 29 focused on Trump and 25 on Clinton. Finally, just over 10 percent (16) of articles discussed *Policy*, of which six had no details, four provided details on Trump's policy only, one on Clinton's policy only, and five made some comparison between the two candidates' policies. The results for the full corpus were similar: Of the 1,433 articles that mentioned Trump or Clinton, 291 were devoted to scandals or other personal matters while only 70 mentioned policy, and of these only 60 mentioned any details of either candidate's positions. In other words, comparing the two datasets, the number of *Personal/Scandal* stories for every *Policy* story ranged from 3.4 (for front-page stories) to 4.2. Further restricting to *Policy* stories that contained some detail about at least one candidate's positions, these ratios rise to 5.5 and 4.85, respectively.

The problem is this: As has become clear since the election, there were profound differences between the two candidates' policies, and these differences are already proving enormously consequential to the American people. Under President Trump, the Affordable Care Act is being actively dismantled, environmental and consumer protections are being rolled back, international alliances and treaties are being threatened, and immigration policy has been thrown into turmoil, among other dramatic changes. In light of the stark policy choices facing voters in the 2016 election, it seems incredible that only five out of 150 front-page articles that the *New York Times* ran over the last, most critical months of the election, attempted to compare the candidate's policies, while only 10 described the policies of either candidate in any detail.

In this context, 10 is an interesting figure because it is also the number of front-page stories the *Times* ran on the Hillary Clinton email scandal in just six days, from October 29 (the day after FBI Director James Comey announced his decision to reopen his investigation of possible wrongdoing by Clinton) through November 3, just five days before the election. When compared with the *Times's* overall coverage of the campaign, the intensity of focus on this one issue is extraordinary. To reiterate, *in just six days,* The New York Times *ran as many cover stories about Hillary Clinton's emails as they did about all policy issues combined in the 69 days leading up to the election* (and that does not include the three additional articles on October 18, and November 6 and 7, or the two articles on the emails taken from John Podesta). This intense focus on the email scandal cannot be written off as inconsequential: The Comey incident and its subsequent impact on Clinton's approval rating among undecided voters could very well have tipped the election.

Turning now to the policy coverage, arguably no policy issue was more important during the election campaign, or more divisive, than the Affordable Care Act (aka Obamacare). It is therefore shocking (if not surprising) how uninformed many Americans were about the mechanics of the law or how successful it had been. In early 2017, for example, The Upshot, the data-centric subsection of the *New*

York Times, published two pieces on Obamacare. The first, "One-Third Don't Know Obamacare and Affordable Care Act Are the Same," published on February 7, described some important misconceptions about Obamacare held by large percentages of the American public—for example, that almost 40 percent (and 47 percent of Republicans) did not know that repealing Obamacare would cause people to lose Medicaid coverage or subsidies for private insurance. The second, "No, Obamacare isn't in a 'Death Spiral,'" published on March 15, 2017, provided readers with some important details about how Obamacare works. For example, it noted that "because of how subsidies work, people were generally shielded from this year's higher prices." It also noted that while prices had gone up recently, they "were lower than expected in the first few years of the program." The article then went on to describe an insurance market that could certainly use improvement, but concluded that the "Obamacare markets will remain stable over the long run, if there are no significant changes."

These articles provide exactly the kind of analysis that would have helped *Times* readers understand the state of the ACA prior to the election. In contrast, the *Times's* pre-election coverage of Obamacare was surprisingly sparse (we counted only four front-page stories between September 1 and November 8) and surprisingly negative. The first article, on October 3, creates almost the opposite impression of the optimistic post-election articles, stating "Mr. Obama's signature domestic achievement will almost certainly have to change to survive." Subsequent articles, appearing over a three-day period from October 25 to 27, were even more negative in tone: "Choices fall in health law as costs rise" declares the October 25 headline; "Growing costs of health law pose a late test;" and finally "Many prefer tax penalties to health law." All four articles emphasized troubles in the insurance market, failing to mention that most policyholders have subsidized capped prices (and are therefore insulated from premium hikes), or that the government was spending less than anticipated, or that premiums were rising slower than before Obamacare. None of the articles mentions the Medicaid expansion, one of the most popular parts of the bill.

Consistent with other studies of media coverage of the election, our analysis finds that the *New York Times* focused much more on "dramatic" issues like the horserace or personal scandals than on substantive policy issues. Moreover, when the paper did write about policy issues, it failed to mention important details, in some cases giving readers a misleading impression of the true state of affairs. If voters had wanted to educate themselves on issues such as healthcare, immigration, taxes, and economic policy—or how these issues would likely be affected by the election of either candidate as president—they would not have learned much from reading the *Times.* What they would have learned was that both candidates were plagued by scandal: Hillary Clinton over her use of a private email server for government business while secretary of state, as well as allegations of possible conflicts of interest in the Clinton Foundation; and Trump over his failure to release his tax returns; his past business dealings; Trump University; the Trump Foundation; accusations of sexual harassment and assault; and numerous misogynistic, racist, and otherwise offensive remarks. What they would also have learned about was the ever-fluctuating state of the horse race: who was up and who was down; who might turn out and who might not; and who was happy or unhappy with whom about what.

To be clear, we do not believe the *Times*'s coverage was worse than other mainstream news organizations, so much as it was typical of a broader failure of mainstream journalism to inform audiences of the very real and consequential issues at stake. In retrospect, it seems clear that the press in general made the mistake of assuming a Clinton victory was inevitable, and were setting themselves as credible critics of the next administration. Possibly this mistake arose from the failure of journalists to get out of their "hermetic bubble." Possibly it was their misinterpretation of available polling data, which showed all along that a Trump victory, albeit unlikely, was far from inconceivable. These were understandable mistakes, but they were still mistakes. Yet, rather than acknowledging the possible impact their collective failure of imagination could have had on the election outcome, the mainstream news community has instead focused its critical attention everywhere but on themselves: fake news, Russian hackers, technology companies, algorithmic ranking, the alt-right, even on the American public.

To be fair, journalists were not the only community to be surprised by the outcome of the 2016 election—a great many informed observers, possibly including the candidate himself, failed to take the prospect of a Trump victory seriously. Also to be fair, the difficulty of adequately covering a campaign in which the "rules of the game" were repeatedly upended must surely have been formidable. But one could equally argue that Facebook could not have been expected to anticipate the misuse of its advertising platform to seed fake news stories. And one could just as easily argue that the difficulties facing tech companies in trading off between complicity in spreading intentional misinformation on the one hand, and censorship on the other hand, are every bit as formidable as those facing journalists trying to cover Trump. For journalists to excoriate the tech companies for their missteps while barely acknowledging their own reveals an important blind spot in the journalistic profession's conception of itself.

We have no doubt that journalists take seriously their mission to provide readers with the information they need in order to make informed decisions about matters of importance. We note, however, that this mission implicitly assumes that journalists are passive observers of events rather than active participants, whose choices about what to cover and how to cover it meaningfully influence the events in question. Given the disruption visited upon the print news business model since the beginning of the 21st century, journalists can perhaps be forgiven for seeing themselves as helpless bystanders in an information ecosystem that is increasingly centered on social media and search. But even if the news media has ceded much of its distribution power to technology companies, its longstanding ability to "set the agenda"—that is, to determine what counts as news to begin with—remains formidable. In sheer numerical terms, the information to which voters were exposed during the election campaign was overwhelmingly produced not by fake news sites or even by alt-right media sources, but by household names like the *New York Times,* the *Washington Post*, and CNN. Without discounting the role played by malicious Russian hackers and naïve tech executives, we believe that fixing the information ecosystem is at least as much about improving the real news as it about stopping the fake stuff.

Methodology
Analysis of front pages

Every front-page article was read by two researchers and coded for the three topline categories and their subcategories, using only the text that appeared on the actual front page (not on what may be continued on future pages). There was very little disagreement between the two researchers; for example, both researchers coded the same set of articles as covering policies of both candidates, and disagreed on only one article with respect to coverage of policy. For simplicity, the authors reviewed all disagreements together, by hand, and we reported from that dataset.

Analysis of the full corpus

What the *New York Times* puts on the front page of its print edition is important, but not necessarily representative of how many readers encounter the news, either because they navigate directly to individual articles from social media sources (mostly Facebook and Twitter), or because articles at nytimes.com can appear in different places at different times. To verify that our conclusions regarding coverage of the campaign on the front page was not totally unrepresentative of the paper as whole, we also coded the entire corpus of all articles published on nytimes.com during the same period. Because this sample is much larger (13,481 vs. 399), we coded them using a combination of machine classification and hand coding.

- First, we scraped the headline and first paragraph, if provided by the API, for each *Times* article from September 1 through November 9, 2016, using the archive API for all articles that included the words "Clinton" or "Trump." Note: This criterion included virtually all campaign-related articles, but may have also included potentially non-campaign related articles (e.g., about Bill Clinton or Ivanka Trump).

- Next, we compiled a list of words (details below) delineating three categories of article: *Campaign* (focused on the horse race and how people react to events); *Policy* (focused on a policy issue); and *Personal/Scandal*. For each article, we checked if any of the words in the article began with one of the stems in our word list. For example, if an article contained the word "immigration," we would first notice that it starts with "immigrat," which is one of our policy words; thus we would mark it as a *Policy* article. For all articles marked as *Policy*, we then hand-coded them into the four subcategories and tossed articles into *Campaign Miscellaneous* if they did not actually cover any policy.

- Finally, we hand-coded the *Policy* articles as *Policy No Details, Policy Clinton*

Details, Policy Trump Details, or *Policy Both Details* using the same criteria as above.

Word list for Clinton/Trump categories:

1. Clinton *Personal/Scandal* words: *email, benghazi, foundation, road*
2. Trump *Personal/Scandal* words: *russia, foundation, university, woman, women, tax, sexual assault, golf, tape, kiss*
3. *Policy* words for both candidates are taken from the list of issues covered by *On the Issues*: *abortion, budget, civil rights, corporation, crime, drug, education, energy, oil, environment, family, families, children, foreign policy, trade, reform, government, gun, health, security, immigra, technology, job, principl, value, social security, war, peace, welfare, poverty, econom, immigrat, immigran*
4. *Campaign* words for both candidates: *fundraise, ads, advertisements, campaign, trail, rally, endors, outreach, ballot, vote, electoral, poll, donat, turnout, margin, swing state*

Print Citations

CMS: Watts, Duncan J., and David M. Rothschild. "Don't Blame the Election on Fake News: Blame It on the Media." In *The Reference Shelf: Alternative Facts, Post-Truth, and the Information War*, edited by Betsy Maury, 78-87. Ipswich, MA: H.W. Wilson, 2018.

MLA: Watts, Duncan J., and David M. Rothschild. "Don't Blame the Election on Fake News: Blame It on the Media." *The Reference Shelf: Alternative Facts, Post-Truth, and the Information War.* Ed. Betsy Maury. Ipswich: H.W. Wilson, 2018. 78-87. Print.

APA: Watts, D.J., & D.M. Rothschild. (2018). Don't blame the election on fake news: Blame it on the media. In Betsy Maury (Ed.), *The reference shelf: Alternative facts, post-truth, and the information war* (pp. 78-87). Ipswich, MA: H.W. Wilson. (Original work published 2017)

Don't Let Liberals End Opinion Diversity Under Cover of 'Fake News' Campaign

by Mike Gonzalez

The Daily Signal, January 19, 2018

The issue of fake news is very much in the news, as it were, and President Donald Trump is being compared to Stalin for his dismissal of journalists who are purveyors of it as "enemies of the American people."

It may be good to jog our memory back to how the term "fake news" arrived among us.

Only then do we remember that it first was intended to be used as a weapon in a sustained campaign by liberals to regain their former monopoly over news delivery, and end one of the most important and hard-won victories by conservatives—the information diversity that arrived with the internet.

Disinformation, of course, has been among us since man first began to use language, sought to conceal something, and lied about it. So a very long time.

Internet searches for "fake news" really kicked up in early November 2016. It is to then that we can trace this Nov. 6, 2016, article by *The New York Times'* media critic, Jim Rutenberg, credited with the first use of the term.

"The internet-borne forces that are eating away at print advertising are enabling a host of faux-journalistic players to pollute the democracy with dangerously fake news items," Rutenberg wrote.

The purpose of Rutenberg's jeremiad was to draw attention to the secular demise of mainstream newspaper outlets and decry the success of conservative outlets.

Rutenberg's evidence was comprised of outrageous examples of conspiracy mongering by alt-right sites—content, he complained, that can "live alongside that of *The Times* or *The Boston Globe* or *The Washington Post* on the Facebook newsfeed and be just as well read, if not more so."

But it is clear from his piece that his real target was opinion diversity.

"If you have a society where people can't agree on basic facts, how do you have a functioning democracy?" Rutenberg quoted *The Washington Post's* executive editor, Martin Baron, as asking.

We heard a very similar version in former President Barack Obama's complaint to David Letterman this month:

One of the biggest challenges we have to our democracy is the degree to which we don't share a common baseline of facts. If you watch Fox News, you are living on a different planet than you are if you are listening to NPR.

We know which planet our 44th president inhabits, and which he thinks is in a galaxy far, far away.

> **This effort to delegitimize conservative outlets went horribly wrong, of course, when Trump appropriated the term and weaponized it.**

We also know whose "basic facts" Rutenberg trusted: In his seminal 2016 column, he mentions the hard-left and equally conspiracy-driven MSNBC as a normal, mainstream network.

The loss of the previous progressive monopoly on the dissemination of news and analysis has poisoned the liberal soul since the internet came on the scene.

The left's "fake news" campaign began, then, as an attempt to smear all legitimate conservative news purveyors, from Fox News Channel to *The Weekly Standard* to the *Washington Examiner* and, of course, *The Daily Signal*, that provide an alternative news selection and interpretation.

This effort to delegitimize conservative outlets went horribly wrong, of course, when Trump appropriated the term and weaponized it. I must admit that when the president started doing it, I thought it wouldn't fly. The current brouhaha proves that I was wrong.

As a former journalist, I don't particularly like calling newsmen "the enemies of the American people." It is indeed a term once used by Stalin. (Though it hardly makes Trump a Stalinist, a distinction that should be reserved for those who actually massacre millions and oppress those who survive.)

My friends in the media are not enemies of the American people. But they are mostly liberal.

Ask the more existential question, "Do liberals like America?" and that's harder to answer. Many liberals don't hide their contempt for the U.S. (there are many, many examples; find them yourself) and many others still proffer to like an America I don't recognize.

Which is why we should all be present in the marketplace of ideas. After gaining this beachhead, conservatives must protect it against what will be sustained attempts to dislodge them.

In 2014, I had a celebrated exchange with Darrell West and Beth Stone at Brookings Institution over their frightening call in a paper for digital platforms such as Facebook, Google, and Twitter to change their algorithms in a manner that would prioritize information from liberal sources.

But West and Stone won, and social networks are now "fact-checking" their content. As my colleague Katrina Trinko points out, this is censoring the news.

Ending opinion diversity this way is the real threat to freedom of the press and the First Amendment, and what should keep those who worry about it awake at night.

Print Citations

CMS: Gonzalez, Mike. "Don't Let Liberals End Opinion Diversity Under Cover of 'Fake News' Campaign." In *The Reference Shelf: Alternative Facts, Post-Truth, and the Information War*, edited by Betsy Maury, 89-90. Ipswich, MA: H.W. Wilson, 2018.

MLA: Gonzalez, Mike. "Don't Let Liberals End Opinion Diversity Under Cover of 'Fake News' Campaign." *The Reference Shelf: Alternative Facts, Post-Truth, and the Information War*. Ed. Betsy Maury. Ipswich: H.W. Wilson, 2018. 89-90. Print.

APA: Gonzalez, M. (2018) Don't Let Liberals End Opinion Diversity Under Cover of "Fake News" Campaign. In Betsy Maury (Ed.), *The reference shelf: Alternative facts, post-truth, and the information war* (pp. 89-90). Ipswich, MA: H.W. Wilson. (Original work published 2017)

News Coverage Says a Study Claimed Fake News on Facebook Didn't Affect the Election

By Morten Bay
Slate, February 1, 2018

In January, it seemed like we got some good news about Facebook for once when three highly regarded political scientists released the results of a study of fake news on Facebook during the 2016 election to the public. The media coverage of the study was extensive and made it seem like all that hand-wringing over fake news—those crazy stories dreamed up by Macedonian teenagers and Russian troll farm workers—was an overreaction. A piece in the *New York Times* claimed the study showed that fake news stories only had "little impact" on voters, because the "false stories were a small fraction of the participants' overall news diet." *Quartz* concluded the study said that "Just a small group of Americans consume fake news." Perhaps unsurprisingly, the conservative website the *Daily Caller* found the study to show that fake news had "considerably less significant impact on voters leading up to the 2016 election than many commentators would have you believe."

But though the news coverage largely presented the study as if it concluded that fake news didn't have much impact on the election, that is not the case. The study had an important limitation: It looked only at Facebook users who actually *clicked* on one of the fake news links littering their news feeds during the election.

For their research, Brendan Nyhan from Dartmouth, Jason Reifler of the University of Exeter, and Andrew Guess of Princeton looked at actual visitors to fake news websites during the last presidential election and concluded that these sites mostly influenced visitors who were already of a certain persuasion. They also found that few undecided voters actively engaged with the same websites. That's an interesting finding, but it "significantly undershoot[s] the true exposure to this material," says Michael Suman, research director at the USC Annenberg School of Communication Center for the Digital Future. "I would argue that *most* exposure to the content of fake news stories is probably incidental, a headline, references in all kinds of places, online discussions." Suman points to the classic media studies concept of the two-step flow model, which he says "showed how news affected voters, but mostly secondhand, through opinion leaders who passed on to others what they got from the media."

Colin Doty teaches courses on misinformation at UCLA and California Lutheran University and is currently writing a book about the phenomenon. He agrees that the study leaves out a substantial amount of people who may be exposed to fake news: "It implies that people who didn't click on the stories were not persuaded by them. The study doesn't really know that, because people might also share the stories without reading them."

Doty is quick to point out, however, that the authors aren't at fault here: "I think the press is overemphasizing the impact, which the paper doesn't actually address," he says. "It talks about who clicked on the stories." The study's authors never claimed that it showed anything about impact, either: "Our study is very clear that we did not measure how much fake news affected an individual's opinions about the election or whether fake news affected the outcome of the election," professors Nyhan, Guess, and Reifler told *Slate* in

> **"Relyng solely on click-thru rates and desktop web browsing data to measure the influence of fake news avoids different ways people engage in mobile social reading."**

an email. They also acknowledge that they only revealed the tip of the misinformation iceberg: "It's important to emphasize that our estimates are likely a lower bound for total fake news consumption."

If that's the "lower bound for total fake news consumption," then exposure could be exponentially larger than what the media gleaned from the study. But it's impossible to study the questions Doty and Suman raise in more detail. Facebook simply isn't willing to part with the data, say the three professors behind the study. Emphasizing the importance of studying indirect exposure to fake news, they make it clear that they "specifically state in the paper that we do not capture other types of exposure. Unless Facebook chooses to share its data with us or other researchers, we cannot observe what happens in the news feed of a proprietary social media platform."

Still, in the news coverage of the study, the influence of fake news was downplayed. *The New York Times* claimed, for instance, that it "paled in influence beside mainstream news coverage." But some researchers disagree about that, too. The Oxford Internet Institute in the U.K. is home to the Computational Propaganda Project, a group of researchers who study, among other things, fake news campaigns in elections. They found that in Michigan, a state that Trump won in 2016 by less than 12,000 votes, fake news stories were shared as frequently as real news in the last days of the election. Stories from news outlets made up two-thirds of all content being shared, and one of those thirds consisted solely of fake news. Nyhan, Guess, and Reifler generally praise the Computational Propaganda Project's work, but they also point out to *Slate* that the Michigan study was based on Twitter users. Facebook, the authors say, is a more reliable platform to study, because it has a much larger reach.

But there's another, perhaps bigger, limitation of the study: It focuses on people who use Facebook on a computer, even though Facebook says that worldwide, about 93 percent of its daily active users in December 2016 accessed the site from a mobile device. (That percentage is probably slightly lower in the U.S., though.)

"Relying solely on click-thru rates and desktop web browsing data to measure the influence of fake news avoids different ways people engage in mobile social reading," says Amelia Acker, professor of information studies at the University of Texas. It isn't just that there are far more mobile users than desktop users; *where* you consume Facebook also changes the experience. "Motivations for reading an article, broadcasting, or reposting stories to your social network will be different across contexts, whether you are sitting at a laptop or looking at your phone while waiting in line," she says. "So, what qualifies as 'exposure' to fake news will also be different." You may be less likely to check the validity of a news story before sharing it on your smartphone than you would on a computer, for instance.

The study's authors agree that lack of mobile data is a limitation. They say that they have included the mobile data in an appendix showing that "the patterns we observe are similar in mobile browsers, but these data are more limited in both panelist coverage and the lack of page-level information."

Nyhan, Guess, and Reifler have now submitted the study to an academic journal, where it is undergoing peer review. In other words, the version of the paper that received all the media attention was not the final product but more of a call for comments. Sharing unpublished research that has yet to undergo review is a process Nyhan believes in for academic reasons: "The feedback makes the work better," he wrote on Twitter last year.

With a seemingly appropriate amount of foresight, his tweet continued: "But the media has to be careful. Essential to consult other experts, explain limitations, and put studies in context of literatures." It's a warning those covering his study would have been wise to heed.

Print citations

CMS: Bay, Morten. "News Coverage Says a Study Claimed Fake News on Facebook Didn't Affect the Election." In *The Reference Shelf: Alternative Facts, Post-Truth, and the Information War,* edited by Betsy Maury, 91-93. Ipswich, MA: H.W. Wilson, 2018.

MLA: Bay, Morten. "News Coverage Says a Study Claimed Fake News on Facebook Didn't Affect the Election." *The Reference Shelf: Alternative Facts, Post-Truth, and the Information War.* Ed. Betsy Maury. Ipswich: H.W. Wilson, 2018. 91-93. Print.

APA: Bay, M. (2018). News coverage says a study claimed fake news on Facebook didn't affect the election. In Betsy Maury (Ed.), *The reference shelf: Alternative facts, post-truth, and the information war* (pp. 91-93). Ipswich, MA: H.W. Wilson. (Original work published 2017)

"Post-Truth" Media Really Is Shifting the News Agenda—And More Subtly Than It Seems

By Precious N. Chatterje-Doody
The Conversation, September 1, 2017

As stories of Russian "information warfare" in various Western countries continue to mount, governments, intelligence agencies and journalists are fretting over the influence of global media outlets funded by autocratic governments. But while these organisations are clearly meant to serve their sponsor governments' agendas in various ways, is the West right to be so worried about them?

Information campaigning in various forms is as old as politics itself, and nor is it the sole province of political bogeymen. Research shows that democracies are better than autocracies at influencing foreign public opinion, and businesses, politicians and states all use the mass media strategically for their information campaigns.

Whether this is public relations, public diplomacy, or propaganda is a matter of perspective. But the names we give a particular information campaign not only reflect our inferences about its aims; they can in fact amplify its power and advance its goals.

A case in point is the Kremlin-funded international broadcaster RT, formerly Russia Today. The network has been sanctioned by media watchdogs for its "misleading" coverage, even as it gathered five Emmy nominations for its investigative reporting. It was even cited by Hillary Clinton in 2011 as an example of an "information war" she said the West was losing—unwittingly describing things to come in her own career.

The network's PR strategy skilfully uses these criticisms to cater to the biases of an anti-establishment generation. Its motto encourages viewers to "Question More", and its various advertising campaigns have successfully exhibited Western contempt and suspicion as a badge of honour.

Yet despite the concerns of high-ranking figures, the US State Department has claimed none of the US$80m recently allocated by Congress for informational countermeasures, and the bulk of the funds will expire if not claimed by the end of September 2017. Some fear that the US is reluctant to risk a Russian backlash by leading a counter-disinformation offensive, leaving the legwork to initiatives like the controversial new Hamilton 68 dashboard, which claims to track Russian-backed influence campaigns across the web and social media.

But just how much influence RT and similar outlets wield is very much open to question.

Fact-checked articles are less influential than the stories they attack, and can actually help disseminate falsehoods to audiences who are prone to misremember them as fact.

Flattering Bias

While many in US intelligence and politics seem to take RT's self-reported audience figures as read, the channel's official data is optimistic compared to its externally verified viewing figures. And despite RT's pride at being "the most watched news network on YouTube", most of its views go to apolitical clickbait human interest stories and coverage of natural disasters.

Some argue that RT's smaller political audience is self-selecting: those who mistrust the mainstream establishment and are partial to conspiracy theories. However, this is all guesswork: so far, there has been little scholarly attention to RT's audience engagement, despite its social media advantage over its competitors during breaking news events. (The University of Manchester and Open University will soon address this knowledge gap with the Reframing Russia project, the first systematic examination of RT's audiences, ethos and multiplatform output.)

While RT may have limited capacity to influence those not already sympathetic to its aims, its reach across social and traditional media, and freedom from any commitment to impartiality, equip it perfectly for an atmosphere of rumour and counter-rumour.

This brings us back to Donald Trump and his ongoing crusade against the mainstream media.

Trump echoes RT's line that all news reporting is biased in some way, and his social media output clearly flatters the views of his followers and allies. Trump's tweets are, intentionally or not, perfectly calibrated to exploit the same effect as RT: audiences seek out content that accords with their political beliefs, and ignore information that does not correspond to their biases.

This effect is even clearer where people have strong political beliefs and ideologically segregated social media networks, because algorithms lock our preferences into our social media experience. Counterintuitively, we're most likely to enter into debate with people with similar views to our own, not those who we perceive as being different and who can offer an alternative world view.

Worst of all, if much of your social media following is made up of automated "bots" primed to repeat, circulate and amplify particular messages—as seems likely in Trump's case—then the volume of echoes increases exponentially. The result? Political opinions are polarised, with completely fabricated stories more widely shared (and believed) than genuine news.

Playing the Mainstream

These patterns are strongest among more ideologically motivated groups, especially those on the political "fringe". While less partisan audiences still look to the mainstream media, the agenda of the mainstream media is nonetheless shifting in response to fringe groups' online interactions. As mainstream outlets report on social media trends, they amplify stories that originated in fringe groups, particularly when the stories reflect their ideological stance.

But the effect is not uniform across the political spectrum. Research on the US media shows that conservative news websites are more likely than liberal ones to propagate fabricated stories, and conservative individuals are more likely to believe them—but that liberal media outlets are more likely to change their agenda in response.

Crucially, fact-checking disputed stories does not help. Fact-checked articles are less influential than the stories they attack, and can actually help disseminate falsehoods to audiences who are prone to misremember them as fact. More than that, merely fact-checking articles on fringe topics only makes those topics objects of mainstream discussion.

Fears about particular outlets' "propaganda" stories are misplaced, since those stories generally only influence self-selecting "fringe" groups. What's really concerning is how these groups repeat and amplify their preferred messages, and how their efforts influence media agendas and shift the parameters of political debate. With trust in the media declining fast, people are increasingly consulting partisan alternatives.

That not only opens the field for players like RT, but polarises social discussion to the point of outright conflict. And as recent events in Charlottesville, Virginia prove, that conflict is not confined to the online world.

Print citations

CMS: "'Post-Truth' Media Really Is Shifting the News Agenda—And More Subtly Than It Seems." In *The Reference Shelf: Alternative Facts, Post-Truth, and the Information War,* edited by Betsy Maury, 94-96. Ipswich, MA: H.W. Wilson, 2018.

MLA: "'Post-Truth' Media Really Is Shifting the News Agenda—And More Subtly Than It Seems." *The Reference Shelf: Alternative Facts, Post-Truth, and the Information War.* Ed. Betsy Maury. Ipswich: H.W. Wilson, 2018. 94-96. Print.

APA: The Conversation. (2018). "Post-truth" media really is shifting the news agenda—And more subtly than it seems. In Betsy Maury (Ed.), *The reference shelf: Alternative facts, post-truth, and the information war* (pp. 94-96). Ipswich, MA: H.W. Wilson. (Original work published 2017)

Trump's "Fake News Awards": Fail to Live Up to the Hype—Or the Hysteria

By W. James Antle III
Washington Examiner, January 18, 2017

President Trump's "Fake News Awards" presentation began not with a bang but a Healthcare.gov-style crash of the Republican National Committee's website.

Anyone expecting a tuxedo-clad Trump to read cards bearing the names of the "failing *New York Times*" and "fake news CNN" or a flurry of new tweets for State Department staffers to print out was bound to be as disappointed as a cable news anchor snubbed by the president's show.

But the end result more closely resembled conservative gripes with the mainstream media that date back to Spiro Agnew, presented in RNC "fact sheet" form, than Joseph Stalin—unless the Media Research Center's regular "disHonors" award dinner constitutes a type of gulag.

Sen. Jeff Flake, R-Ariz., made a number of valid points in his speech criticizing Trump for engaging in this kind of media-bashing, especially when he pointed to more oppressive regimes that are luxuriating in the craze of calling unflattering headlines "fake news," and the White House's description of the retiring senator as a "mouthpiece of the Cuban government" over a perfectly legitimate policy difference was an unconscionably low blow.

Nevertheless, while Trump's tweeting out of the RNC webpage taking predictable, and often well-deserved, shots at various media outlets might indeed be a "spectacle" beneath the dignity of the office, it also "beggars belief" to describe it as an "assault on the constitutionally-protected free press."

To be singled out by Trump may invite a torrent of abuse from the president's supporters, especially on Twitter. All other things being equal, it does not make any journalist on the receiving end of Trump's tirades worse off career-wise. Most would eagerly wear the presidential opprobrium as a badge of honor.

Indeed, CNN's Jim Acosta used that very phrase after an Oval Office confrontation with Trump. He was recently promoted to chief White House correspondent. MSNBC's Katy Tur has seen her career take off after a series of contentious interviews with the future president on the campaign trail, including some uncomfortable—some feared dangerous—encounters with "Make America Great Again" rally-goers.

> **Trump himself accentuates all these problems. He is a serial exaggerator and fabulist.**

None of this justifies shabby treatment from the president or his supporters and it is perfectly legitimate for Trump-skeptical voices to ascend in the press, although Acosta frequently carries himself like a Ted Baxter-style parody of a pompous news anchor. Trump does not deserve an award himself for merely being rude while refraining from sending reporters to Guantanamo Bay.

But it ought to put Trump's transparently political campaign against the media in perspective. It mainly takes the form of silly publicity stunts rather than fearsome attacks on the First Amendment. Threat inflation is rampant in Washington and here is no different.

It is precisely because Trump entertains, though so far does little to implement, unhealthy ideas about "opening up" libel laws to make it harder to criticize the famous and the powerful—and because he has escalated the rhetoric of Republican press criticisms far beyond isolated, hot-mic barbs against this or that "major-league asshole" at a top newspaper—that it is important to not conflate even over-the-top media-bashing with real interference.

Trump's latest salvo against the media comes the day after reporters descended unto a briefing about the president's health and as a group appeared overeager and ill-informed, unprepared to deal in basic medical terms but skeptical of an examination that did not comport with their armchair diagnoses.

Maybe that skepticism is warranted. Speculation about Hillary Clinton's health, for example, was allowed some days. Other days it wasn't. You'll note these days weren't very far apart.

There is, however, an eagerness to get Trump that is too often resulting in stories that are too good to check. It results in errors that overwhelmingly run in one direction.

After Trump told the *Washington Examiner* last year that he was willing to entertain proposals to break up the 9th Circuit after some unfavorable court rulings, one cable news network ran the chyron: "Trump threatens to break up 9th circuit (he can't)."

Yet the full context involved legislation Congress could in fact pass, and Trump could actually sign it into law; it was not some unilateral, presidential court-smashing. Maybe it is not likely; maybe it is not wise. It is not constitutionally impossible or absurd.

Reporters are predominantly liberal. Even many of the conservative journalists working in New York and Washington opposed Trump, some all the way to Election Day. Many in the press feel they weren't hard enough on Trump in 2016 or were too hard on Clinton, offering too much coverage to her emails or flaws as a candidate while ignoring her Republican opponent because he was considered a sure loser.

The good reporting on Trump's scandals seemed to have little impact, with the significant exception of the "Access Hollywood" tape, which wound up being overtaken by email investigation-related events. On top of that, Trump routinely disparages journalists to the enthusiastic cheers of supporters who like how hard he hits back compared to previous Republicans—which really just eggs on the press.

All these tendencies have been magnified by the rapid news cycle, social media, and the political polarization of information sources into self-affirming echo chambers on all sides, in which all nuance is quickly stripped out of the discussion and errors seem to travel faster than corrections.

Trump himself accentuates all these problems. He is a serial exaggerator and fabulist. He conflates promptly corrected, if easily avoidable, mistakes with deliberately false information disseminated for propaganda, profit, or even fun—the original definition of "fake news"—while some of his own media boosters exercise minimal standards.

Perhaps this will erode norms in ways that come back to haunt press freedoms to a greater degree later. Or maybe such erosions will prove easier under a president who enjoys much chummier relations with the media.

In the war between Trump and the media, most of the casualties piling up on both sides are self-inflicted wounds.

Print Citations

CMS: Antle, W. James III. "Trump's 'Fake News Awards' Fail to Live Up to the Hype—Or the Hysteria." In *The Reference Shelf: Alternative Facts, Post-Truth, and the Information War*, edited by Betsy Maury, 97-99. Ipswich, MA: H.W. Wilson, 2018.

MLA: Antle, W. James III. "Trump's 'Fake News Awards' Fail to Live Up to the Hype—Or the Hysteria." *The Reference Shelf: Alternative Facts, Post-Truth, and the Information War*. Ed. Betsy Maury. Ipswich: H.W. Wilson, 2018. 97-99. Print.

APA: Antle, W. J. III. (2018). Trump's "fake news awards" fail to live up to the hype—or the hysteria. In Betsy Maury (Ed.), *The reference shelf: Alternative facts, post-truth, and the information war* (pp. 97-99). Ipswich, MA: H.W. Wilson. (Original work published 2017)

4

Fake News and Your Health

A Prescription bottle labeled Fake News: Helps Create a New Reality. Disinformation Supplement.

Fallacies, Bias, and the Post-Truth Mind

Is fake news dangerous? Is the flood of fake news and misinformation changing human psychology? These are some of the interesting questions that psychologists and other health professionals have been asking about the media environment. Coupled with concerns about the overall impact of social media and new modes of media engagement, some perceive a unique and growing threat to the quality and legitimacy of the American world view.

Social Media and Instinct

Humans are social animals and the ways that other social animals manage their interactions can therefore be illustrative when analyzing human behavior. For instance, like chimpanzees (*Pan troglodytes*), with whom humans share 98 percent of their genes, humans create gender and social hierarchies that dictate access to resources and to the benefits of society membership. Humans also share 85 percent of their genes with fish and, like social fish, human interaction and thought are dictated by sometimes simple social rules.[1]

In schooling fish, each fish reacts and acts so as to maintain an optimized place within the school. If Fish B perceives a wide gap between itself and Fish A, it will speed up, or if it feels it is too close to Fish A, it will slow its movement, so as to find a comfortable amount of space. These interactions aren't linear but occur in four dimensions, with Fish B reacting to other fish in front, behind, and all around in its environment. In a closed environment, like a barrel, the interactions that each fish uses to try and govern its position become more intense, with the fish rapidly rotating in a circle as their collective efforts to find a comfortable position and reactions to their environment create a repetitive system. The smaller the environment, the less space between the fish and the more uncomfortable each fish becomes.

This metaphor represents a person's social and media news environment. Information that a person consumes defines that person's distance from one or more other people, ideas, ways of thinking, etc. Media has evolved so as to better gauge consumer preference. In the social media world, consumers demonstrate their preference with symbols reflecting instinctual emotional reactions. Therefore, sad faces, angry faces, thumbs down, and cartoons of feces signify negative reactions, while happy faces, thumbs up, and hearts signify positive reactions. These various signifiers indicate interest and, whether good or bad, interest can be used to shape one's behavior.

A person motivated to be liked might behave in ways that maximize positive interest, while a person looking to provoke, might maximize negative interest. Individuals and companies therefore developed ways of maximizing interest and simplifying interactions such that interest, positive or negative, could be transformed into a simple quantity doling out instant rewards for those who participate. As the digital age allows everyone to become a content creator, this reward and punishment environment (the barrel that transcribes the schooling fishes' circle) is open to anyone.

Since the dawn of social media, psychologists and media analysts have been looking at the way that the changing media environment has impacted psychology. For one thing, researchers have found that the social media environment tends to make people more vulnerable to peer pressure because the simplified reward and punishment environment provides a far more concentrated effect for relatively minor behaviors than occurs, typically, in face-to-face interactions. This can lead to impulsive interactions and impulsive behavior overall, with social media use having been linked to problems with anger management and impulse control. Studies have shown that anger spreads more rapidly in social media than more positive emotions and so the promulgation of anger-eliciting media constitutes a large share of social media content.[2]

Social media turns interaction, artistic production, and news into a game in which persons seek rewards. Some seek out positive reactions (likes) while some seek out negative interactions for entertainment or to express their own anger. Whether negative or positive, all reactions are attention and thus have an encouraging effect for some consumers and content creators, while the only truly negative situation in the environment is to generate no interest at all. Relationships between persons also offer rewards, but the rewards are more diffuse and nuanced. Thus, forming direct relationships requires a different type of behavior that is not as readily reinforced as the multi-pronged reactionary environment of social media. Person-to-person relationships are more banal, but ultimately more developmentally impactful.[3]

The Evolutionary Psychology of Bias

When attempting to decipher information all humans have instinctual biases. For one thing, humans display a "confirmation bias," which means that people are more willing to accept information that confirms what the individual already feels or believes. Second, humans tend to exhibit "proportionality bias" in which a person is more likely to believe statements or ideas proportional to how impactful or important a person sees a certain issue. Thus, a big event, like the 9-11 terrorist attacks or the assassination of John F. Kennedy become the subject of conspiracy theories purporting a shadowy collection of actors engaged in secretive social manipulation and cover-ups. These explanations appealed to some because the magnitude of the event was seen as necessitating an explanation of similar magnitude, such as a global conspiracy. Further, humans tend to use "projection" when reasoning, in which a person projects his or her motivations or emotions onto others. Thus, if a person feels violently about a person or type of person, he or she is more likely to believe that that person or type of person feels the same about them.[4]

A 2017 article from the *European Journal of Psychology*, entitled "Too Special to Be Duped," explains how an instinctual desire to be unique creates another level of bias in the way people reason. Individuals with a more acute desire to see themselves as unique gravitate away from mainstream consensus and towards groups, behaviors, and beliefs that they see as more unique or unusual. Individuals who demonstrate an interest in body modification or tattoos, or in unusual clothing, tend to display a higher than average desire to be unique in psychological testing. This is also true of belief, with those displaying a higher desire to be unique more likely to believe conspiracy theories and other types of misinformation.[5] Thus, a person who believes that climate change is not occurring, despite the consensus of global scientists and experts in the field, might see him or herself as part of a small, special group that is, as the paper's title suggests, "too special to be duped" by the misinformation that has pervaded mainstream thought.

The evolutionary history of humanity has, in fact, left humans highly susceptible to many different types of flawed reasoning. For instance, generalizations are typically a poor tool to use in reasoning, and yet, in the distant past those who developed quick ideas about potential dangers by generalizing from the specific to the global might avoid danger where a more carefully considerate human would not.

The logical fallacy known as *post hoc ergo propter hoc* is another example and occurs when a person assumes a causal connection between two things without evidence. So, one might say, the economy is doing well, President X is president, so President X is responsible for the state of the economy. However, economic research reveals that the current state of an economy lags behind the policies and economic initiatives put into place typically several years before. Therefore, if President X recently assumed the presidency, then he or she likely had little to no actual impact on the state of the current economy, but rather, the policies of President X will be evident in the state of the economy two or more years later. The post hoc ergo propter hoc fallacy leads to poor reasoning, but, in the distant past, this type of flawed reasoning might have had survival value. A person who sees someone die after eating a certain type of berry and then decides that the berries are poisonous might be wrong about this connection and so might miss out on a delicious snack. However, if the berries really *are* poisonous, the decision to avoid them could potentially be life-saving.[6]

All of the various biases and fallacious reasoning errors play a role in "motivated reasoning," in which a person thinking about an issue is motivated to find an answer that confirms what the person already believes or wants to be true. Thus, when a mass shooting occurs in the United States in 2018, some individuals typically claim that the shooter is connected to "radical Islam," without evidence to confirm this belief. Even if this belief is quickly disproven by a police investigation, the belief is likely to continue within some circles both because this belief confirms existing biases and attitudes and because some see this type of explanation as proportional to the danger posed from Islamic philosophy.

The Post-Truth Label

The election of Donald Trump ushered in what some have called a "post-truth" era, nebulously defined by the perception that the narratives dominating the news, social media, and political avenues of discourse have been shaped by actors pursuing agendas and not by legitimate data. This perception has been motivated by the well-documented fact that Donald Trump has a tendency to either believe or at least make false claims about a variety of issues. Trump did not create a new era in human history, nor is he the primary architect of any current social transformation in the United States. It has been noted by historians that all presidents and perhaps all politicians occasionally lie to support their careers. Ronald Reagan told the public that he wasn't aware of the controversy regarding US federal funding of violent regimes in Central America, but it has since been revealed that he was well aware of how US action fueled the wars in the part of Central America still sometimes called the "Violent Triangle."

However, the frequency with which Donald Trump advances false narratives is unusual. The non-partisan fact-checking website *Politifact* found that full 70 percent of all the claims made by Trump were false, in that they were unable to locate data to support those claims. *Politifact* found that a further 11 percent of Trump's claims were mostly true, but misleading, and that only 4 percent were entirely credible. A full fifteen percent of claims made by Donald Trump were ranked by *Politifact* as "pants on Fire," which means that not even gross reinterpretation of the statement can create any semblance of truth.[7] By contrast, 51 percent of the claims made by Hillary Clinton were verifiably true, with about 24 percent being false and 2 percent rated as "pants on fire." So, while all presidents and perhaps all politicians lie, Trump's tendencies are unusual and have fueled an intense level of concern about his fitness as a leader.[8] While polls indicate that a majority of Americans view Trump as dishonest overall, the effects of his tendency to repeat false claims remain unclear.[9]

Psychologist Daniel Gilbert, in a 1991 research paper, "How Mental Systems Believe," explained that every time a person hears a lie, the brain's instinctual process means that, for a moment, the lie must first be accepted as true before the person engages in a deeper, fact-checking process that either confirms or rejects the information presented.[10] This underlying predisposition in the human mind, coupled with the rapidity of data in the modern information environment might explain why people like Trump are apparently failing to effectively reason regarding the validity of various claims. A 2018 study by Marcelle Tambuscio and colleagues found that the overload of information means that individuals do not dwell on a specific claim long enough to engage in a process of verification. Thus, a new claim comes along so quickly that the instinctual embrace of false claims remains rooted in the brain.[11] These studies suggest that the proliferation of lies can be exacerbated by the rapid flow of information in the Digital Age and by the tendency of consumers to switch between issues in the competitive media environment.

The "post-truth" label may itself be a reactionary response to the perception that inaccurate information is more frequently coming from top-tiers of the nation's political hierarchy as well as to the fact that this same faction has repeatedly questioned both the legitimacy of the mainstream media and the popular consensus on a variety of issues. On the importance of climate change, the effect of immigration, and the benefit of net neutrality, among other issues, the Trump administration's positions are well outside of the consensus of experts and also run opposed to public opinion. Why the administration has chosen to pursue policies not supported by professional research or reflecting public consensus is unclear but this tendency has fueled the perception that the administration actively ignores "truth" in pursuance of its own goals. Attitudes about Trump's dishonesty might be different in a more favorable environment, but Trump has not managed to achieve majority support among the public and so criticisms of his perceptively negative qualities are more intense and frequent because those criticisms reflect the views of a majority.

The modern information environment is not, of course, Trump's doing. Issue entrepreneurs, recreational provocateurs, and those duped into spreading misinformation themselves, all contribute to the legitimacy of modern media. It is worth noting that humans are still adjusting to digital data as the primary channel for discourse and to the more diverse information environment that has resulted from the digital revolution. It is likely that, as humans adjust, many of these issues will become less pronounced, but this process will also require research and investigation to show how inaccurate information is created and spreads through the social networks of the world.

Micah L. Issitt

Works Used

Buckley, Thea. "Why Do Some People Believe in Conspiracy Theories?" *Scientific American*. MIND. 2018. Web. 24 Feb 2018.

Bustamante, Thomas and Christian Dahlman, eds. *Argument Types and Fallacies in Legal Argumentation*. New York: Springer. 2015. Print.

Crist, Carolyn. "On the Mind: Your Brain on Social Media." *Paste*. Paste Media Group. Feb 28, 2017. Web. 24 Feb. 2018.

Crollius, Hughes Roesst and Jean Weissenbach. "Fish Genomics and Biology." *Genome Research*. No. 15. (2005): 1675–82. Print.

" Donald Trump's File." *Politifact*. Politifact. 2018. Web. 25 Feb 2018.

Fan, Rui, Xu, Ke, and Jichang Zhao. "High Contagion and Weaker Ties Mean Anger Spreads Faster Than Joy in Social Media." *arXiv*. Web. 25 Feb 2018.

Gilbert, Daniel T. "How Mental Systems Believe." *American Psychologist*. Vol. 46, No. 2. Feb 1991. Web. 25 Feb 2018.

Guess, Andrew, Nyhan, Brenadan, and Jason Reifler. "Selective Exposure to Misinformation: Evidence from the Consumption of Fake News during the 2016 Presidential Campaign." *Dartmouth University*. Web. 24 Feb 2018.

" Hillary Clinton's File." *Politifact*. Politifact. 2018. Web. 25 Feb 2018.

Imhoff, Roland and Pia Karoline Lamberty. "Too Special to Be Duped: Need for Uniqueness Motivates Conspiracy Beliefs." *European Journal of Social Psychology*. Vol. 47, No. 6 (Oct 2017): 724–34. Web. 24 Feb 2018.

Malloy, Tim and Pat Smith Rubenstein, " Trump Is Intelligent, but Not Fit or Level Headed, U.S. Voters Tell Quinnipiac University National Poll; First Year Was 'Disaster,' 'Chaotic,' 'Successful'." *Quinnipiac University Poll*. Jan 10, 2018. Web. 25 Feb 2018.

Nordquist, Richard. "Logical Fallacy Defined with Examples." *Thought Co*. Web. 25 Feb 2018.

Panko, Ben. "How Fake News Breaks Your Brain." *Smithsonian*. Smithsonian Institution. Jun 30, 2017. Web. 24 Feb 2018.

Notes

1. Crollius and Weissenbach, "Fish Genomics and Biology."
2. Fan, Xu, and Zhao, "Higher Contagion and Weaker Ties Mean Anger Spreads Faster Than You in Social Media."
3. Crist, "On the Mind: Your Brain on Social Media."
4. Buckley, "Why Do Some People Believe in Conspiracy Theories?"
5. Imhoff and Lamberty, "Too Special to Be Duped: Need for Uniqueness Motivates Conspiracy Beliefs."
6. Nordquist, "Logical Fallacy Defined with Examples."
7. "Donald Trump's File," *Politifact*.
8. "Hillary Clinton's File," *Politifact*.
9. Malloy and Smith, " Trump Is Intelligent, But Not Fit or Level Headed, U.S. Voters Tell Quinnipiac University National Poll; First Year Was 'Disaster,' 'Chaotic,' 'Successful'."
10. Gilbert, "How Mental Systems Believe."
11. Panko, "How Fake News Breaks Your Brain."

Post-Truth: The Dark Side of the Brain

By Sebastian Dieguez

Scientific American, **September 2017**

It may seem surprising that after being elected president, Donald Trump continued to insist that the elections were rigged. Or that he accused his predecessor of having tapped his phone—without any proof. Or that one of his advisers claimed that the inauguration ceremony had shattered the record for attendance, which clearly it had not. But that would underestimate the new and baffling phenomenon of "post-truth," of which Trump is the most striking example.

Post-truth triumphed the day after the U.K. voted in favor of Brexit. That's when its defenders acknowledged that they had misled the public about the health care benefits of leaving Europe. It triumphed again when François Fillon's center-right campaign for the French presidency rushed to exaggerate the number of supporters who turned out for a campaign rally in the Place du Trocadéro in Paris. And again when the Spanish government expressed pride in having strategically placed many researchers abroad in scientific collaborations, when in fact they had left as a result of relentless budget cuts. Further examples include the Turkish government, which complains of being censored in Europe—while imprisoning its journalists. And Russia, which supplies the whole world with dubious information through clever use of media propaganda.

Leaving aside politicians, "alternative facts" are created and disseminated at all levels. It is this planetary tsunami of false information that has driven many experts to refer to the era of "post-truth." But what exactly is it? Derived from the title of a book published by journalist Ralph Keyes in 2004, the term achieved its 15 minutes of fame after being selected in 2016 as the Oxford Dictionaries Word of the Year. The Oxford Dictionaries defines post-truth as an adjective "relating to or denoting circumstances in which objective facts are less influential in shaping public opinion than appeals to emotion and personal belief." This definition reflects a profound lack of confidence in the "legitimate" dispensers of facts (particularly the media and experts), making any truth, or any claim to the truth, suspect. Falsehood, in all its forms, thus takes on a routine character, becomes omnipresent and overwhelming, and enjoys virtually complete immunity. The sciences, unfortunately, are not spared, as shown by the climate controversy and the categorical rejection of vaccines by a segment of the population. Some people will even assert (as former NBA player Shaquille O'Neal did recently) that Earth is flat and defend their right to say it.

The term "post-truth," however, is not without its detractors. Some observers point out that the phenomenon of disinformation has always existed and that, consequently, there is nothing new or "post" under the sun. Because when have we ever really known an "era of truth"? Or been perfectly and impartially informed? Or bothered to listen to points of view contrary to ours and argued solely on the basis of facts? Others dispute the idea that "truth" is even a relevant concept, given that it most often is left to certain dominant elites to determine what is false and what is true, according to their own interests.

An Unholy Alliance?

The lack of consensus notwithstanding, there does seem to be something new about the current phenomenon. Many experts see it as the monstrous fruit of the encounter between our ancestral psychological propensities and technological progress.

In fact, our good old Homo sapiens brain is not as concerned with objectivity as one might think. Its priority is rather to safeguard its own regime of truth. The "argumentative theory of reasoning" of French researchers Hugo Mercier and Dan Sperber postulates that our very ability to reason is constrained and shaped by our need to be right and to convince. This explains our numerous errors of reasoning, which far from being anarchic or random, often stroke our ego. Thus, we more readily accept and retain information that suits us and that reinforces our beliefs—a tendency known as confirmation bias. According to a recent study by Jonas Kaplan of the University of Southern California and his colleagues, an entire cerebral network is involved in ego representation (called the default mode network). This network is activated when we receive information contrary to our political ideas, as if our very identity were being attacked.

In another study, Micah Edelson of the Weizmann Institute in Rehovot, Israel, and his colleagues showed that changing one's mind depends on increased activity in a small region called the anterior lateral prefrontal cortex. Yet this activity is inhibited by the combined action of the amygdala and the hippocampus, or the centers of emotion and memory, respectively. The memories and beliefs recorded in our brain appear to have the power to prevent us from changing our mind, especially if they are emotionally laden.

Rise of Individualism

Yet another factor—this one sociopolitical—is involved in maintaining false beliefs: economic progress goes hand in hand with a rise in individualism. This link was recently shown by Henri Santos of the University of Waterloo in Ontario and his colleagues. The researchers looked at data from 77 countries over 51 years, using behavioral criteria (such as the percentage of people living alone) and values associated with individualism (for example, using data from surveys assessing the importance of independence). In an individualist society, personal expression and forming opinions are highly valued. Truth and memory are thus perceived less as a common, shared legacy than in traditional societies and more as strictly sacrosanct, private goods.

Consequently, when partisans of François Fillon or Donald Trump believed they saw larger crowds than were truly present, their brain is blocking both the information that contradicts their beliefs and the brain regions that would allow them to change their mind. The sociopolitical context then reinforces their right to maintain their beliefs—a perverse outcome of what begins as a positive impulse, namely, to form an individual opinion.

But individual blindness is hardly the whole story. Another key characteristic of the era of post-truth is the way in which false information spreads. Here is where new technologies, and in particular social networks, come into play: the ability to share and disseminate makes it possible for any belief to turn into "information," especially as the distinction between them tends to disappear. Walter Quattrociocchi and his team at the IMT School for Advanced Studies in Lucca, Italy, showed how Facebook amplifies the confirmation bias through its "personalized" algorithms. In fact, these algorithms lead to the creation of isolated communities that tend to become polarized, ones whose beliefs are reinforced and become ever more extreme.

Buzz Neurons

A study done in 2017 shows how much our lack of ancestral concern for objectivity is reflected on social networks. Using functional MRI, researchers at the University of Pennsylvania analyzed the brain activity of subjects reading *New York Times* articles and then asked them to rate their likelihood of sharing the articles later. The question the researchers wanted to answer was: Does this brain activity predict whether information will become viral on social networks? By comparing the number of actual sharing generated by the article with the participants' fMRI scans, the researchers concluded that this was indeed the case. The key was the activity of a "judgment system" comprising the ventral striatum and the ventromedial prefrontal cortex: the more these regions were activated during reading, the more success the article had on the Internet. The ventral striatum is involved in motivation and pleasure, and the ventromedial prefrontal cortex in self-representation and social cognition.

> **We more readily accept and retain information that suits us and that reinforces our beliefs—a tendency known as confirmation bias.**

These results suggest that the choice of sharing an article is based on anticipating the reactions of others ("Will my social network like it and respond?") and on the hope for increased personal prestige (being picked up and "liked" is a reward in itself that undoubtedly contributes to the success of social networks). It is not, however, based on the veracity of the information.

Consequently, even information that is false spreads. Conditions seem ripe for a threshold effect: drowning in a mess of falsehoods and vagaries, the truth loses all prescriptive power to lay out a course of action. This is an unprecedented situation that leaves observers perplexed. How can we fight against post-truth when there is no recognition of the difference between objective reality and personal opinion? Fortunately, remedies are at hand: never before have we seen so much analysis and fact-checking. Even sales of *1984* by George Orwell, a forerunner in the denunciation of disinformation, are surging.

The Hydra Head of Post-Truth

But to what effect? Unfortunately, post-truth possesses formidable self-defense mechanisms. Disseminating corrective updates, however factual they may be, often reinforces false information, simply because it is thus repeated and propagated. Attacking an alternative fact also gives it weight, making it more credible and memorable than it deserves. Another difficulty arises from the fact that "official" sources evoke a certain degree of mistrust. Vaccination campaigns therefore tend to reinforce the hostility of people who oppose vaccines—in other words, precisely those whose behavior should be changed (the so-called boomerang effect). Why? Because they feel that their convictions are being attacked, one of which is that an unnamed "they" seeks to silence them by any means.

Worse, a recent study shows that even if we succeed in changing false beliefs, this does not guarantee a change in behavior. Briony Swire of the Massachusetts Institute of Technology and her collaborators interviewed subjects of all political stripes during the presidential campaign of 2016, before Trump was elected. They were asked to rate whether the billionaire's statements were true or false. Not surprisingly, Trump's supporters were more likely to believe them. After they were presented with corrections of objectively false statements, however, an amazing thing happened: participants reduced their belief in the falsehoods, regardless of the source of the explanation—whether from a pro- or anti-Trump expert—but they did not change their voting preferences.

In short, all signs indicate that we expect to be lied to and that deep down many of us find it normal or hardly realize it. As the authors concluded, "Something other than the truth [of his statements] accounted for his success."

End of Cognitive Dissonance

In principle, being directly contradicted by the facts should create a form of dissonance, an uncomfortable cognitive state that must be resolved one way or another, at the very least by acknowledging bad faith—basic postulates of a theory put forward by psychologist Leon Festinger in the mid-1950s. Here, too, we may be looking at an unprecedented phenomenon deserving of study: post-truth could be killing cognitive dissonance, which had the virtue at least of signaling some kind of incoherence.

How, then, are we to resist? Tried-and-true methods are obviously of paramount importance: to reestablish truth in all circumstances, to gain confidence by being rigorous and impartial, to teach critical thinking at school. Yet perhaps the truth is ill equipped to win this battle alone. Perhaps it is also worth rehabilitating fiction by invoking its distinctiveness: after all, "post-truth" could well imply a "post-fiction" world. Today the boundaries are blurred: Trump was, after all, a champion of reality TV, the genre that introduced the idea that one could film unscripted day-to-day life and live a fairy tale. In this context, Françoise Lavocat, professor of comparative literature at the New Sorbonne University, Paris, advocates reestablishing a clear distinction between truth and fiction. As a species, we are particularly fond of stories. Of that there is no doubt. But it only increases the urgency of resolving to defend truth and facts. We are at a critical juncture. It may never be more important to make the most of our extraordinary ability to invent alternative worlds and to learn to enjoy them without confusing them with reality.

In Brief

• Many political leaders have recently taken to making fanciful statements. These assertions combine with the mass of false information circulating on the Internet and influence public opinion. People no longer seem to care about objective reality. We have gotten to the point where experts now refer to the era of post-truth.

• Although "truth" is discussed all the time, it has never had as little currency as it does now. Researchers explain this development as the product of our ancestral brain encountering modern individualism and new technologies. Studies show that what we find interesting about information is not so much its veracity as the social prestige it brings, especially on social networks.

• The phenomenon is difficult to control because it is armed with formidable mechanisms of self-defense. But fact-checking and education in critical thinking initiatives must continue to develop. We may also need to rehabilitate fiction, emphasizing its capacity to give us pleasure without needing to make it into reality.

Print Citations

CMS: Dieguez, Sebastian. "Post-Truth: The Dark Side of the Brain." In *The Reference Shelf: Alternative Facts, Post-Truth, and the Information War*, edited by Betsy Maury, 109-113. Ipswich, MA: H.W. Wilson, 2018.

MLA: Dieguez, Sebastian. "Post-Truth: The Dark Side of the Brain." *The Reference Shelf: Alternative Facts, Post-Truth, and the Information War*. Ed. Betsy Maury. Ipswich: H.W. Wilson, 2018. 109-113. Print.

APA: Dieguez, S. (2018). Post-truth: The dark side of the brain. In Betsy Maury (Ed.), *The reference shelf: Alternative facts, post-truth, and the information war* (pp. 109-113). Ipswich, MA: H.W. Wilson. (Original work published 2017)

The New Psychology of Fake News

By Vinita Mehta

Psychology Today, June 29, 2017

Last year, an armed man entered a neighborhood restaurant called Comet Ping Pong in Washington, DC. He fired his assault rifle multiple times inside the family-friendly establishment. Thankfully, police apprehended the gunman and no one was hurt. This well-known eatery is not far from where I both live and practice, and I've been there on a number of occasions myself.

Needless to say it was far too close for comfort. And the man's explanation of his actions was particularly disturbing: He was investigating a conspiracy theory about Hillary Clinton operating a child sex ring out of the restaurant. Since fake news has been essentially been waging war on truth and democracy, perhaps it's unsurprising that it would eventually lead to an event with real guns.

But why is fake news so believable—despite that it's so often preposterous? New research led by Gordon Pennycook of Yale University helps explain why it's so easy to judge fake news as the real deal.

The research extends work on the illusory truth effect, which has demonstrated that familiarity increases the perceived accuracy of plausible statements, even if they are untrue. This is because we cognitively process material that is familiar to us with much greater ease, and this familiarity subsequently serves as a heuristic (a cognitive method of problem solving). For example, one study found that when participants repeated the false statement, "Chemosynthesis is the name of the process by which plants make their food," they evaluated it as more accurate even though they reported that they knew the right answer.

Building on this body of work, Pennycook and his team conducted a series of three studies based on the 2016 election that investigated whether the illusory truth effect can help explain the phenomenon of fake news.

Study 1: Familiarity Makes Fake News Seem Accurate

In the first study, Pennycook and his collaborators examined the relationship between familiarity and the perceived accuracy of news stories. To that end, they had participants view actual news headlines. Five stories were real news, and five were fake news (i.e., five items were factually accurate, and five items were complete falsehoods). The fake news headlines were sensational and highly partisan. For example, "Donald Trump Sent His Own Plane To Transport 200 Stranded Marines," and "FBI Agent Suspected in Hillary Email Leaks Found Dead In Apparent Murder-Suicide." Quite cleverly, the team used the same format as postings on Facebook—that is, a headline with a corresponding photograph and byline.

Participants then rated each headline for both familiarity and accuracy, and the researchers crunched the numbers. The results were striking. In line with expectations, familiar news headlines were much more likely to be perceived as accurate by comparison to unfamiliar news headlines. What's more, even though the real news headlines were generally viewed as more accurate than the fake ones, familiarity was an overriding factor in that participants rated familiar fake news to be more accurate than unfamiliar real news.

Study 2: We Use Low-Level Thinking When We Encounter Fake News

In their second study, Pennycook and his collaborators explored the cognitive mechanisms that underlie the relationship between familiarity and the perception of accuracy of news headlines. More specifically, they wanted to see if participants engaged low-level rather than high-level thinking processes. In other words, are people engaging reasoned and deliberative thought processes when reading headlines?

The investigators designed a three-stage experiment. In stage one, the familiarization stage, participants viewed equal numbers of real and fake news headlines and were asked whether they would share each headline on social media (of note, some were collected from *Snopes.com*, a website that fact-checks news stories). In stage two, the distractor stage, participants completed a questionnaire that asked about their demographic background. This was done to temporarily refocus their attention. In stage three, the assessment stage, participants were presented with the 12 news headlines they viewed in the familiarization stage and 12 new headlines (six fake news, six real news). Participants rated each headline for familiarity and accuracy.

The authors tested lower-level vs. higher level thinking processes in two ways. First, they analyzed the effect of providing participants with explicit information about accuracy as they would experience it in real life. Half of the participants were assigned to a "warning condition," in which the fake news stories were flagged with a caution emoji and the text "Disputed by 3rd Party Fact-Checkers." Facebook specifically developed this warning in order to stanch the spread of fake news.

The authors reasoned that if the familiarity effect is driven by high-level thinking processes, a warning should weaken its influence. According to this logic, a participant's thinking would change from "I saw this before so it's probably true" to "I saw this before and it's probably not true." Put another way, a direct warning should make participants question the accuracy of a fake news headline when seen in the familiarization stage.

However, if low-level thinking processes are being used, then an explicit warning would have no influence—and familiar headlines would still lead participants to perceive them as accurate, regardless of whether they were real or fake news. What were the results? The familiarity effect was found for fake news headlines in both the warning and no-warning conditions. That is, participants rated familiar fake news headlines that they were explicitly warned about as more accurate than unfamiliar fake news headlines that they were not warned about.

Pennycook and his team also examined the influence of "political concordance," or agreement, on the familiarity effect. A sizable body of work has demonstrated that politically charged material can give rise to what's known as motivated reasoning. This is reasoning that is biased in favor of conclusions that match one's already established view. To test for the possible impact of motivated reasoning, the researchers presented participants with equal numbers of pro-Republican and pro-Democrat news headlines. In particular, they wanted to see if participants would be more likely to assess news headlines as being accurate if they were concordant with their views.

> **This series of studies helps to explain the pernicious reach of fake news, and how misinformation can fold into our memories with such disturbing ease.**

The authors contend that politically discordant headlines should activate high-level reasoning. What did they find? Low-level thinking processes were again at play, as the familiarity effect was found for both politically concordant and discordant headlines. In other words, participants judged familiar headlines to be more accurate, whether or not the stories matched their political views.

Study 3: Familiarity Makes Fake News Seem More Accurate, Even after a Week

In the third study, Pennycook and his team followed the same three-stage procedure they used in Study 2. Yet the researchers made key changes. First, they increased the amount of time between the familiarization stage and the accuracy stage to assess the persistence of the familiarity effect. They also increased the length of the distractor stage by adding 20 more unrelated items to the demographics questionnaire. And the participants were invited to return for a follow-up session one week later, at which they were presented with the same headlines they had seen in the assessment stage as well as a set of new headlines not included in the first session. By designing the study this way, the researchers could look at how time influenced the stability of the familiarity effect over both the course of a testing session and the span of a week.

Again, headlines presented in the familiarization stage were rated as more accurate than novel headlines. And one week later, the investigators found a clear effect of familiarity on accuracy ratings. Moreover, the perceived accuracy of a story rose linearly with the number of times the participants had been exposed to that particular story, suggesting a sort of compounding effect. The relationship between number of exposures and accuracy remained when only fake news stories were under consideration. And it was found yet again for fake news in both the warning condition and the no-warning condition.

This series of studies helps to explain the pernicious reach of fake news, and how misinformation can fold into our memories with such disturbing ease. As the findings reveal, familiarity can breed trust. Though an explicit warning that a news item may be fake did help curb the problem to some degree, we clearly need to do more to stop the spread of fake news and falsehoods.

Print Citations

CMS: Mehta, Vinita. "The New Psychology of Fake News." In *The Reference Shelf: Alternative Facts, Post-Truth, and the Information War*, edited by Betsy Maury, 114-117. Ipswich, MA: H.W. Wilson, 2018.

MLA: Mehta, Vinita. "The New Psychology of Fake News." *The Reference Shelf: Alternative Facts, Post-Truth, and the Information War*. Ed. Betsy Maury. Ipswich: H.W. Wilson, 2018. 114-117. Print.

APA: Mehta, V. (2018). The new psychology of fake news. In Betsy Maury (Ed.), *The reference shelf: Alternative facts, post-truth, and the information war* (pp. 114-117). Ipswich, MA: H.W. Wilson. (Original work published 2017)

Yes, I'd Lie to You

The Economist, September 10, 2016

When Donald Trump, the Republican presidential hopeful, claimed recently that President Barack Obama "is the founder" of Islamic State and Hillary Clinton, the Democratic candidate, the "co-founder", even some of his supporters were perplexed. Surely he did not mean that literally? Perhaps, suggested Hugh Hewitt, a conservative radio host, he meant that the Obama administration's rapid pull-out from Iraq "created the vacuum" that the terrorists then filled?

"No, I meant he's the founder of ISIS," replied Mr Trump. "He was the most valuable player. I give him the most valuable player award. I give her, too, by the way, Hillary Clinton."

Mr Hewitt, who detests Mr Obama and has written a book denouncing Mrs Clinton's "epic ambition", was not convinced. "But he's not sympathetic to them. He hates them. He's trying to kill them," he pushed back.

Again, Mr Trump did not give an inch: "I don't care. He was the founder. The way he got out of Iraq was, that, that was the founding of ISIS, OK?"

For many observers, the exchange was yet more proof that the world has entered an era of "post-truth politics". Mr Trump appears not to care whether his words bear any relation to reality, so long as they fire up voters. *PolitiFact*, a fact-checking website, has rated more of his statements "pants-on-fire" lies than of any other candidate—for instance his assertion that "inner city crime is reaching record levels", which plays on unfounded fears that crime rates are rising.

And he is not the only prominent practitioner of post-truth politics. Britons voted to leave the European Union in June on the basis of a campaign of blatant misinformation, including the "fact" that EU membership costs their country £350m ($470m) a week, which could be spent instead on the National Health Service, and that Turkey is likely to join the EU by 2020.

Hang on, though. Don't bruised elites always cry foul when they fail to persuade the masses of their truth? Don't they always say the other side was peddling lies and persuaded ignoramuses to vote against their interest? Perhaps, some argue, British Remainers should accept the vote to leave the EU as an expression of justified grievance and an urge to take back control—not unlike the decision by many Americans to support Mr Trump.

There may have been some fibbing involved but it is hardly as though politics has ever been synonymous with truthfulness. "Those princes who do great things,"

Machiavelli informed his readers, "have considered keeping their word of little account, and have known how to beguile men's minds by shrewdness and cunning." British ministers and prime ministers have lied to the press and to Parliament, as Anthony Eden did during the Suez affair. Lyndon Johnson misinformed the American people about the Gulf of Tonkin incident, thus getting the country into Vietnam. In 1986 Ronald Reagan insisted that his administration did not trade weapons for hostages with Iran, before having to admit a few months later that: "My heart and my best intentions still tell me that's true, but the facts and evidence tell me it is not."

Fact or Fiction

It is thus tempting to dismiss the idea of "post-truth" political discourse—the term was first used by David Roberts, then a blogger on an environmentalist website, *Grist*—as a modish myth invented by *de-haut-en-bas* liberals and sore losers ignorant of how dirty a business politics has always been. But that would be complacent. There is a strong case that, in America and elsewhere, there is a shift towards a politics in which feelings trump facts more freely and with less resistance than used to be the case. Helped by new technology, a deluge of facts and a public much less given to trust than once it was, some politicians are getting away with a new depth and pervasiveness of falsehood. If this continues, the power of truth as a tool for solving society's problems could be lastingly reduced.

Reagan's words point to an important aspect of what has changed. Political lies used to imply that there was a truth—one that had to be prevented from coming out. Evidence, consistency and scholarship had political power. Today a growing number of politicians and pundits simply no longer care. They are content with what Stephen Colbert, an American comedian, calls "truthiness": ideas which "feel right" or "should be true." They deal in insinuation ("A lot of people are saying..." is one of Mr Trump's favourite phrases) and question the provenance, rather than accuracy, of anything that goes against them ("They would say that, wouldn't they?"). And when the distance between what feels true and what the facts say grows too great, it can always be bridged with a handy conspiracy theory.

This way of thinking is not new. America saw a campaign against the allegedly subversive activities of the "Bavarian Illuminati" in the early 19th century, and Senator Joseph McCarthy's witch-hunt against un-American activities in the 1950s. In 1964 a historian called Richard Hofstadter published *The Paranoid Style in American Politics*. When George W. Bush was president, the preposterous belief that the attacks of September 11th 2001 were an "inside job" spread far and wide among left-wingers, and became conventional wisdom in the Arab world.

The Lie of the Lands

Post-truth politics is advancing in many parts of the world. In Europe the best example is Poland's ultranationalist ruling party, Law and Justice (PiS). Among other strange stories, it peddles lurid tales about Poland's post-communist leaders plotting with the communist regime to rule the country together. In Turkey the protests at Gezi Park in 2013 and a recent attempted coup have given rise to all kinds of conspiracy theories, some touted by government officials: the first was financed by Lufthansa, a German airline (to stop Turkey from building a new airport which would divert flights from Germany), the second was orchestrated by the CIA.

Then there is Russia, arguably the country (apart from North Korea) that has moved furthest past truth, both in its foreign policy and internal politics. The Ukraine crisis offers examples aplenty: state-controlled Russian media faked interviews with "witnesses" of alleged atrocities, such as a child being crucified by Ukrainian forces; Vladimir Putin, Russia's president, did not hesitate to say on television that there were no Russian soldiers in Ukraine, despite abundant proof to the contrary.

Such *dezinformatsiya* may seem like a mere reversion to Soviet form. But at least the Soviets' lies were meant to be coherent, argues Peter Pomerantsev, a journalist whose memoir of Mr Putin's Russia is titled *Nothing Is True and Everything Is Possible*. In a study in 2014 for the Institute of Modern Russia, a think-tank, he quotes a political consultant for the president saying that in Soviet times, "if they were lying they took care to prove what they were doing was 'the truth'. Now no one even tries proving 'the truth'. You can just say anything. Create realities."

In such creation it helps to keep in mind—as Mr Putin surely does—that humans do not naturally seek truth. In fact, as plenty of research shows, they tend to avoid it. People instinctively accept information to which they are exposed and must work actively to resist believing falsehoods; they tend to think that familiar information is true; and they cherry-pick data to support their existing views. At the root of all these biases seems to be what Daniel Kahneman, a Nobel-prizewinning psychologist and author of a bestselling book, *Thinking, Fast and Slow*, calls "cognitive ease": humans have a tendency to steer clear of facts that would force their brains to work harder.

In some cases confronting people with correcting facts even strengthens their beliefs, a phenomenon Brendan Nyhan and Jason Reifler, now of Dartmouth College and the University of Exeter, respectively, call the "backfire effect". In a study in 2010 they randomly presented participants either with newspaper articles which supported widespread misconceptions about certain issues, such as the "fact" that America had found weapons of mass destruction in Iraq, or articles including a correction. Subjects in both groups were then asked how strongly they agreed with the misperception that Saddam Hussein had such weapons immediately before the war, but was able to hide or destroy them before American forces arrived.

As might be expected, liberals who had seen the correction were more likely to disagree than liberals who had not seen the correction. But conservatives who had seen the correction were even more convinced that Iraq had weapons of mass destruction. Further studies are needed, Mr Nyhan and Mr Reifler say, to see whether conservatives are indeed more prone to the backfire effect.

Given such biases, it is somewhat surprising that people can ever agree on facts, particularly in politics. But many societies have developed institutions which allow some level of consensus over what is true: schools, science, the legal system, the media. This truth-producing infrastructure, though, is never close to perfect: it can establish as truth things for which there is little or no evidence; it is constantly prey to abuse by those to whom it grants privileges; and, crucially, it is slow to build but may be quick to break.

Trust Your Gut

Post-truth politics is made possible by two threats to this public sphere: a loss of trust in institutions that support its infrastructure and deep changes in the way knowledge of the world reaches the public. Take trust first. Across the Western world it is at an all-time low, which helps explain why many prefer so-called "authentic" politicians, who "tell it how it is" (i.e., say what people feel), to the wonkish type. Britons think that hairdressers and the "man in the street" are twice as trustworthy as business leaders, journalists and government ministers, according to a recent poll by Ipsos MORI. When Michael Gove, a leading Brexiteer, said before the referendum that "people in this country have had enough of experts" he may have had a point.

This loss of trust has many roots. In some areas—dietary advice, for example—experts seem to contradict each other more than they used to; governments get things spectacularly wrong, as with their assurances about the wisdom of invading Iraq, trusting in the world financial system and setting up the euro. But it would be a mistake to see the erosion of trust simply as a response to the travails of the world. In some places trust in institutions has been systematically undermined.

Mr Roberts first used the term "post-truth politics" in the context of American climate-change policy. In the 1990s many conservatives became alarmed by the likely economic cost of a serious effort to reduce carbon emissions. Some of the less scrupulous decided to cast doubt on the need for a climate policy by stressing to the point of distortion uncertainties in the underlying science. In a memo Frank Luntz, a Republican pollster, argued: "Should the public come to believe that the scientific issues are settled, their views about global warming will change accordingly. Therefore, you need to continue to make the lack of scientific certainty a primary issue in the debate." Challenging—and denigrating—scientists in order to make the truth seem distant and unknowable worked pretty well. One poll found that 43% of Republicans believe climate change is not happening at all, compared to 10% of Democrats.

Some conservative politicians, talk-show hosts and websites, have since included the scientific establishment in their list of institutions to bash, alongside the government itself, the courts of activist judges and the mainstream media. The populist wing of the conservative movement thus did much to create the conditions for the trust-only-your-prejudices world of Mr Trump's campaign. Some are now having second thoughts. "We've basically eliminated any of the referees, the gatekeepers… There is nobody: you can't go to anybody and say: 'Look, here are the facts'" said Charlie Sykes, an influential conservative radio-show host, in a recent interview, adding that "When this is all over, we have to go back. There's got to be a reckoning on all this."

Yet gatekeepers would be in much less trouble without the second big factor in post-truth politics: the internet and the services it has spawned. Nearly two-thirds of adults in America now get news on social media and a fifth do so often, according to a recent survey by the Pew Research Centre, a polling outfit; the numbers continue to grow fast.

On Facebook, Reddit, Twitter or WhatsApp, anybody can be a publisher. Content no longer comes in fixed formats and in bundles, such as articles in a newspaper, that help establish provenance and set expectations; it can take any shape—a video, a chart, an animation. A single idea, or "meme", can replicate shorn of all context, like DNA in a test tube. Data about the spread of a meme has become more important than whether it is based on facts.

The mechanisms of these new media are only now beginning to be understood. One crucial process is "homophilous sorting": like-minded people forming clusters. The rise of cable and satellite television channels in the 1980s and 1990s made it possible to serve news tailored to specific types of consumer; the internet makes it much easier. According to Yochai Benkler of Harvard University in his book *The Wealth of Networks*, individuals with shared interests are far more likely to find each other or converge around a source of information online than offline. Social media enable members of such groups to strengthen each other's beliefs, by shutting out contradictory information, and to take collective action.

Fringe beliefs reinforced in these ways can establish themselves and persist long after outsiders deem them debunked: see, for example, online communities devoted to the idea that the government is spraying "chemtrails" from high-flying aircraft or that evidence suggesting that vaccines cause autism is being suppressed. As Eric Oliver of the University of Chicago points out in a forthcoming book, *Enchanted America: The Struggle between Reason and Intuition in US Politics*, this is the sort of thinking that comes naturally to Mr Trump: he was once devoted to the "birther" fantasy that Mr Obama was not born an American.

Following Mr Oliver's ideas about the increasing role of "magical thinking" on the American populist right, *The Economist* asked YouGov to look at different elements of magical thinking, including belief in conspiracies and a fear of terrible things, like a Zika outbreak or a terrorist attack, happening soon. Even after controlling for party identification, religion and age, there was a marked correlation with support for Mr Trump: 55% of voters who scored positively on our conspiracism index favoured him, compared with 45% of their less superstitious peers. These measures were not statistically significant predictors of support for Mitt Romney, the far more conventional Republican presidential candidate in 2012.

From Fringe to Forefront

Self-reinforcing online communities are not just a fringe phenomenon. Even opponents of TTIP, a transatlantic free-trade agreement, admit that the debate over it in Austria and Germany has verged on the hysterical, giving rise to outlandish scare stories—for instance that Europe would be flooded with American chickens treated with chlorine. "Battling TTIP myths sometimes feels like taking on Russian propaganda," says an EU trade official.

The tendency of netizens to form self-contained groups is strengthened by what Eli Pariser, an internet activist, identified five years ago as the "filter bubble". Back in 2011 he worried that Google's search algorithms, which offer users personalised results according to what the system knows of their preferences and surfing behaviour, would keep people from coming across countervailing views. Facebook subsequently became a much

> **Helped by new technology, a deluge of facts and a public much less given to trust than once it was, some politicians are getting away with a new depth and pervasiveness of falsehood. If this continues, the power of truth as a tool for solving society's problems could be lastingly reduced.**

better—or worse—example. Although Mark Zuckerberg, the firm's founder, insists that his social network does not trap its users in their own world, its algorithms are designed to populate their news feeds with content similar to material they previously "liked". So, for example, during the referendum campaign Leavers mostly saw pro-Brexit items; Remainers were served mainly pro-EU fare.

But though Facebook and other social media can filter news according to whether it conforms with users' expectations, they are a poor filter of what is true. Filippo Menczer and his team at Indiana University used data from *Emergent*, a now defunct website, to see whether there are differences in popularity between articles containing "misinformation" and those containing "reliable information". They found that the distribution in which both types of articles were shared on Facebook are very similar. "In other words, there is no advantage in being correct," says Mr Menczer.

If Facebook does little to sort the wheat from the chaff, neither does the market. Online publications such as *National Report*, *Huzlers* and the *World News Daily Report* have found a profitable niche pumping out hoaxes, often based on long-circulating rumours or prejudices, in the hope that they will go viral and earn clicks. Newly discovered eyewitness accounts of Jesus's miracles, a well-known ice-tea brand testing positive for urine, a "transgender woman" caught taking pictures of an underage girl in the bathroom of a department store—anything goes in this parallel news world. Many share such content without even thinking twice, let alone checking to determine if it is true.

Weakened by shrinking audiences and advertising revenues, and trying to keep up online, mainstream media have become part of the problem. "Too often news organisations play a major role in propagating hoaxes, false claims, questionable rumours and dubious viral content, thereby polluting the digital information stream," writes Craig Silverman, now the editor of *BuzzFeed Canada*, in a study for the Tow

Centre for Digital Journalism at the Columbia Journalism School. It does not help that the tools to keep track of and even predict the links most clicked on are getting ever better. In fact, this helps explain why Mr Trump has been getting so much coverage, says Matt Hindman of George Washington University.

Equally important, ecosystems of political online publications have emerged on Facebook—both on the left and the right. Pages such as Occupy Democrats and Make America Great can have millions of fans. They pander mostly to the converted, but in these echo chambers narratives can form before they make it into the wider political world. They have helped build support for both Bernie Sanders and Mr Trump, but it is the latter's campaign, friendly media outlets and political surrogates that are masters at exploiting social media and its mechanisms.

A case in point is the recent speculation about the health of Mrs Clinton. It started with videos purporting to show Mrs. Clinton suffering from seizures, which garnered millions of views online. *Breitbart News*, an "alt-right" web publisher that gleefully supports Mr. Trump—Stephen Bannon, the site's boss, took over as the Trump campaign's "chief executive officer" last month—picked up the story. "I'm not saying that, you know, she had a stroke or anything like that, but this is not the woman we're used to seeing," Mr Bannon said. Mr Trump mentioned Mrs Clinton's health in a campaign speech. Rudy Giuliani, a former mayor of New York, urged people to look for videos on the internet that support the speculation. The Clinton campaign slammed what it calls "deranged conspiracy theories", but doubts are spreading and the backfire effect is in full swing.

Such tactics would make Dmitry Kiselyov proud. "The age of neutral journalism has passed," the Kremlin's propagandist-in-chief recently said in an interview. "It is impossible because what you select from the huge sea of information is already subjective." The Russian government and its media, such as Rossiya Segodnya, an international news agency run by Mr Kiselyov, produce a steady stream of falsehoods, much like fake-news sites in the West. The Kremlin deploys armies of "trolls" to fight on its behalf in Western comment sections and Twitter feeds. Its minions have set up thousands of social-media "bots" and other spamming weapons to drown out other content.

"Information glut is the new censorship," says Zeynep Tufekci of the University of North Carolina, adding that other governments are now employing similar tactics. China's authorities, for instance, do not try to censor everything they do not like on social media, but often flood the networks with distracting information. Similarly, in post-coup Turkey the number of dubious posts and tweets has increased sharply. "Even I can no longer really tell what is happening in parts of Turkey," says Ms Tufekci, who was born in the country.

This plurality of voices is not in itself a bad thing. Vibrant social media are often a power for good, allowing information to spread that would otherwise be bottled up. In Brazil and Malaysia social media have been the conduit for truth about a corruption scandal involving Petrobras, the state oil company, and the looting of 1MDB, a state-owned investment fund. And there are ways to tell good information from bad. Fact-checking sites are multiplying, and not just in America: there are now nearly 100, according to the Reporters' Lab at Duke University. Social media have started to police their platforms more heavily: Facebook recently changed the algorithm that decides what users see in their newsfeeds to filter out more clickbait. Technology will improve: Mr Menczer and his team at Indiana University are building tools that can, among other things, detect whether a bot is behind a Twitter account.

The Truth Is Out There

The effectiveness of such tools, the use of such filters and the impact of such sites depends on people making the effort to seek them out and use them. And the nature of the problem—that the post-truth strategy works because it allows people to forgo critical thinking in favour of having their feelings reinforced by soundbite truthiness—suggests that such effort may not be forthcoming. The alternative is to take the power out of users' hands and recreate the gatekeepers of old. "We need to increase the reputational consequences and change the incentives for making false statements," says Mr Nyhan of Dartmouth College. "Right now, it pays to be outrageous, but not to be truthful."

But trying to do this would be a tall order for the cash-strapped remnants of old media. It is not always possible or appropriate for reporters to opine as to what is true or not, as opposed to reporting what is said by others. The courage to name and shame chronic liars—and stop giving them a stage—is hard to come by in a competitive marketplace the economic basis of which is crumbling. Gatekeeping power will always bring with it a temptation for abuse—and it will take a long time for people to come to believe that temptation can be resisted even if it is.

But if old media will be hard put to get a new grip on the gates, the new ones that have emerged so far do not inspire much confidence as an alternative. Facebook (which now has more than 1.7 billion monthly users worldwide) and other social networks do not see themselves as media companies, which implies a degree of journalistic responsibility, but as tech firms powered by algorithms. And putting artificial intelligence in charge may be a recipe for disaster: when Facebook recently moved to automate its "trending" news section, it promoted a fake news story which claimed that Fox News had fired an anchor, Megyn Kelly, for being a "traitor".

And then there is Mr Trump, whose Twitter following of over 11m makes him a gatekeeper of a sort in his own right. His moment of truth may well come on election day; the odds are that he will lose. If he does so, however, he will probably claim that the election was rigged—thus undermining democracy yet further. And although his campaign denies it, reports have multiplied recently that he is thinking about creating a "mini-media conglomerate", a cross of Fox and Breitbart News, to make money from the political base he has created. Whatever Mr Trump comes up with next, with or without him in the White House, post-truth politics will be with us for some time to come.

Print citations

CMS: "Yes, I'd Lie to You." In *The Reference Shelf: Alternative Facts, Post-Truth, and the Information War*, edited by Betsy Maury, 118-126. Ipswich, MA: H.W. Wilson, 2018.

MLA: "Yes, I'd Lie to You." *The Reference Shelf: Alternative Facts, Post-Truth, and the Information War*. Ed. Betsy Maury. Ipswich: H.W. Wilson, 2018. 118-126. Print.

APA: The Economist. (2018). Yes, I'd lie to you. In Betsy Maury (Ed.), *The reference shelf: Alternative facts, post-truth, and the information war* (pp. 118-126). Ipswich, MA: H.W. Wilson. (Original work published 2016)

5

Next Generation News Consumers

This April 10, 2016 photo taken in Washington shows a woman reading an online version of a mockup of what a frontpage might look like should Republican frontrunner Donald Trump win the presidency, as it condemned his 'deeply disturbing' and 'profoundly un-American' vision. 'Deportations to begin, President Trump calls for tripling of ICE (immigration and customs enforcement); riots continue,' read The Boston Globe's fake headline, dated April 9, 2017. It was posted on the editorial page, accompanied by a ruthless editorial article saying Trump's campaign 'demands an active and engaged opposition.'

Solutions to the Misinformation Age

Is fake news a problem that needs to be corrected? Does the social media industry need to be regulated or to create new policies that mitigate the proliferation of inaccurate information presented as news? Does media literacy need to be part of a standard educational curriculum? Some would answer "yes" to all of these questions while others might see less of a problem with the way that the media and public views have evolved. The problem is a matter of perception, as are the various solutions that have been proposed.

Media Detectives

Reality television isn't real. Shows like *House Hunters* or *Judge Judy* don't give viewers any insight into the legal process or the real estate and home improvement industry. Judge Judy is free to quip about the perceived faults of whatever person she sees fit because there are no stakes. Persons ordered to pay "damages" on the program actually have their fees paid by the network, and the rulings that Judge Judy delivers are neither legal nor binding. Judge Judy herself has been criticized for her treatment of the poor and moralizing beyond the scope of what a legitimate judge would be allowed to do in a courtroom, but this type of behavior is popular with consumers. However, some judges and lawyers have long complained that courtroom dramas create unrealistic beliefs about the legal process that affect the behavior of both lawyers and jurors.[1]

Reality television and fake news are two sides of the same coin, presenting readers or viewers with versions of reality that confirm what they want to be true or fear is true. Those who most eagerly embrace fake news and those who believe that reality television isn't scripted fall into the category of consumers who have difficulty telling the difference between truth and fiction. In some ways, this is a manifestation of media literacy.

Consider the following statements:

1) Cats are condescending and evil.

2) Experts in feline behavior say that cats are more malicious in their behavior than dogs.

Neither of these statements is true and neither provides legitimate information for a person who wants to understand the complex behavior of the domestic feline, though the two statements may appear to differ in legitimacy. The first statement is entirely opinion-based and ascribes characteristics to cats that are subjective reflections on the morality of human behavior. The second statement appears to cite reference to an authority, by stating that the findings presented are from "experts," and increases the perception of legitimacy by using the term "malicious" in place of a term like "evil," which may appear more obviously subjective to a reader.

In a 2012 article in *Slate Magazine*, author Rob Dunn describes research regarding how popular opinions and attitudes about felines reflect the evolutionary history of the human species. In the distant past, humans were hunted by predatory cats and so being suspicious of cats or believing that cats are malicious, reflects this ancient human survival instinct.[2] The idea that cats are standoffish creatures whose apparent affection for their owners is simply a tactic to get food has become widespread, but has rarely been tested, and the tendency to believe this might be a result of that ancient evolutionary suspicion of the feline temperament. Therefore, an individual might be willing to accept one or both of the above false claims due to internal biases and evolutionary predispositions ingrained in the human psyche.

However, consider this statement:

A study by animal behaviorists in a 2016 issue of the journal *Behavioral Processes* found that domestic cats prefer human interaction to either food, toys, or interesting scents when given a choice between these stimuli.[3]

The above statement presents accurate information. Notice that the statement not only claims an expert source but describes that source to facilitate the process of judging whether or not the expert cited should be considered an expert. The claim is also not imparting value, but simply describing a finding by a group of experts in a field. Notice too that the accurate statement is more specific and detailed than the inaccurate statements. This is characteristic of valid information, because many issues are complex and presenting valid data often necessitates imparting more information that when presenting an opinion or belief. In the case of feline behavior, the accurate information conflicts with "common knowledge" and the widespread biases that shape belief and this then provides an example of how the information obtained through accurate information can be vastly different than that imparted through opinion-based discourse.

In the fast-paced world of media bytes and social media, news producers are more often opting for fast, incomplete information over longer, more expository coverage. Thankfully, digital media has also created a short cut that enables journalists to have it "both ways." By creating links within an article that takes readers directly to the source, a news writer can quickly cover a topic without needing to describe data so as to legitimize the data's source. Providing hyperlinks has become common in online print media and is a major benefit to consumers, enabling any reader who wishes to fact check the article for him or herself.

Developing media literacy is a process that involves learning how to identify problems and decipher information presented in various types of media. In general, media literacy is also about cultivating a healthy skepticism, patience, and the ability to think critically when making decisions. Fact checking news articles can be time-intensive and difficult, especially in an environment where individuals are willing to present themselves as legitimate while trying to mislead. Fake news sites, for instance, often occupy web addresses similar to legitimate news sites so that individuals might accidentally be led astray by the false claims they present.

One way to view media literacy and critical thinking is to imagine approaching news as a detective might investigate a crime. Each claim made in the media symbolizes a statement given by a witness or a piece of evidence and the detective evaluates each until she or he feels they have arrived as a robust hypothesis. This mindset is not infallible, but makes it less likely that a person can be duped and enables a person to become an active player in the information market, rather than the passive target for the overlapping goals of those creating content.

The Socialist Media Machine

Journalists are individuals and have their own biases and beliefs that affect the ways in which they report information to consumers. Journalists also make mistakes that can result in unintentionally misleading information. A 2005 study from UCLA found that many of the major media outlets "tilt to the left"[4] and studies like these have been used as evidence to suggest that the mainstream media is not balanced and only supports liberal or progressive views. While bias is evident in news coverage, the situation is not such that the coverage of mainstream media is in any way comparable to actual "fake news."

The results of a 2014 study of journalists found that the nature of the industry creates the "bias" so often perceived by conservative critics, as shown by the following demographic characteristics:

1) A majority describe themselves as independent politically (50.2) or as Democrats (28.1), while only 7.1 percent described themselves as Republican.

2) Journalists are, on average, more highly educated than the average American.

3) The vast majority of journalists live in middle- to low-class income brackets and few become wealthy by working in their profession.

4) Journalists are driven by morals and ethics to a higher degree than most Americans.[5]

What's also important are professional motivations. Journalists and writers do not typically enter their industries out of a desire for personal gain, but rather out of a desire to root out injustices or problems in the world and to, in general, try and make the world a better place. Many journalists see their careers as a way to try and move the world "forward" and thus, journalists tend to be progressive by nature. What this means, is that a person who identifies as conservative may have a different set of biases and prejudices to the journalists creating news for mainstream outlets. If careers in journalism appealed to more conservatives, there would be more examples of bias towards both sides of the ideological spectrum.

The perception of bias is intensified by the fact that networks like *Fox News* and *MSNBC* not only produce news, but also produce punditry, which is a form of informational advertising. A pundit, like Bill O'Reilly, his tongue-in-cheek rival Stephen Colbert, or *National Review* columnist Heather MacDonald, is a person who espouses authoritative opinions on political issues. Some, like Colbert, do this openly as a form of comedic entertainment. Others, like MacDonald purport to be delivering expert information on a topic, but use charged language, disparaging and inaccurate depictions, and misleading statistics to pursue an agenda. Punditry has always been an important part of American media but is not the same as journalism. Punditry, like fake news, is not an effort to inform, it is an effort to direct, shape, or control opinion. For entertainment purposes, punditry can be harmless and enjoyable, but when pundits are not open about their goals and present themselves as journalists, punditry can cloud the informational environment.

Bias in news typically manifests in a couple of ways. Individuals will, often unknowingly, emphasize aspects of a story that fit with the author's views, and de-emphasize aspects of a story that contrast with his or her views. A journalist may intentionally or unintentionally inject bias into his or her articles but the essential feature that separates journalists from pundits or "content creators," is intention. Journalists are bound by a set of ethical principles and their performance can be judged by how well they adhere to these principles. Journalism thrives by hewing close to legitimacy and so must constantly try to police itself to excise egregious failures to produce realistic or legitimate information on a topic. What this means is that journalism, like scientific research, tends to be self-correcting. If a journalist makes a mistake or presents information in an overly biased or misleading way, another journalist can benefit by pointing out this mistake, thereby attracting readers to his or her publication and making it appear that the publication that identified the mistake is the more legitimate. This also means that managers and editors within a paper are motivated to identify mistakes within their own papers before the public or other journalists do so.

Consider Donald Trump's recent "fake news" awards in January of 2018. The social media event was far less popular than Trump may have hoped and less impactful than many of the journalists and news outlets Trump has called "fake" might have feared.

On January 17, Glenn Kessler of the *Washington Post*, went through the claims that Trump made during his awards and fact-checked each claim. In the article, Kessler also provides hyperlinks to the sources that he used to fact-check Trump's claims such that any reader could, if he or she wanted, check Kessler's facts in the same way that he was checking Trump's claims. Fact-checking Trump's "fake news" claims actually produces the opposite result, demonstrating a media in which there are mistakes and bias, but in which the institutions involved police themselves and typically, whether bias exists or not, present the public with the information needed to make their own decisions.

For instance, Trump claimed that CNN falsely reported that Trump and his son had accessed hacked documents from WikiLeaks. Long before Trump claimed this was fake news, however, the *Washington Post* and *NBC News*, other outlets called "fake news" by Trump, had already pointed out the mistake and CNN had already issued a correction on the story as originally reported. In another example, Trump stated that the *Washington Post* reported that the President's Pensacola, Florida rally was empty. The "fake news" reported in this instance was a tweet from the reporter, which did not appear in an article about the incident, and which was corrected minutes after the first tweet by the same reporter who made the mistake to begin with.[6]

Bubbles, Echoes, and Skeptics

One of the problems that some critics see in the modern media environment is the increasing tendency for consumers to fall into what some have called "media bubbles" or "echo chambers," relatively closed environments in which all of the information that a person receives is shaped by his or her consumer habits and like-minded friends. Some believe that these echo chambers are destructive, concealing more nuanced, fact-based information that might otherwise help people to develop realistic views. A number of solutions to this have been put forward, such as encouraging individuals to step outside of their media environments or to try and look at things from other perspectives.

A metaphor from fiction may help to illustrate how various facets of the modern media environment create illusory perspectives. In the Stanislav Lem novel *Solaris*, the captain of a spacecraft visiting a strange alien planet begins to see what is apparently the return of his deceased wife. However, as he interacts with her, he begins to understand that the person before him is not a recreation of his wife as she was, but only as she existed in his mind and thus, not a person, but merely a reflection of his desires and emotions. Because the replica was created out of what he remembered or felt he knew about his wife, the illusion was convincing and it was not until he engaged in introspective evaluation of himself that he began to see the truth.

A person's beliefs are like the replicas in *Solaris*, less a representation of truth than a manifestation of a person's hopes, dreams, desires, and fears; a reflection of the believer, rather than the belief. If belief is personal than any solution to mistaken beliefs might also need to begin with personal motivations. Therefore, if the "echo chamber" of one's social media environment, or the belief that most media is "fake" fits with a person's personal desires and fears, such facets of the media environment will likely remain unchallenged for that person. Critical thinking is not a requirement but is an optional strategy that one can choose to use when evaluating his or her environment. For those who value self-determination, media legitimacy and the various forces manipulating data for their own interests, are not insignificant concerns but rather are challenges that must be met in order to assume an active role in the formation of one's identity.

Micah L. Issitt

Works Used

Dunn, Rob. "What Are You So Scared Of? Saber-Toothed Cats, Snakes, and Carnivorous Kangaroos." *Slate*. Slate Group. Oct 15, 2012. Web. 25 Feb 2018.

Holcomb, Jesse. "5 Facts about Fox News." *Pew Research Center*. Facttank. Jan 14, 2014. Web. 25 Feb 2018.

Kessler, Glenn. "Fact-Checking President Trump's 'Fake News Awards'." *The Washington Post*. The Washington Post Co. Jan 17, 2018. Web. 25 Feb 2018.

Mayyasi, Alex. "The Hypocrisy of 'Judge Judy'." *Priceonomics*. Jan 14, 2016. Web. 25 Feb 2018.

Shreve, Kristyn R., Mehrkam, Lindsay R., and Monique A.R. Udell, "Social Interaction, Food, Scent or Toys? A Formal Assessment of Domestic Pet and Shelter Cat (*Felis silvestris catus*) Preferences." *Behavioral Processes*. Vol. 141, Part 3 (August 2017),: 322–28. Print.

Sullivan, Meg. "Media Bias Is Real, Finds UCLA Political Scientist." *UCLA*. UCLA Newsroom. Dec 14, 2005. Web. 25 Feb 2018.

Thompson, Derek. "Report: Journalists Are Miserable, Liberal, Over-Educated, Under-Paid, Middle-Aged Men." *The Atlantic*. Atlantic Monthly Group. May 8, 2014. Web. 25 Feb 2018.

Notes

1. Mayyasi, "The Hypocrisy of 'Judge Judy'."
2. Dunn, "What Are You So Scared Of? Saber-Toothed Cats, Snakes, and Carnivorous Kangaroos."
3. Shreve, Mehrkam, and Udell, "Social Interaction, Food, Scent or Toys? A Formal Assessment of Domestic Pet and Shelter Cat (*Felis silvestris catus*) preferences."
4. Sullivan, "Media Bias Is Real, Finds UCLA Political Scientist."
5. Thompson, "Report: Journalists are Miserable, Liberal, Over-Educated, Under-Paid, Middle-Aged Men."
6. Kessler, "Fact-Checking President Trump's 'Fake News Awards'."

Echo Chambers Are Dangerous—We Must Try to Break Free of Our Online Bubbles

By David Robert Grimes

The Guardian, December 4, 2017

It has been little over a year since Donald Trump stunned the world by becoming US president. His election marked a severe upset to conventional wisdom, with his startling use of social media drawing particular attention.

A new nadir came last week, with Trump sharing videos from far-right group Britain First via Twitter. These were also shared by conservative Ann Coulter, one of only 45 people the president follows on Twitter. When asked by the BBC's Nick Robinson to explain why the president might have retweeted videos from a far-right group, Coulter responded that Trump could not be expected to check the biography of people he retweeted and that "the video is the video, it's not a faked video".

This ugly incident perfectly illustrates a deeper problem: the alarming ease with which social media and the internet as a whole can be abused, and used to prop up dubious narratives.

This abuse is an ubiquitous problem, but perhaps one that might have surprised the pioneers of the web. The early days of the internet promised a mind-expanding utopia, where we could freely exchange new ideas and contemplate other points of view. Even in those days of heady optimism, there were already a few academics who worried that this vision pivoted on too high-minded a picture of human nature. In 2017, after a year of revelations involving cyberbullying, troll factories, campaigns of misinformation and more, we should urgently be questioning our use of online space. And to counter these threats we need to examine the greatest one: our own cosy online bubble.

In 1996, MIT researchers Marshall Van Alstyne and Erik Brynjolfsson warned of a potential dark side to our newly interconnected world:

> Individuals empowered to screen out material that does not conform to their existing preferences may form virtual cliques, insulate themselves from opposing points of view, and reinforce their biases. Internet users can seek out interactions with like-minded individuals who have similar values, and thus become less likely to trust important decisions to people whose values differ from their own."

Van Alstyne and Brynjolfsson dubbed this fracturing of the online community Cyberbalkanization. Ominously, they warned that "the loss of shared experiences and values may be harmful to the structure of democratic societies as well as decentralized organizations."

Their foresight appears to have been uncomfortably close to the mark. An analysis of the 2016 US presidential election by the *Columbia Journalism Review* noted that "… a right-wing media network anchored around Breitbart developed as a distinct and insulated media system, using social media as a backbone to transmit a hyper-partisan perspective to the world." The consequence? "This pro-Trump media sphere appears to have not only successfully set the agenda for the conservative media sphere, but also strongly influenced the broader media agenda, in particular coverage of Hillary Clinton."

Of course, some degree of ideological bias is inescapable, and can hardly be blamed solely on the internet. Newspapers, for example, have always catered to their audience. Nowhere is this clearer than in the UK, which has arguably the most partisan press in the world. But, despite whatever editorial leanings publications may have, a robust legal and—in some cases regulatory—framework places media outlets under compulsion to at least report facts when it comes to news. Whatever the faults of the mainstream media, they do not have carte blanche to concoct fictions, libel or slander.

But what the internet has done is facilitate the emergence of alternative news sites. And here, factual accuracy can no longer be taken for granted. Untethered from journalistic ethics, some outlets thrive by telling their audience precisely what they want to hear. And social media allows the rapid growth and spread of everything from the ludicrous Pizzagate conspiracy theory to rampant climate-change denial—and exists across the political spectrum.

This proliferation of urban myths and conspiracies would perhaps be laughable if it weren't so uniquely dangerous. An estimated 61% of millennials garner news primarily through social media. But in the process, we trigger algorithms that curate our feeds. These cherry-picked things with which we are likely to agree cause up to jettison information that does not appear to fit our preferences—often at the cost of accuracy and balance. As the Knight Center observed in 2016, "… through social media, professional and other qualified news is mixed with un-checked information and opinions. Rumours

> The echo chamber may be comforting, but ultimately it locks us into perpetual tribalism, and does tangible damage to our understanding. To counteract this, we need to become more discerning at analyzing our sources—something we are currently poor at doing.

and gossip get in the flow." They also noted this tended to increase political polarisation, and warned: "people may be losing the skills to differentiate information from opinion."

So why does this happen? Part of the problem is our reliance on internet giants— and their vested interest in rewarding us with what we like to see. Everything from our Google searches to our Facebook news feeds are tailored to keep us engaged and generate profit. But while there is limited evidence that filter bubbles might reduce diversity, the data suggests that we play the lead role in driving our own polarisation. We are much more homogeneous than we think, and tend to interact more with people who echo our beliefs. A recent study in Science found that we tend to engage most with information that flatters our ideological preconceptions, and that this accounted for much more selection bias than algorithmic filtering.

Such findings probably won't be overly surprising to psychologists, who have long been aware of the human tendency towards confirmation bias. But such polarisation has consequences far beyond politics—it has alarming implications for science, and our collective wellbeing. For example, climate-change denial is strongly linked to political belief. Yet despite the overwhelming evidence of anthropogenic climate change, the proliferation of outlets publishing claims attempting to counter the scientific consensus means those unwilling to face reality have no shortage of media sources to bolster their view—to our collective detriment.

These divisions run deep, creating walled communities that reinforce their own beliefs in a feedback loop. A 2015 study in *PNAS* found that misinformation flourished online, because users "… aggregate in communities of interest, which causes reinforcement and fosters confirmation bias, segregation, and polarisation". These online echo chambers cement dubious notions, giving them an air of legitimacy and fuel increasing separation from reality.

Targeted individuals (TIs), for example, believe their every action is being shadowed by some sinister collective, convening online to discuss it. Many claim to hear sinister voices in their head, suggesting delusional disorders might be at play, a view supported by research to date. Yet on forums for those affected, the strongly-enforced message that those suggesting a psychological cause are agents of deception. As psychologist Dr. Lorraine Sheridan laments, "there are no counter sites that try and convince targeted individuals that they are delusional. They end up in a closed-ideology echo chamber." With victims discouraged from getting help, tragic consequences can ensue. In 2014, Myron May uploaded a video to YouTube outlining his agony as a TI, hours before opening fire at Florida State University, dying in a shoot-out with police.

Echo chambers abound for many other conditions which are not medically recognised, from chronic Lyme disease to electromagnetic hypersensitivity. But perhaps most worrisome is the advance of anti-vaccine narratives across the web. The explosion of dubious sources has allowed them to propagate wildly, undeterred by debunking in the popular press. We might take the current drastic fall in HPV vaccine uptake in Ireland, driven by anti-vaccine groups like REGRET, despite its life-saving efficacy. While organisations including the Health Service Executive have valiantly tried to counter these myths, these claims are perpetuated across social media with little to stop them.

It doesn't have to be this way. The echo chamber may be comforting, but ultimately it locks us into perpetual tribalism, and does tangible damage to our understanding. To counteract this, we need to become more discerning at analysing our sources—something we are currently poor at doing. More difficult perhaps is that we must learn not to cling to something solely because it chimes with our beliefs, and be willing to jettison any notion when it is contradicted by evidence—no matter how comforting the disproven idea may be. As the great physicist Richard Feynman once observed, we ourselves are "the easiest person to fool." This adage should never be far from our minds in our interconnected world. From the dying embers of 2017, we must resolve to make 2018 the year of questioning not only our opponents' sources, but our own.

Print Citations

CMS: Grimes, David Robert. "Echo Chambers Are Dangerous—We Must Try to Break Free of Our Online Bubbles." In *The Reference Shelf: Alternative Facts, Post-Truth, and the Information War*, edited by Betsy Maury, 135-138. Ipswich, MA: H.W. Wilson, 2018.

MLA: Grimes, David Robert. "Echo Chambers Are Dangerous—We Must Try to Break Free of Our Online Bubbles." *The Reference Shelf: Alternative Facts, Post-Truth, and the Information War*. Ed. Betsy Maury. Ipswich: H.W. Wilson, 2018. 135-138. Print.

APA: Grimes, D.R. (2018). Echo chambers are dangerous—We must try to break free of our online bubbles. In Betsy Maury (Ed.), *The reference shelf: Alternative facts, post-truth, and the information war* (pp. 135-138). Ipswich, MA: H.W. Wilson. (Original work published 2017)

Making Media Literacy Great Again

By Michael Rosenwald

Columbia Journalism Review, Fall 2017

Professor Carl T. Bergstrom began his first lecture for INFO198 at the University of Washington with a declaration about America. "There is so much bullshit," he said, looking up at 160 students last spring. "We are drowning in it." Bergstrom's audience didn't seem surprised or outraged by his phraseology. They had surely heard that word before, but they no doubt also recognized it from the title in the course catalog: "Calling Bullshit in the Age of Big Data."

As Bergstrom spoke, a picture of Hillary Clinton and Donald Trump appeared on a screen behind him, followed moments later by a photo of a young woman typing on her phone. "The average American spends nearly an hour a day on Facebook," he said. "Doing what? Mostly spreading bullshit." The students laughed. Then Bergstrom shouted, "Enough! Enough bullshit! We are tired of this."

That roughly explains how Bergstrom, an evolutionary biologist, wound up in a lecture hall declaring war on fake news. He and his colleague Jevin West, a data science professor, launched the class this past spring, not long after hoax stories, Russian bots, and clickbait headlines wreaked havoc on the US electoral process. The professors were also concerned about misleading science stories, journalism by press release, and the way interest groups and corporations twist data. The class filled up in less than a minute, with several hundred students turned away.

"We wanted to teach students how to evaluate the onslaught of information in their lives," West tells *CJR*. "There's information warfare going on right now."

As a data expert, West lives in a world where algorithms and machine learning solve human problems. He is encouraged that Facebook, Google, and Twitter are rolling out such tools to eradicate fake news and surface trustworthy content. But he knows that ones and zeros alone can't solve the problem.

Later in the semester, West and Bergstrom offered students a striking reason why, examining a fake news story about vaccines causing shaken baby syndrome. The claim was so absurd that literally no content existed online to refute it. Searching Google for this phrase—"do vaccinations cause shaken baby syndrome?"—only turned up links to other bogus websites that repeated and expanded on the invented data.

"We need a cultural solution as well," West tells *CJR*. "That's why we're doing this."

At least a dozen universities around the country have launched or are planning similar classes, using "Calling Bullshit" and curriculum from Stony Brook University's Center for News Literacy as templates. There has been a burst of interest in secondary education as well, with legislators in at least 15 states introducing or recently passing laws mandating digitally focused media literacy instruction in public schools.

"This can get real," West said that first day of class, taking over the mic from Bergstrom. "And when the shit gets real, that's when we should care as a society."

Fake News Is Not New

Humans have manipulated and fabricated information for centuries—to persuade, confuse, entertain. There was Yellow Journalism, of course. During World War II, the United States used propaganda on American citizens to rally the country. And Adolf Hitler was a master of fake news.

Also not a new idea: media literacy. In the 1930s, an ex-journalist named Clyde Miller started the Institute for Propaganda Analysis, which designed curriculum for educators to teach students to recognize seven different propaganda devices. One was "glittering generalities," defined as "[a]n attempt to sway emotions through the use of shining ideals or virtues, such as freedom, justice, truth, education, democracy in a large, general way."

Schools have taught media literacy concepts for decades, but obviously never in an environment like this one, where owning a printing press or TV satellite isn't needed to quickly and widely disseminate information. That, combined with hyperpartisan politics, has led to the weaponization of news by individuals, political groups, and foreign countries.

The old tools of media literacy—source checking, relying on known outlets—aren't enough when a hacker in Macedonia can easily create a website that looks legitimate, then quickly make thousands of dollars from advertising as bogus stories circulate. Scrolling through social media feeds produces one challenge after another, from the serious to the mundane.

Just ask the "Calling Bullshit" students.

"So many people just see stuff and share it," says Conner Ardman, 19, who took the class and plans to major in Informatics with a concentration in data science. "They don't even look at it. They have no idea what it is."

Early in the semester, the professors displayed several memes that had been circulating online. The students voted electronically on whether the claims were true.

"You need to be careful on the toilet, you guys," West said, showing a widely shared picture of a toilet with text reading, "No one tells you, but more than 30,000 Americans are injured each year in the process of using the toilet."

Much laughter.

"Bullshit," West said. "Or not bullshit?"

The students voted. Roughly 65 percent thought it was bullshit.

"It's not bullshit," West said. "This one is really true. People really do get injured on toilets."

The truth of toilet danger raises a rather profound question for our time: If something online that sounds ridiculous is true, how can internet users know if something that sounds potentially plausible is actually false? That's what classes like "Calling Bullshit" are trying to address. Though fake news might seem like a know-it-when-you-see-it nuisance, students say that social networks make it exactly the opposite.

> **Humans have manipulated and fabricated information for centuries—to persuade, confuse, entertain.**

"It's hard because you normally trust your friends when they tell you something," says Jessica Basa, 20, a University of Washington computer science and informatics major who took the class. "They're not trying to trick you when they post stuff they think is interesting but isn't true."

Some of the instruction seems old and obvious, yet also newly relevant. As a first line of defense, the "Calling Bullshit" professors instructed students to ask themselves three questions when encountering a news story, scientific study, or complicated data: Who is telling me this? How do they know it? What's in it for them?

"If you were going to a car dealership, you would be asking these types of questions," West said during a lecture. "We want you to have that kind of frame of mind going forward....You should put your skeptical hat on, especially when you're in these digital environments."

West and Bergstrom introduced theoretical defenses as well, such as Occam's Razor, a 14th century principle that says the simplest explanation is usually correct. They paired this with the so-called "Bullshit Asymmetry Principle," an idea tweeted by an Italian software developer in 2013. It states, "The amount of energy needed to refute bullshit is an order of magnitude bigger than to produce it." For evidence, the professors offered the Comet Ping Pong saga—allegations that Hillary Clinton ran a child sex ring in the basement of a Washington, DC, pizza shop. The fiction took months to dislodge, and references still pop up on social networks, shared by those who believe it or simply want to use it as ammo against the opposition.

Other detection tactics, such as the ones taught at Stony Brook, are more technical and workmanlike, but equally important. Students are taught how to look up domain name registration records. Though these records can be fudged, any English-language news site originating in Eastern Europe—the vast majority of fake news is manufactured there—is likely to be bogus. Another tool: image searches. To track down a photo's origins, simply drop the questionable image into the search bar on Google Images. Definite warning signs: poor grammar and cheap-looking design.

Stony Brook became a leader in media literacy soon after Howard Schneider, a former *Newsday* editor, founded the university's journalism school in 2006. Besides training the next generation of journalists, Schneider was prophetic in recognizing that there should be, as he put it in a 2007 *Nieman Reports* article, an additional mission "of equal—perhaps greater—importance: to educate the next generation of news consumers."

"The digital revolution might bring the promise of enlightenment, but in its pathological lack of accountability might just as easily spread a virus of confusion and disinformation," Schneider wrote. "The ultimate check against an inaccurate or irresponsible press never would be just better-trained journalists, or more press critics and ethical codes."

What Was the Answer?

"Consumers who could differentiate between raw, unmediated information coursing through the Internet and independent, verified journalism," Schneider wrote.

More than 10,000 students have taken Stony Brook's news literacy course, which is constantly updated to help students identify the latest ways bogus news and information are created. For instance, there are dozens of websites that let anyone easily produce counterfeit social media posts, then retweet them, post them on Facebook, or embed them in a news story. But fake tweets seem positively quaint compared to an even newer threat: Using artificial intelligence to make videos of people saying things they didn't say. Researchers recently made a video of Barack Obama speaking very earnestly about his priorities for the waning days of his administration.

"The single most important thing I can do now," Obama said, according to the doctored audio track, "is to play golf."

The following sentence is not fake news, nor does it rely on bullshit data: Media literacy works, and it just might save humanity. At least part of that sentence is backed up by a recent study that examines how people judge the accuracy of claims about controversial subjects. Researchers from the University of California, Riverside, and Santa Clara University provided more than 2,000 teenagers and adults up to age 27 with fake assertions connected to stories on highly charged topics such as economic inequality and tax policy. The study found that claims about controversial topics, whether true or false, were more often than not identified as accurate if they aligned with the person's prior views. That's essentially confirmation bias, seeking out and believing information that strengthens your worldview. Sobering. Also, not surprising.

Then the researchers dug further into the data, producing remarkable findings. They looked at two subsets of study subjects: those with higher than average political knowledge but no media literacy training, and those who had little or no political knowledge but took media literacy courses. Having political knowledge "did not improve judgments of accuracy," the authors wrote. Media literacy education did. Other recent studies have hinted at similar success, but it's unknown whether these lessons carry as much weight once students enter the real world.

The University of California authors were cautiously optimistic, noting the results seem to advance the notion of so-called "critical loyalty." "Those with critical loyalty still hold strong values and beliefs," the authors write, "but they adopt a critical stance when evaluating an argument—even when that argument aligns with their partisan preferences." In other words, those with media literacy training can still be fiercely committed to their world view, but they can also successfully question flimsy claims. They can call bullshit. Maybe they can even stop spreading it.

Some caution about these results is warranted. People don't just share fake news because they don't know any better. A Pew Research Center survey last year found that 14 percent of US adults shared news they knew was fake. In many cases, researchers say, it's an identity thing—to show what groups and ideas they agree with, to feel part of a movement, even for entertainment. Then there's the problem of volume. Researchers have recently used complicated mathematical models to show that the sheer amount of information shared online—both real and fake—creates a sort of whack-a-mole situation, in which many moles survive to surface another day.

Nevertheless, media literacy educators are excited by this moment. For one thing, they hope it leads to more resources. This past summer, the Knight Foundation awarded $1 million in grants to 20 media literacy projects around the country, including "Calling Bullshit." But educators also hope the enthusiasm will lead to meaningful changes in how students and adults deal with the onslaught of digital information. They are especially encouraged that both red and blue states are passing or considering laws mandating new digitally focused media literacy initiatives at the secondary school level. California, a liberal bastion, passed one such measure. Texas, at the other end of the political spectrum, is contemplating one.

At the last lecture of "Calling Bullshit," Bergstrom focused on a future in which the course's inaugural students go out into the world with their new skills, share what they know, and stop bullshit in its tracks.

"Starting with this class and spreading out further," he said, "I'm hoping we can make a difference."

Ardman, the computer science major, is already trying. Not long ago, a friend on Facebook posted a story saying an FBI agent investigating Hillary Clinton's private email server had killed his wife, then himself.

"This can't be right," Ardman thought.

He checked it out and posted a comment with his findings: fake news.

"It's important to call it out," Ardman says. "It's your civic duty."

Back to School

For today's college students, a dubious story, photo, or video shared by a friend on social media can enter the bloodstream faster than a Jello shot. Here are some key takeaways from students enrolled in some of the growing number of media literacy classes at colleges and universities around the country.

SARA SCHABE

Junior, Stony Brook University; major: Journalism
"I was like, 'I'm such an idiot.'"

Before Hurricane Sandy hit New Jersey a few years ago, Schabe saw a photo online of an eerie storm cloud looming over New York City. "I thought it was a real picture," she says. In class, she learned it was doctored from a movie. "I was like, 'I'm such an idiot.'"

Lesson learned: Use Google's reverse image search to check whether photos are legit.

NAVID AZODI

Senior, University of Washington; major: Business and information systems
"Just liking one fake story can become this huge downward spiral."

"Some of these fake news sites look totally real," Azodi says, pointing to the widely shared fake news story about the Pope's endorsement of Donald Trump. "Just liking one fake story can become this huge downward spiral."

Lesson learned: If a news outlet is unfamiliar, look up domain records and use online fact-checkers such as Snopes.

STARLA SAMPACO

Senior, University of Washington; major: Video journalism
"Debunking fake news is really hard."

A surprising but fundamental research finding about fake news is that the more a claim is refuted, the harder it is to debunk, particularly among those with strong ideological views. "You can't just keep saying something isn't true," Sampaco says. "That's why debunking fake news is really hard."

Lesson learned: People don't just share fake news because they've been duped— it's a way to strengthen their own beliefs and position.

GARY GHAYRAT

Junior, Stony Brook University; major: Journalism
"You have to use multiple sources."

"It was really shocking to learn what a rigorous process it is to publish a story," Ghayrat says. "You have to have multiple sources [and] corroborate them with other sources to make sure you're getting everything right."

Lesson learned: Look for the basics of journalism in every story. Are the sources named? Who provided the information? Is there an opposing viewpoint? Is it too good to be true?

Print Citations

CMS: Rosenwald, Michael. "Making Media Literacy Great Again." In *The Reference Shelf: Alternative Facts, Post-Truth, and the Information War*, edited by Betsy Maury, 139-144. Ipswich, MA: H.W. Wilson, 2018.

MLA: Rosenwald, Michael. "Making Media Literacy Great Again." *The Reference Shelf: Alternative Facts, Post-Truth, and the Information War*. Ed. Betsy Maury. Ipswich: H.W. Wilson, 2018. 139-144. Print.

APA: Rosenwald, M. (2018). Making media literacy great again. In Betsy Maury (Ed.), *The reference shelf: Alternative facts, post-truth, and the information war* (pp. 139-144). Ipswich, MA: H.W. Wilson. (Original work published 2017)

The Remedy for the Spread of Fake News? History Teachers

By Kevin M. Levin

Smithsonian.com, December 6, 2016

Few people would approach a complete stranger on the street for information about the pressing issues of the day, and yet that is just how many behave on the Internet. In the wake of the 2016 election, reporting from *Buzzfeed* and other outlets has made it increasingly clear that the American voter is woefully lacking in the skills needed to judge the veracity of a news website. Among the many headlines from fake news websites were reports that Pope Francis endorsed President-elect Trump, that Hillary Clinton used a body double throughout the campaign and sold weapons to ISIS. The founders and authors of these fake news promulgators craft their stories for the sole purpose of maximizing visitor hits to in turn generate massive revenue. Their deceptions play to readers' worst fears regardless of whether the writers themselves subscribe to the political leanings of the article's content. "It is not intended to pose an alternative truth," writes author Neal Gabler, "as if there could be such a thing, but to destroy truth altogether, to set us adrift in a world of belief without facts, a world where there is no defense against lies." In comparison with news outlets (and other sites) that offer ideologically biased takes on the most pressing issues of the day, fake news operations occupy a unique place on the web and constitute an obvious and menacing threat to unsuspecting visitors. The inability of so many readers to distinguish between the two, and knowing when to steer clear of a website altogether, is undoubtedly concerning.

For those of us on the frontlines of education, especially for history teachers, this problem is nothing new, given the ways in which the rise of the Internet has transformed the teaching of the subject over the past 15 years. Students and teachers now have access to a vast amount of information about the past, but few know how to discern what is reliable and what is not.

The problem surfaced for me in 2001 when a student handed in a research paper on the early history of the Ku Klux Klan that minimized the level of racial violence during Reconstruction and characterized their relationship with black Southerners as overall positive. The sources were drawn almost entirely from websites published by individual Klan chapters. The student had not thought about the obvious bias of the website or whether it constituted a legitimate historical source. The experience served as an important learning experience for the students, but even more so for me.

Even as late as 2001, my students still relied primarily on printed materials compared to Internet sources. Librarians maintained control over new additions to the stacks, allowing for a certain level of quality control, but with each passing year the availability of faster personal computers, handheld devices and increased access to the web provided students with easier access to information about an ever-expanding number of historical subjects. Students and teachers benefited immensely from this increased access. Teachers could now introduce their students to a deep well of primary sources and historical figures that never made it into textbooks. Opportunities for students to conduct their own research through primary and secondary sources was soon limitless, defined only by the time they are willing to spend researching.

On the other hand, the technology quickly outpaced educators' ability to police or even guide students as to how best to search and assess online information. An unsubstantiated narrative, perpetuated by the media, that children are digital natives, naturally hardwired to understand how to use computers, helped to exacerbate the problem even further. Students were left to figure it out on their own as schools gradually cut back on the purchase of additional printed sources or purged their

Fake news operations occupy a unique place on the web and constitute an obvious and menacing threat to unsuspecting visitors.

collections entirely. Where once librarians taught students how to research, few schools appreciated the important role they could play in educating students how to search and assess information on the web. A recent study of Internet literacy among students by the Stanford History Education Group shows that they are incapable of "distinguishing advertisements from news articles or identifying where information came from."

There is no denying that access to primary sources from the Library of Congress and other research institutions, along with secondary sources from the scholarly community, has enriched the teaching of history, but their availability means little if they cannot be accessed or distinguished from the vast amount of misinformation that awaits the uneducated user online.

In 2008, George Mason University professor T. Mills Kelly created a course called "Lying About the Past" in which students were encouraged to create fake websites about a historical subject. Students worked on creating a fake Wikipedia page, blog, and videos about Edward Owens, a fictitious Virginia oyster fisherman who took up piracy in the Chesapeake Bay in the 1870s. This fake historical narrative was complemented by fake primary sources, including Owens's "legal will." Although the project was met with some skepticism and even more serious charges by Wikipedia founder Jimmy Wales, Kelly hoped his students "would become much more skeptical consumers of online information."

It's difficult to imagine a more effective method of driving home such an important lesson. In the years since Mills first taught the class, opportunities to publish and share information online has expanded even further through Facebook, YouTube and Twitter and blogging platforms such as WordPress and Medium. Opportunities to publish can be an empowering experience. History teachers who embrace these digital tools can shift from assignments that would never see the outside of their classroom's walls to projects that have the potential to reach a wide public audience. Educators can engage students about the ethical responsibilities related to how information should be published on the web.

But if the public is left unprepared and without the skills needed to determine what is real and what is suspect, there can be real consequences. Consider for instance the publication of *Our Virginia: Past and Present* a fourth-grade textbook written by Joy Masoff. First discovered by William and Mary historian Carol Sheriff, whose child was then in the fourth grade, the chapter on the Civil War included a statement that "thousands of Southerner blacks fought in Confederate ranks, including two battalions under the command of Stonewall Jackson." The myth of the Confederate black soldier is an insidious one, traced back to the late 1970s and a small group of Confederate heritage advocates who hoped to distance the history of the Confederacy from slavery. If black men fought as soldiers in the army, they argued, than it would be difficult to maintain that the Confederacy fought to protect and expand the institution of slavery. Not a single academic historian came forward in support of the textbook's claim. Later it was learned that Masoff had discovered the information on a website published by the Sons of Confederate Veterans.

There are thousands of websites published by individuals and organizations who believe black Confederate soldiers existed. Websites such as the *Petersburg Express*, for example, includes photographs and even primary sources that to the uneducated may appear legitimate. The purveyors of these stories often insist that they are providing a public service by uncovering accounts that academic historians have intentionally ignored. Regardless of the motivation for publishing the material in question, these websites present visitors with some of the same challenges as fake news sites.

The history classroom is an ideal place in which to teach students how to search and evaluate online information given the emphasis that is already placed on the careful reading and analysis of historical documents. Even the most basic guidelines can steer students away from misinformation. Consider the following questions next time you are researching online:

- Is the site associated with a reputable institution like a museum, historical society or university?

- Can you identify the individual or organization responsible for the site, and are the proper credentials displayed?

- Then, finally, you have to examine the material itself. Is the information provided on the website, including text and images, properly cited? What can you discern from both the incoming and outgoing links to the site? Only then can you approach it with the same level of trust that you would a scholarly journal or piece of archival material.

History classrooms that emphasize the critical evaluation of bias and perspective in primary sources, along with the questions above, will also provide students of all ages with the necessary skills to evaluate the links that regularly appear in their Twitter and Facebook feeds. Healthy and well-deserved skepticism can go a long way.

The ease with which we can access and contribute to the web makes it possible for everyone to be his or her own historian, which is both a blessing and a curse. The Internet is both a goldmine of information as well as a minefield of misinformation and distortion. Teaching our students how to discern the difference will not only help them steer clear of fake history and fake news, but reinforce the importance of a responsible and informed citizenry. In doing so, we strengthen the very pillars of democracy.

Print Citations

CMS: Levin, Kevin M. "The Remedy for the Spread of Fake News? History Teachers." In *The Reference Shelf: Alternative Facts, Post-Truth, and the Information War*, edited by Betsy Maury, 145-148. Ipswich, MA: H.W. Wilson, 2018.

MLA: Levin, Kevin M. "The Remedy for the Spread of Fake News? History Teachers." *The Reference Shelf: Alternative Facts, Post-Truth, and the Information War.* Ed. Betsy Maury. Ipswich: H.W. Wilson, 2018. 145-148. Print.

APA: Levin, K. (2018). The remedy for the spread of fake news? History teachers. In Betsy Maury (Ed.), *The reference shelf: Alternative facts, post-truth, and the information war* (pp. 145-148). Ipswich, MA: H.W. Wilson. (Original work published 2016)

Can AI Win the War Against Fake News?

By Jackie Snow

MIT Technology Review, December 13, 2017

It may have been the first bit of fake news in the history of the Internet: in 1984, someone posted on Usenet that the Soviet Union was joining the network. It was a harmless April's Fools Day prank, a far cry from today's weaponized disinformation campaigns and unscrupulous fabrications designed to turn a quick profit. In 2017, misleading and maliciously false online content is so prolific that we humans have little hope of digging ourselves out of the mire. Instead, it looks increasingly likely that the machines will have to save us.

One algorithm meant to shine a light in the darkness is AdVerif.ai, which is run by a startup of the same name. The artificially intelligent software is built to detect phony stories, nudity, malware, and a host of other types of problematic content. AdVerif.ai, which launched a beta version in November, currently works with content platforms and advertising networks in the United States and Europe that don't want to be associated with false or potentially offensive stories.

The company saw an opportunity in focusing on a product for companies as opposed to something for an average user, according to Or Levi, AdVerif.ai's founder. While individual consumers might not worry about the veracity of each story they are clicking on, advertisers and content platforms have something to lose by hosting or advertising bad content. And if they make changes to their services, they can be effective in cutting off revenue streams for people who earn money creating fake news. "It would be a big step in fighting this type of content," Levi says.

AdVerif.ai scans content to spot telltale signs that something is amiss—like headlines not matching the body, for example, or too many capital letters in a headline. It also cross-checks each story with its database of thousands of legitimate and fake stories, which is updated weekly. The clients see a report for each piece the system considered, with scores that assess the likelihood that something is fake news, carries malware, or contains anything else they've ask the system to look out for, like nudity. Eventually, Levi says he plans to add the ability to spot manipulated images and have a browser plugin.

Testing a demo version of the AdVerif.ai, the AI recognized the *Onion* as satire (which has fooled many people in the past). *Breitbart* stories were classified as "unreliable, right, political, bias," while *Cosmopolitan* was considered "left." It could tell when a Twitter account was using a logo but the links weren't associated

> **Developers are working on tools that can help spot suspect stories and call them out, but it may be the beginning of an automated arms race.**

with the brand it was portraying. AdVerif.ai not only found that a story on Natural News with the headline "Evidence points to Bitcoin being an NSA-engineered psyop to roll out one-world digital currency" was from a blacklisted site, but identified it as a fake news story popping up on other blacklisted sites without any references in legitimate news organizations.

Some dubious stories still get through. On a site called Action News 3, a post headlined "NFL Player Photographed Burning an American Flag in Locker Room!" wasn't caught, though it's been proved to be a fabrication. To help the system learn as it goes, its blacklist of fake stories can be updated manually on a story-by-story basis.

AdVerif.ai isn't the only startup that sees an opportunity in providing an AI-powered truth serum for online companies. Cybersecurity firms in particular have been quick to add bot- and fake news-spotting operations to their repertoire, pointing out how similar a lot of the methods look to hacking. Facebook is tweaking its algorithms to deemphasize fake news in its newsfeeds, and Google partnered with a fact-checking site—so far with uneven results. The Fake News Challenge, a competition run by volunteers in the AI community, launched at the end of last year with the goal of encouraging the development of tools that could help combat bad-faith reporting.

Delip Rao, one of its organizers and the founder of Joostware, a company that creates machine-learning systems, said spotting fake news has so many facets that the challenge is actually going to be done in multiple steps. The first step is "stance detection," or taking one story and figuring out what other news sites have to say about the topic. This would allow human fact checkers to rely on stories to validate other stories, and spend less time checking individual pieces.

The Fake News Challenge released data sets for teams to use, with 50 teams submitting entries. Talos Intelligence, a cybersecurity division of Cisco, won the challenge with an algorithm that got more than 80 percent correct—not quite ready for prime time, but still an encouraging result. The next challenge might take on images with overlay text (think memes, but with fake news), a format that is often promoted on social media, since its format is harder for algorithms to break down and understand.

"We want to basically build the best tools for the fact checkers so they can work very quickly," Rao said. "Like fact checkers on steroids."

Even if a system is developed that is effective in beating back the tide of fake content, though, it's unlikely to be the end of the story. Artificial-intelligence systems are already able to create fake text, as well as incredibly convincing images and video. Perhaps because of this, a recent Gartner study predicted that by 2022, the majority of people in advanced economies will see more false than true information.

The same report found that even before that happens, fake content will outpace AI's ability to detect it, changing how we trust digital information.

What AdVerif.ai and others represent, then, looks less like the final word in the war on fake content than the opening round of an arms race, in which fake content creators get their own AI that can outmaneuver the "good" AIs. As a society, we may yet have to reevaluate how we get our information.

Print Citations

CMS: Snow, Jackie. "Can AI Win the War Against Fake News?" In *The Reference Shelf: Alternative Facts, Post-Truth, and the Information War*, edited by Betsy Maury, 149-151. Ipswich, MA: H.W. Wilson, 2018.

MLA: Snow, Jackie. "Can AI Win the War Against Fake News?" *The Reference Shelf: Alternative Facts, Post-Truth, and the Information War*. Ed. Betsy Maury. Ipswich: H.W. Wilson, 2018. 149-151. Print.

APA: Snow, J (2017). Can AI Win the War Against Fake News? In Betsy Maury (Ed.), *The reference shelf: Alternative facts, post-truth, and the information war* (pp. 149-151). Ipswich, MA: H.W. Wilson. (Original work published 2016)

The Problem with Facts

By Tim Harford
Financial Times, March 8, 2017

Just before Christmas 1953, the bosses of America's leading tobacco companies met John Hill, the founder and chief executive of one of America's leading public relations firms, Hill & Knowlton. Despite the impressive surroundings—the Plaza Hotel, overlooking Central Park in New York—the mood was one of crisis.

Scientists were publishing solid evidence of a link between smoking and cancer. From the viewpoint of Big Tobacco, more worrying was that the world's most read publication, the *Reader's Digest*, had already reported on this evidence in a 1952 article, "Cancer by the Carton." The journalist Alistair Cooke, writing in 1954, predicted that the publication of the next big scientific study into smoking and cancer might finish off the industry.

It did not. PR guru John Hill had a plan—and the plan, with hindsight, proved tremendously effective. Despite the fact that its product was addictive and deadly, the tobacco industry was able to fend off regulation, litigation and the idea in the minds of many smokers that its products were fatal for decades.

So successful was Big Tobacco in postponing that day of reckoning that their tactics have been widely imitated ever since. They have also inspired a thriving corner of academia exploring how the trick was achieved. In 1995, Robert Proctor, a historian at Stanford University who has studied the tobacco case closely, coined the word "agnotology." This is the study of how ignorance is deliberately produced; the entire field was started by Proctor's observation of the tobacco industry. The facts about smoking—indisputable facts, from unquestionable sources—did not carry the day. The indisputable facts were disputed. The unquestionable sources were questioned. Facts, it turns out, are important, but facts are not enough to win this kind of argument.

Agnotology has never been more important. "We live in a golden age of ignorance," says Proctor today. "And Trump and Brexit are part of that."

In the UK's EU referendum, the Leave side pushed the false claim that the UK sent £350m a week to the EU. It is hard to think of a previous example in modern western politics of a campaign leading with a transparent untruth, maintaining it when refuted by independent experts, and going on to triumph anyway. That performance was soon to be eclipsed by Donald Trump, who offered wave upon shameless wave of demonstrable falsehood, only to be rewarded with the presidency. The

Oxford Dictionaries declared "post-truth" the word of 2016. Facts just didn't seem to matter any more.

The instinctive reaction from those of us who still care about the truth—journalists, academics and many ordinary citizens—has been to double down on the facts. Fact-checking organisations, such as Full Fact in the UK and PolitiFact in the US, evaluate prominent claims by politicians and journalists. I should confess a personal bias: I have served as a fact checker myself on the BBC radio programme *More or Less*, and I often rely on fact-checking websites. They judge what's true rather than faithfully reporting both sides as a traditional journalist would. Public, transparent fact checking has become such a feature of today's political reporting that it's easy to forget it's barely a decade old.

Mainstream journalists, too, are starting to embrace the idea that lies or errors should be prominently identified. Consider a story on the NPR website about Donald Trump's speech to the CIA in January: "He falsely denied that he had ever criticised the agency, falsely inflated the crowd size at his inauguration on Friday...—" It's a bracing departure from the norms of American journalism, but then President Trump has been a bracing departure from the norms of American politics.

Facebook has also drafted in the fact checkers, announcing a crackdown on the "fake news" stories that had become prominent on the network after the election. Facebook now allows users to report hoaxes. The site will send questionable headlines to independent fact checkers, flag discredited stories as "disputed," and perhaps downgrade them in the algorithm that decides what each user sees when visiting the site.

We need some agreement about facts or the situation is hopeless. And yet: will this sudden focus on facts actually lead to a more informed electorate, better decisions, a renewed respect for the truth? The history of tobacco suggests not. The link between cigarettes and cancer was supported by the world's leading medical scientists and, in 1964, the US surgeon general himself. The story was covered by well-trained journalists committed to the values of objectivity. Yet the tobacco lobbyists ran rings round them.

In the 1950s and 1960s, journalists had an excuse for their stumbles: the tobacco industry's tactics were clever, complex and new. First, the industry appeared to engage, promising high-quality research into the issue. The public were assured that the best people were on the case. The second stage was to complicate the question and sow doubt: lung cancer might have any number of causes, after all. And wasn't lung cancer, not cigarettes, what really mattered? Stage three was to undermine serious research and expertise. Autopsy reports would be dismissed as anecdotal, epidemiological work as merely statistical, and animal studies as irrelevant. Finally came normalisation: the industry would point out that the tobacco-cancer story was stale news. Couldn't journalists find something new and interesting to say?

Such tactics are now well documented—and researchers have carefully examined the psychological tendencies they exploited. So we should be able to spot their re-emergence on the political battlefield.

"It's as if the president's team were using the tobacco industry's playbook," says Jon Christensen, a journalist turned professor at the University of California, Los Angeles, who wrote a notable study in 2008 of the way the tobacco industry tugged on the strings of journalistic tradition.

One infamous internal memo from the Brown & Williamson tobacco company, typed up in the summer of 1969, sets out the thinking very clearly: "Doubt is our product." Why? Because doubt "is the best means of competing with the 'body of fact' that exists in the mind of the general public. It is also the means of establishing a controversy." Big Tobacco's mantra: keep the controversy alive.

Doubt is usually not hard to produce, and facts alone aren't enough to dispel it. We should have learnt this lesson already; now we're going to have to learn it all over again.

Tempting as it is to fight lies with facts, there are three problems with that strategy. The first is that a simple untruth can beat off a complicated set of facts simply by being easier to understand and remember. When doubt prevails, people will often end up believing whatever sticks in the mind. In 1994, psychologists Hollyn Johnson

> **The facts need a champion. Facts rarely stand up for themselves—they need someone to make us care about them, to make us curious.**

and Colleen Seifert conducted an experiment in which people read an account of an explosive warehouse fire. The account mentioned petrol cans and paint but later explained that petrol and paint hadn't been present at the scene after all. The experimental subjects, tested on their comprehension, recalled that paint wasn't actually there. But when asked to explain facts about the fire ("why so much smoke?"), they would mention the paint. Lacking an alternative explanation, they fell back on a claim they had already acknowledged was wrong. Once we've heard an untrue claim, we can't simply unhear it.

This should warn us not to let lie-and-rebuttal take over the news cycle. Several studies have shown that repeating a false claim, even in the context of debunking that claim, can make it stick. The myth-busting seems to work but then our memories fade and we remember only the myth. The myth, after all, was the thing that kept being repeated. In trying to dispel the falsehood, the endless rebuttals simply make the enchantment stronger.

With this in mind, consider the Leave campaign's infamous bus-mounted claim: "We send the EU £350m a week." Simple. Memorable. False. But how to rebut it? A typical effort from the *Guardian* newspaper was headlined, "Why Vote Leave's £350m weekly EU cost claim is wrong," repeating the claim before devoting hundreds of words to gnarly details and the dictionary definition of the word "send." This sort of fact-checking article is invaluable to a fellow journalist who needs the issues set out and hyperlinked. But for an ordinary voter, the likely message would be: "You can't trust politicians but we do seem to send a lot of money to the EU." Doubt suited the Leave campaign just fine.

This is an inbuilt vulnerability of the fact-checking trade. Fact checkers are right to be particular, to cover all the details and to show their working out. But that's why the fact-checking job can only be a part of ensuring that the truth is heard.

Andrew Lilico, a thoughtful proponent of leaving the EU, told me during the campaign that he wished the bus had displayed a more defensible figure, such as £240m. But Lilico now acknowledges that the false claim was the more effective one. "In cynical campaigning terms, the use of the £350m figure was perfect," he says. "It created a trap that Remain campaigners kept insisting on jumping into again and again and again."

Quite so. But not just Remain campaigners—fact-checking journalists too, myself included. The false claim was vastly more powerful than a true one would have been, not because it was bigger, but because everybody kept talking about it.

Proctor, the tobacco industry historian turned agnotologist, warns of a similar effect in the US: "Fact checkers can become Trump's poodle, running around like an errand boy checking someone else's facts. If all your time is [spent] checking someone else's facts, then what are you doing?"

There's a second reason why facts don't seem to have the traction that one might hope. Facts can be boring. The world is full of things to pay attention to, from reality TV to your argumentative children, from a friend's Instagram to a tax bill. Why bother with anything so tedious as facts?

Last year, three researchers—Seth Flaxman, Sharad Goel and Justin Rao—published a study of how people read news online. The study was, on the face of it, an inquiry into the polarisation of news sources. The researchers began with data from 1.2 million internet users but ended up examining only 50,000. Why? Because only 4 per cent of the sample read enough serious news to be worth including in such a study. (The hurdle was 10 articles and two opinion pieces over three months.) Many commentators worry that we're segregating ourselves in ideological bubbles, exposed only to the views of those who think the same way we do. There's something in that concern. But for 96 per cent of these web surfers the bubble that mattered wasn't liberal or conservative, it was: "Don't bother with the news."

In the war of ideas, boredom and distraction are powerful weapons. A recent study of Chinese propaganda examined the tactics of the paid pro-government hacks (known as the "50 cent army," after the amount contributors were alleged to be paid per post) who put comments on social media. The researchers, Gary King, Jennifer Pan and Margaret Roberts, conclude: "Almost none of the Chinese government's 50c party posts engage in debate or argument of any kind...they seem to avoid controversial issues entirely...the strategic objective of the regime is to distract and redirect public attention."

Trump, a reality TV star, knows the value of an entertaining distraction: simply pick a fight with Megyn Kelly, the *New York Times* or even Arnold Schwarzenegger. Isn't that more eye-catching than a discussion of healthcare reform?

The tobacco industry also understood this point, although it took a more highbrow approach to generating distractions. "Do you know about Stanley Prusiner?" asks Proctor.

Prusiner is a neurologist. In 1972, he was a young researcher who'd just encountered a patient suffering from Creutzfeldt-Jakob disease. It was a dreadful degenerative condition then thought to be caused by a slow-acting virus. After many years of study, Prusiner concluded that the disease was caused instead, unprecedentedly, by a kind of rogue protein. The idea seemed absurd to most experts at the time, and Prusiner's career began to founder. Promotions and research grants dried up. But Prusiner received a source of private-sector funding that enabled him to continue his work. He was eventually vindicated in the most spectacular way possible: with a Nobel Prize in Medicine in 1997. In his autobiographical essay on the Nobel Prize website, Prusiner thanked his private-sector benefactors for their "crucial" support: RJ Reynolds, maker of Camel cigarettes.

The tobacco industry was a generous source of research funds, and Prusiner wasn't the only scientist to receive both tobacco funding and a Nobel Prize. Proctor reckons at least 10 Nobel laureates are in that position. To be clear, this wasn't an attempt at bribery. In Proctor's view, it was far more subtle. "The tobacco industry was the leading funder of research into genetics, viruses, immunology, air pollution," says Proctor. Almost anything, in short, except tobacco. "It was a massive 'distraction research' project." The funding helped position Big Tobacco as a public-spirited industry but Proctor considers its main purpose was to produce interesting new speculative science. Creutzfeldt-Jakob disease may be rare, but it was exciting news. Smoking-related diseases such as lung cancer and heart disease aren't news at all.

The endgame of these distractions is that matters of vital importance become too boring to bother reporting. Proctor describes it as "the opposite of terrorism: trivialism". Terrorism provokes a huge media reaction; smoking does not. Yet, according to the US Centers for Disease Control, smoking kills 480,000 Americans a year. This is more than 50 deaths an hour. Terrorists have rarely managed to kill that many Americans in an entire year. But the terrorists succeed in grabbing the headlines; the trivialists succeed in avoiding them.

Tobacco industry lobbyists became well-practised at persuading the media to withhold or downplay stories about the dangers of cigarettes. "That record is scratched," they'd say. Hadn't we heard such things before?

Experienced tobacco watchers now worry that Trump may achieve the same effect. In the end, will people simply start to yawn at the spectacle? Jon Christensen, at UCLA, says: "I think it's the most frightening prospect."

On the other hand, says Christensen, there is one saving grace. It is almost impossible for the US president not to be news. The tobacco lobby, like the Chinese government, proved highly adept at pointing the spotlight elsewhere. There are reasons to believe that will be difficult for Trump.

There's a final problem with trying to persuade people by giving them facts: the truth can feel threatening, and threatening people tends to backfire. "People respond in the opposite direction," says Jason Reifler, a political scientist at Exeter University. This "backfire effect" is now the focus of several researchers, including Reifler and his colleague Brendan Nyhan of Dartmouth.

In one study, conducted in 2011, Nyhan, Reifler and others ran a randomised trial in which parents with young children were either shown or not shown scientific information debunking an imaginary but widely feared link between vaccines and autism. At first glance, the facts were persuasive: parents who saw the myth-busting science were less likely to believe that the vaccine could cause autism. But parents who were already wary of vaccines were actually less likely to say they'd vaccinate their children after being exposed to the facts—despite apparently believing those facts.

What's going on? "People accept the corrective information but then resist in other ways," says Reifler. A person who feels anxious about vaccination will subconsciously push back by summoning to mind all the other reasons why they feel vaccination is a bad idea. The fear of autism might recede, but all the other fears are stronger than before.

It's easy to see how this might play out in a political campaign. Say you're worried that the UK will soon be swamped by Turkish immigrants because a Brexit campaigner has told you (falsely) that Turkey will soon join the EU. A fact checker can explain that no Turkish entry is likely in the foreseeable future. Reifler's research suggests that you'll accept the narrow fact that Turkey is not about to join the EU. But you'll also summon to mind all sorts of other anxieties: immigration, loss of control, the proximity of Turkey to Syria's war and to Isis, terrorism and so on. The original lie has been disproved, yet its seductive magic lingers.

The problem here is that while we like to think of ourselves as rational beings, our rationality didn't just evolve to solve practical problems, such as building an elephant trap, but to navigate social situations. We need to keep others on our side. Practical reasoning is often less about figuring out what's true, and more about staying in the right tribe.

An early indicator of how tribal our logic can be was a study conducted in 1954 by Albert Hastorf, a psychologist at Dartmouth, and Hadley Cantril, his counterpart at Princeton. Hastorf and Cantril screened footage of a game of American football between the two college teams. It had been a rough game. One quarterback had suffered a broken leg. Hastorf and Cantril asked their students to tot up the fouls and assess their severity. The Dartmouth students tended to overlook Dartmouth fouls but were quick to pick up on the sins of the Princeton players. The Princeton students had the opposite inclination. They concluded that, despite being shown the same footage, the Dartmouth and Princeton students didn't really see the same events. Each student had his own perception, closely shaped by his tribal loyalties. The title of the research paper was "They Saw a Game."

A more recent study revisited the same idea in the context of political tribes. The researchers showed students footage of a demonstration and spun a yarn about what it was about. Some students were told it was a protest by gay-rights protesters outside an army recruitment office against the military's (then) policy of "don't ask, don't tell." Others were told that it was an anti-abortion protest in front of an abortion clinic.

Despite looking at exactly the same footage, the experimental subjects had sharply different views of what was happening—views that were shaped by their political loyalties. Liberal students were relaxed about the behaviour of people they thought were gay-rights protesters but worried about what the pro-life protesters were doing; conservative students took the opposite view. As with "They Saw a Game," this disagreement was not about the general principles but about specifics: did the protesters scream at bystanders? Did they block access to the building? We see what we want to see—and we reject the facts that threaten our sense of who we are.

When we reach the conclusion that we want to reach, we're engaging in "motivated reasoning". Motivated reasoning was a powerful ally of the tobacco industry. If you're addicted to a product, and many scientists tell you it's deadly, but the tobacco lobby tells you that more research is needed, what would you like to believe? Christensen's study of the tobacco public relations campaign revealed that the industry often got a sympathetic hearing in the press because many journalists were smokers. These journalists desperately wanted to believe their habit was benign, making them ideal messengers for the industry.

Even in a debate polluted by motivated reasoning, one might expect that facts will help. Not necessarily: when we hear facts that challenge us, we selectively amplify what suits us, ignore what does not, and reinterpret whatever we can. More facts mean more grist to the motivated reasoning mill. The French dramatist Molière once wrote: "A learned fool is more foolish than an ignorant one." Modern social science agrees.

On a politically charged issue such as climate change, it feels as though providing accurate information about the science should bring people together. The opposite is true, says Dan Kahan, a law and psychology professor at Yale and one of the researchers on the study into perceptions of a political protest. Kahan writes: "Groups with opposing values often become more polarised, not less, when exposed to scientifically sound information."

When people are seeking the truth, facts help. But when people are selectively reasoning about their political identity, the facts can backfire.

All this adds up to a depressing picture for those of us who aren't ready to live in a post-truth world. Facts, it seems, are toothless. Trying to refute a bold, memorable lie with a fiddly set of facts can often serve to reinforce the myth. Important truths are often stale and dull, and it is easy to manufacture new, more engaging claims. And giving people more facts can backfire, as those facts provoke a defensive reaction in someone who badly wants to stick to their existing world view. "This is dark stuff," says Reifler. "We're in a pretty scary and dark time." Is there an answer? Perhaps there is.

We know that scientific literacy can actually widen the gap between different political tribes on issues such as climate change—that is, well-informed liberals and well-informed conservatives are further apart in their views than liberals and conservatives who know little about the science. But a new research paper from Dan Kahan, Asheley Landrum, Katie Carpenter, Laura Helft and Kathleen Hall Jamieson explores the role not of scientific literacy but of scientific curiosity.

The researchers measured scientific curiosity by asking their experimental subjects a variety of questions about their hobbies and interests. The subjects were offered a choice of websites to read for a comprehension test. Some went for ESPN, some for Yahoo Finance, but those who chose Science were demonstrating scientific curiosity. Scientifically curious people were also happier to watch science documentaries than celebrity gossip TV shows. As one might expect, there's a correlation between scientific knowledge and scientific curiosity, but the two measures are distinct.

What Kahan and his colleagues found, to their surprise, was that while politically motivated reasoning trumps scientific knowledge, "politically motivated reasoning...appears to be negated by science curiosity." Scientifically literate people, remember, were more likely to be polarised in their answers to politically charged scientific questions. But scientifically curious people were not. Curiosity brought people together in a way that mere facts did not. The researchers muse that curious people have an extra reason to seek out the facts: "To experience the pleasure of contemplating surprising insights into how the world works."

So how can we encourage curiosity? It's hard to make banking reform or the reversibility of Article 50 more engaging than football, *Game of Thrones* or baking cakes. But it does seem to be what's called for. "We need to bring people into the story, into the human narratives of science, to show people how science works," says Christensen.

We journalists and policy wonks can't force anyone to pay attention to the facts. We have to find a way to make people want to seek them out. Curiosity is the seed from which sensible democratic decisions can grow. It seems to be one of the only cures for politically motivated reasoning but it's also, into the bargain, the cure for a society where most people just don't pay attention to the news because they find it boring or confusing.

What we need is a Carl Sagan or David Attenborough of social science—somebody who can create a sense of wonder and fascination not just at the structure of the solar system or struggles of life in a tropical rainforest, but at the workings of our own civilisation: health, migration, finance, education and diplomacy.

One candidate would have been Swedish doctor and statistician Hans Rosling, who died in February. He reached an astonishingly wide audience with what were, at their heart, simply presentations of official data from the likes of the World Bank.

He characterised his task as telling people the facts— "to describe the world." But the facts need a champion. Facts rarely stand up for themselves—they need someone to make us care about them, to make us curious. That's what Rosling did. And faced with the apocalyptic possibility of a world where the facts don't matter, that is the example we must follow.

Print Citations

CMS: Harford, Tim. "The Problem with Facts." In *The Reference Shelf: Alternative Facts, Post-Truth, and the Information War*, edited by Betsy Maury, 152-160. Ipswich, MA: H.W. Wilson, 2018.

MLA: Harford, Tim. "The Problem with Facts." *The Reference Shelf: Alternative Facts, Post-Truth, and the Information War*. Ed. Betsy Maury. Ipswich: H.W. Wilson, 2018. 152-160. Print.

APA: Harford, T. (2018). The problem with facts. In Betsy Maury (Ed.), *The reference shelf: Alternative facts, post-truth, and the information war* (pp. 152-160). Ipswich, MA: H.W. Wilson. (Original work published 2017)

We Already Have a Solution to Fake News: It's Called the First Amendment

By Jarrett Stepman

Heritage.org, October 9, 2017

Fake news isn't suddenly ruining America, but putting government in charge of deciding what news is fake will.

In the wake of President Donald Trump's victory in the 2016 election, numerous media outlets ran stories claiming that many websites had published false stories that helped Trump beat Hillary Clinton.

Since then Left-leaning opinion writers have called for a solution to this alleged epidemic. *The New York Times* reported in January that Silicon Valley giants Facebook and Google will team up with legacy media outlets to fact-check stories and curtail the proliferation of "fake news."

However, intentionally misleading news has been around since before the invention of the printing press. In fact, our Founding Fathers grappled with this very issue when they created our system of government. They saw that while it was tempting to censor fake stories, ultimately the truth was more likely to be abused by an all-powerful government arbiter than the filter of unimpeded popular debate. Attempts to weed out factually incorrect news reports can quickly morph into fact-checking and manipulating differences in opinion.

Fortunately, there have been few serious calls in the United States for official censoring of political news or media, in contrast to most of the world, including Europe. Freedom of thought, freedom of the press, and even the freedom to be wrong make America great and exceptional. In addition to preserving liberty, our free-wheeling tradition gives the United States an edge in adapting to the increasingly decentralized media landscape that is a natural product of the Internet Age. Most importantly, it produces a more critically informed populace in the long term.

The Founders and the Free Press

The Founding Fathers were well aware of the power of the press, for good or ill. After all, many of them, such as Samuel Adams, Benjamin Franklin, and Thomas Paine, were newspapermen and pamphleteers. The revolutionary ideas they disseminated throughout the colonies found eager readers, putting them high on King George III's enemies list.

Three years after the Constitution was ratified, the American people amended it by adding the Bill of Rights, which included the First Amendment and its protections of the media. However, the Founders understood that a free press was not an entirely unqualified blessing; some had reservations.

Elbridge Gerry, who was present at the Constitutional Convention, lamented how con artists in his home state were manipulating the people. "The people do not [lack] virtue, but are the dupes of pretended patriots," Gerry said at the convention. "In Massachusetts it had been fully confirmed by experience, that they are daily misled into the most baneful measures and opinions, by the false reports circulated by designing men, and which no one on the spot can refute."

Benjamin Franklin also warned about the power of the press, which the public must put so much trust in. In a short essay, Franklin explained how the press acted as the "court" of public opinion and wielded enormous unofficial power.

For an institution with so much influence, Franklin noted that the bar for entry into journalism is remarkably low, with no requirement regarding "Ability, Integrity, Knowledge." He said the liberty of the press can easily turn into the "liberty of affronting, calumniating, and defaming one another."

The Founders wrote constitutional protections for the press with open eyes, as their written remarks record. Yet, the evils that come through the occasional problems of a free press are heavily outweighed by its benefits. Lies may proliferate, but the truth has a real chance to rise to the top.

Thomas Jefferson said that the most effectual way for a people to be governed by "reason and truth" is to give freedom to the press. There was simply no other way. He wrote in a letter to Gerry:

> I am [...] for freedom of the press, and against all violations of the Constitution to silence by force and not by reason the complaints or criticisms, just or unjust, of our citizens against the conduct of their agents.

Liars and scandal mongers may occasionally have success in a system without censorship, but truth was ultimately more likely to be found when passed through the people as a whole. Jefferson wrote:

> It is so difficult to draw a clear line of separation between the abuse and the wholesome use of the press, that as yet we have found it better to trust the public judgment, rather than the magistrate, with the discrimination between truth and falsehood. And hitherto the public judgment has performed that office with wonderful correctness.

Despite full knowledge of the media's often unscrupulous power over public opinion, the Founders chose to grant broad protections to a decentralized press, opting to place their faith in newspapers checking one another with more efficacy and less risk of bias than heavy-handed government crackdowns.

When the Federalist Party passed the infamous Alien and Sedition Acts under President John Adams to clamp down on "false, scandalous and malicious writing" against the government in the midst of the "Quasi War" with France, there was an immense backlash. A few journalists were arrested, but the governing party was crushed in future elections and ceased to exist shortly thereafter. In the United States, press freedom would become an almost unquestioned element of American culture and policy.

Things worked out differently across the Atlantic. In France, a popular uprising, stoked by a rabid press, led to mob violence, tyranny, and oppressive censorship. Revolutionary scribblers initially brought an end to the Old Regime and the royal restrictions on speech, but freedom of the press didn't last. After the monarchy was crushed, the revolutionaries censored the press even more ruthlessly than had the Bourbon kings. The radicals argued that press freedom was leading people astray and impeding their revolution.

Maximilien Robespierre, leader of the Jacobin party, called journalists "the most dangerous enemies of liberty." Robespierre and his allies in the French government created a state-sponsored newspaper to counter what they saw as the media's lies. Then, seeing that even that was not enough to prevent alternative opinions from growing, began to arrest and execute those who opposed the policies of the government. Robespierre's "Reign of Terror" gripped France for more than a year, during which 16,594 official death sentences were handed out.

Calls for liberty ended with censorship and ultimately the guillotine for unbelievers. Clearly there was a difference between the American and French regimes and cultures, both nominally standing for liberty, but arriving at radically different ends.

A Frenchman who was a keen observer of both systems explained why freedom of the press worked out so differently in these sister republics.

Tocqueville, the United States, and France

Alexis de Tocqueville caught on to why liberty of the press worked so much better in the United States than in his home country. One system was almost entirely free from suggestions of government censorship and the other perpetually in danger of falling prey to the "instincts of the pettiest despots."

Americans understood, wrote Tocqueville in his book *Democracy in America*, that creating a government body with the power to assess the truth in media would be far more dangerous than any system of press freedom. They instinctively knew that:

> Whoever should be able to create and maintain a tribunal of this kind would waste his time in prosecuting the liberty of the press; for he would be the absolute master of the whole community and would be as free to rid himself of the authors as of their writings.

In other words, the creation of such an official "court" to oversee media truth would logically end in absolute tyranny. Tocqueville concluded that "in order to enjoy the inestimable benefits that the liberty of the press ensures, it is necessary to submit to the inevitable evils that it creates."

Fortunately, America had a diverse and highly decentralized press from the beginning. Not so in France, which had a highly centralized press both in terms of geography and number of media organizations. Therefore, Tocqueville wrote, in a centralized media environment such as France, "[t]he influence upon a skeptical nation of a public press thus constituted must be almost unbounded. It is an enemy with whom a government may sign an occasional truce, but which it is difficult to resist for any length of time."

France never really changed. It continued a cycle of crackdowns on the free press as new regimes took power. Instead of decentralizing the press of the monarchical regime, each successive set of revolutionaries seized the central apparatus for their own purposes. In 1852, when the Second Empire under Napoleon III took power, the government said that censorship would be implemented for public safety.

> **The Founders saw that while it was tempting to censor fake stories, ultimately the truth was more likely to be abused by an all-powerful government arbiter than the filter of unimpeded popular debate.**

A petition message to the legislative body concluded: "As long as there exists in France parties hostile to the Empire, liberty of the press is out of the question, and the country at large has no wish for it."

Though President Trump has caused concern by calling members of the press "enemies of the people," his threats against the press come through mockery and rebuke rather than official sanctions. Presidential media hating has been around since George Washington was in office, but there have been few serious proposals to actually crack down on reporting.

By contrast, the press is treated quite differently in France, where citizens are placed on a 44-hour legal media blackout on the eve of elections. As *USA Today* reported, in the days leading up to the French presidential election, the media were warned not to report on data leaks from candidate Emmanuel Macron's campaign. The French election commission said that the leaks likely contained some fraudulent data, i.e. "fake news," and any reporting on it or even passing it along on social media could lead to criminal charges.

Jim Swift of *The Weekly Standard* pointed out the obvious: "This is censorship, plain and simple. In the Internet Age, reporters and citizens around the globe can share information—be it about the Macron hack or not—on Twitter, Facebook, or on their websites. The French press and citizenry? Repressed."

But *The New York Times* praised the reporting ban, and emphasized the benefits of the centralized French system over the more freewheeling ones in Britain and the United States. In a recent article, The *Times* noted:

> The contrast may have been amplified further by the absence of a French equivalent to the thriving tabloid culture in Britain or the robust right-wing broadcast media in the United States, where the Clinton hacking attack generated enormous negative coverage.

"We don't have a Fox News in France," said Johan Hufnagel, managing editor of the Left-wing daily *Libération*, according to *The New York Times*. "There's no broadcaster with a wide audience and personalities who build this up and try to use it for their own agendas."

A similar scandal occurred in the United States when Wikileaks published thousands of emails from the Democratic National Committee that cast the Clinton campaign in a negative light. Yet, there was no censorship of the information; the American people would not have stood for it.

Who has the better system? Since the adoption of the U.S. Constitution, France has gone through five republics, two empires, and four monarchies. Despite the bumptious nature of American politics and media, it would be foolish to bet on France's fifth republic outlasting America's first.

Americans have been lucky to have a decentralized media through most of their history and a culture that strongly embraces the idea of a truly free press. Those arrangements have had a long-lasting impact on American institutions and have made the country resistant to authoritarian impulses. However, in the mid-20th century, the American press became more centralized and the country opened its media sector to many of the same problems that had plagued European media.

Some glamorize the era in which a few television companies and big newspapers became media gatekeepers, similar to the model that currently exists in France. This nostalgia for "more responsible" journalism ignores the fact that some of the most egregious fake news blunders were perpetrated by an unchecked centralized press. Perhaps the worst offense of all came from *The New York Times*.

The New York Times and the Fraud of the Century

Today, a 30-foot-long bronze wall stands in Northwest Washington, D.C., and on this wall is the simple image of a wheat field. It is a monument to the victims of The Holodomor, a monstrous genocide committed by one of the most ruthless and authoritarian regimes in human history.

In 1932, Soviet dictator Joseph Stalin, frustrated that he could not crush Ukrainian nationalism, ordered that grain quotas for Ukrainian fields be raised so high that the peasants working the fields would not be left with enough food to feed themselves. NKVD troops collected the grain and watched over the populace to prevent them from leaving to find nourishment elsewhere.

As a result of these policies, as many as 7 million Ukrainians died of starvation in 1932 and 1933.

But while Stalin was conducting an atrocity with few equals in human history, *The New York Times* was reporting on the regime's triumphs of modernization.

Walter Duranty, the *Times* Moscow bureau chief, won the 1932 Pulitzer Prize for Correspondence for his 1931 series of articles on the Soviet Union. Pulitzer in hand, he proceeded to perpetrate perhaps the worst incident of fake news in American media history at a time when Americans relied on the *Times* and a handful of other large media outlets to bring them news from around the world.

Duranty's motivation for covering up the crimes taking place in Ukraine has never been fully ascertained. However, it undoubtedly gave the Bolshevik sympathizer better access to Stalin's regime, which routinely fed him propaganda.

While privately admitting that many Ukrainians had starved to death, Duranty sent numerous reports back to the United States praising the good work of the Soviet government. He reported that there had been some deaths from "diseases due to malnutrition," but called the suggestion that a widespread famine was taking place "malignant propaganda."

These reports were highly influential in the United States and had enormous impact on U.S.-Soviet relations. Historian Robert Conquest wrote in his book, *The Harvest of Sorrow: Soviet Collectivization and the Terror-Famine*, that due to the perceived credibility of *The New York Times*, the American people accepted the fraudulent accounts as true.

Sally J. Taylor wrote in her book *Stalin's Apologist* that Duranty's reports helped convince President Franklin D. Roosevelt to extend official diplomatic recognition to the Soviet government in November of 1933. She wrote: "[A]lmost single-handedly did Duranty aid and abet one of the world's most prolific mass murderers, knowing all the while what was going on but refraining from saying precisely what he knew to be true."

Though Duranty's reporting was a lie, *The New York Times* never questioned its authenticity and dismissed charges that their reporter was cooking up false reports. Famed British journalist Malcolm Muggeridge wrote of this willful self-deception in his autobiography:

> If the *New York Times* went on all those years giving great prominence to Duranty's messages, building him and them up when they were so evidently nonsensically untrue [...] this was not, we may be sure, because the Times was deceived. Rather it wanted to be so deceived, and Duranty provided the requisite deception material.

In the more centralized national media landscape of the mid-20th century, a fraudulent story like that published in the *Times* was both more likely to be believed and less likely to be debunked.

The Truth Cannot Be Centrally Planned

But America's evolving media landscape is again moving toward decentralization. And, fortunately, the First Amendment is a mighty weapon against the suffocating and stultifying suppression of speech that frequently occurs in other nations.

The system the Founders created and intended for the United States was one that they hoped would lead our civilization to the truth. We have acquiesced to the fact that there will always be a great deal that the smartest and the wisest simply don't know. No earthly, impartial arbiter has the capacity, or *should* have the capacity, to determine absolute fact for us—especially in the realm of politics, philosophy, and man's relation to man.

For all the uncertainty and chaos that an unfettered media seem to engender, Americans have been best at ultimately veering closer to the truth than any other people. The First Amendment is one of the greatest of many gifts the Founding generation bequeathed us and has been a truly defining feature of American exceptionalism with few comparisons around the globe.

Through all the angst over fake news, fraudulent journalists, and media hyperbole, the American republic will survive. In the end, fake news peddlers will only damage their own reputations and bring doubt on their reporting. Fortunately, our freedom isn't dependent on the musings of the White House press corps. It hinges on the Constitution and the liberty it was created to protect.

Print Citations

CMS: Stepman, Jarrett. "We Already Have a Solution to Fake News: It's Called the First Amendment." In *The Reference Shelf: Alternative Facts, Post-Truth, and the Information War*, edited by Betsy Maury, 161-167. Ipswich, MA: H.W. Wilson, 2018.

MLA: Stepman, Jarrett. "We Already Have a Solution to Fake News: It's Called the First Amendment." *The Reference Shelf: Alternative Facts, Post-Truth, and the Information War*. Ed. Betsy Maury. Ipswich: H.W. Wilson, 2018. 161-167. Print.

APA: Stepman, J. (2018). We already have a solution to fake news: It's called the first amendment. In Betsy Maury (Ed.), *The reference shelf: Alternative facts, post-truth, and the information war* (pp. 161-167). Ipswich, MA: H.W. Wilson. (Original work published 2017)

Bibliography

"2016 Presidential Campaign Hacking Fast Facts." *CNN*. CNN News. Feb 21, 2018. Web. 26 Feb 2018.

Anand, Bharat N. "The U.S. Media's Problems Are Much Bigger Than Fake News and Filter Bubbles." *Harvard Business Review*. Jan 5, 2017. Web. 26 Feb 2018.

Bartlett, Bruce. "How Fox News Changed American Media and Political Dynamics." *SSRN*. Elsevier. June 4, 2015. Web. 23 Feb 2018.

Beaujon, Andrew. "Survey: NPR's Listeners Best-Informed, Fox Viewers Worst-Informed." *Poynter*. The Poynter Institute. May 23, 2012. Web. 23 Feb 2018.

Beckwith, Ryan Teague. "President Trump Made 1,950 Untrue Claims in 2017: That's Making His Job Harder." *Time*. Time Inc. Jan 2, 2018. Web. 26 Feb 2018.

Breiner, Andrew. "Pizzagate, Explained: Everything You Want to Know about the Comet Ping Pong Pizzeria Conspiracy Theory but Are Too Afraid to Search for on Reddit." *Salon*. Salon Media Group, Inc. Dec 10, 2016. Web. 26 Feb 2018.

Buckley, Thea. "Why Do Some People Believe in Conspiracy Theories?" *Scientific American*. MIND. 2018. Web. 24 Feb 2018.

Bustamante, Thomas and Christian Dahlman, eds. *Argument Types and Fallacies in Legal Argumentation*. New York: Springer. 2015. Print.

Crist, Carolyn. "On the Mind: Your Brain on Social Media." *Paste*. Paste Media Group. Feb 28, 2017. Web. 24 Feb. 2018.

Crollius, Hughes Roesst and Jean Weissenbach. "Fish Genomics and Biology." *Genome Research*. No. 15. (2005): 1675–82. Print.

"Donald Trump's File." *Politifact*. Politifact. 2018. Web. 25 Feb 2018.

Douthat, Ross. "The Trolling of the American Mind." *The New York Times*. The New York Times, Co. Feb 21, 2018. Web. 23 Feb 2018.

Dunn, Rob. "What Are You So Scared Of? Saber-Toothed Cats, Snakes, and Carnivorous Kangaroos." *Slate*. Slate Group. Oct 15, 2012. Web. 25 Feb 2018.

"Ecclesiastes 1:9." *Biblehub*. Bible Hub. 2017. Web.

Edwards-Levy, Ariel. "Most Americans Think Legal Immigrants Are Good For The Country." *Huffington Post*. Aug 10, 2017. Web. 26 Feb 2018.

"Ethics of Algorithms." *CIHR*. Centre For Internet and Human Rights. Frankfurt University. Web. 26 Feb 2018.

Fan, Rui, Xu, Ke, and Jichang Zhao. "High Contagion and Weaker Ties Mean Anger Spreads Faster Than Joy in Social Media." *arXiv*. Web. 25 Feb 2018.

Farley, "Trump: Jobs Returning 'Because of Me'." *Factcheck*. Annenberg Public Policy Center. The Wire. Jan 21, 2017. Web. 23 Feb 2018.

Friedman, Marcelle. "Why It Matters That House Hunters Is Fake." *Slate*. Slate Group. Jun 14, 2012. Web.

Ghonim and Rashbass, "It's Time to End the Secrecy and Opacity of Social Media."

The Washington Post. The Washington Post Co. Oct 31, 2017. Web. 26 Feb 2018.

Gilbert, Daniel T. "How Mental Systems Believe." *American Psychologist*. Vol. 46, No. 2. Feb 1991. Web. 25 Feb 2018.

Grieco, Elizabeth and Jeffrey Gottfried. "In Trump's First 100 Days, News Stories Citing His Tweets Were More Likely to Be Negative." *Pew Research*. Pew Research Center. Oct 18, 2017. Web. 26 Feb 2018.

Guess, Andrew, Nyhan, Brenadan, and Jason Reifler. "Selective Exposure to Misinformation: Evidence from the Consumption of Fake News during the 2016 Presidential Campaign." *Dartmouth University*. Web. 24 Feb 2018.

Guess, Andrew, Nyhan, Brendan, and Jason Reifler. "Selective Exposure to Misinformation: Evidence from the Consumption of Fake News during the 2016 Presidential Campaign." *Dartmouth University*. Web. 24 Feb 2018.

"Have We a Dusky Peril?" *SAADA*. South Asian American Digital Archive. 2017. Web.

"Hillary Clinton's File." *Politifact*. Politifact. 2018. Web. 25 Feb 2018.

Imhoff, Roland and Pia Karoline Lamberty. "Too Special to Be Duped: Need for Uniqueness Motivates Conspiracy Beliefs." *European Journal of Social Psychology*. Vol. 47, No. 6 (Oct 2017): 724–34. Web. 24 Feb 2018.

Johnson, Jenna and Abigail Hauslohner. "'I Think Islam Hates Us': A Timeline of Trump's Comments about Islam and Muslims." *The Washington Post*. The Washington Post Co. May 20, 2017. Web. 26 Feb 2018.

Kessler, Glenn, Kelly, Meg, and Nicole Lewis. "President Trump Has Made 1,950 False or Misleading Claims over 347 Days." *The Washington Post*. The Washington Post Co. Jan 2, 2018. Web. 26 Feb 2018.

Kessler, Glenn. "Fact-Checking President Trump's 'Fake News Awards'." *The Washington Post*. The Washington Post Co. Jan 17, 2018. Web. 25 Feb 2018.

Kessler, Glenn. "In a 30-Minute Interview, President Trump Made 24 False or Misleading Claims." *The Washington Post*. The Washington Post Co. Dec 29, 2017. Web. 26 Feb 2018.

Kirby, Emma Jane. "The City Getting Rich from Fake News." *BBC News*. BBC. Dec 5, 2016. Web.

Maheshwari, Sapna. "10 Times Trump Spread Fake News." *The New York Times*. The New York Times Co. Jan 18, 2017. Web. 23 Feb 2018.

Malloy, Tim and Pat Smith Rubenstein, "Trump Is Intelligent, but Not Fit or Level Headed, U.S. Voters Tell Quinnipiac University National Poll; First Year Was 'Disaster,' 'Chaotic,' 'Successful'." *Quinnipiac University Poll*. Jan 10, 2018. Web. 25 Feb 2018.

Mariani, Mike. "Nativism, Violence, and the Origins of the Paranoid Style." *Slate*. Slate Group. Mar 22, 2017. Web.

Mayyasi, Alex. "The Hypocrisy of 'Judge Judy'." *Priceonomics*. Jan 14, 2016. Web. 25 Feb 2018.

Mitchell, Amy, Simmons, Katie, Matsa, Katerina Eva, and Laura Silver. "Publics Globally Want Unbiased News Coverage, but are Divided on Whether Their

News Media Delivers." *Pew Research*. Pew Research Center. Jan 11 2018. Web. 26 Feb 2018.

Mooney, Chris. "What Is Motivated Reasoning? How Does It Work? Dan Kahan Answers." *Discover Magazine*. The Intersection. May 5, 2011. Web. 23 Feb 2018.

Narayanan, Vidya, et al. "Polarization, Partisanship and Junk News Consumption over Social Media in the US." *Comprop Data Memo*. Oxford University. February 6, 2018. Web. 23 Feb 2018.

Nordquist, Richard. "Logical Fallacy Defined with Examples." *Thought Co*. Web. 25 Feb 2018.

Panko, Ben. "How Fake News Breaks Your Brain." *Smithsonian*. Smithsonian Institution. Jun 30, 2017. Web. 24 Feb 2018.

Patterson, Thomas E. "News Coverage of the 2016 General Election: How the Press Failed the Voters." *Shorenstein Center*. Harvard Kennedy School. Dec 7, 2016. Web. 26 Feb 2018.

Rainie, Lee and Janna Anderson. "The Future of Privacy." *Pew Research*. Pew Research Center Internet & Technology. Dec 18 2014. Web. 26 Feb 2018.

Rainie, Lee. "The State of Privacy in Post-Snowden America." *Pew Research*. Facttank. Sep 21, 2016. Web. 26 Feb 2018.

Sandomir, Richard. "Albert Freedman, Producer of Rigged 1950s Quiz Show, Dies at 95." *The New York Times*. The New York Times, Co. Apr 22, 2017. Web.

Shreve, Kristyn R., Mehrkam, Lindsay R., and Monique A.R. Udell, "Social Interaction, Food, Scent or Toys? A Formal Assessment of Domestic Pet and Shelter Cat (*Felis silvestris catus*) Preferences." *Behavioral Processes*. Vol. 141, Part 3 (August 2017),: 322–28. Print.

Shuster, Simon and Sandra Ifraimova. "A Former Russian Troll Explains How to Spread Fake News." *Time*. Time, Inc. Feb 21, 2018. Web. 23 Feb 2018.

Soll, Jacob. "The Long and Brutal History of Fake News." *Politico*. Politico Magazine. Dec 18, 2016. Web.

Standage, Tom. "The True History of Fake News." *The Economist*. Economist 1843. June/July 2017. Web.

Stepman, Jarrett. "The History of Fake News in the United States." *The Daily Signal*. The Heritage Foundation. Jan 1, 2018. Web. 26 Feb 2018.

Subramanian, Samanth. "Inside the Macedonian Fake-News Complex." *Wired*. Condé Nast. Feb 15, 2017. Web. 23 Feb 2018.

Sullivan, Meg. "Media Bias Is Real, Finds UCLA Political Scientist." *UCLA*. UCLA Newsroom. Dec 14, 2005. Web. 25 Feb 2018.

Thompson, Derek. "Report: Journalists Are Miserable, Liberal, Over-Educated, Under-Paid, Middle-Aged Men." *The Atlantic*. Atlantic Monthly Group. May 8, 2014. Web. 25 Feb 2018.

Umberti, David. "The Real History of Fake News." *CJR*. Columbia Journalism Review. Dec 15, 2016. Web. 26 Feb 2018.

Walton, Alice G. "6 Ways Social Media Affects Our Mental Health." *Forbes*. Forbes, Inc. Jun 30, 2017. Web. 26 Feb 2018.

Wines, Michael. "All This Talk of Voter Fraud? Across U.S., Officials Found Next to None." *The New York Times*. The New York Times, Co. Dec 18, 2016. Web. 23 Feb 2018.

Websites

Society of Professional Journalists (SPJ)

www.spj.org

The Society of Professional Journalists is a professional organization and standards group for professional journalists in the United States. Created in 1909, the society developed from the Sigma Delta Chi foundation. SPJ provides professional resources for journalists and also formulates the SPJ Code of Ethics that helps guide and govern the ethical policies put in place by many of the nation's media organizations.

Center for Journalism Ethics

www.ethics.journalism.wisc.edu

The Center for Journalism Ethics from the University of Wisconsin-Madison school of journalism and mass communication is one of the nation's leading research and academic institutions supporting studies of ethics in journalism. The department's webpage provides a variety of articles and information about journalism and ethics and research from the department has been part of shaping national standards for the industry.

Center for Media Literacy

www.medialit.org

The Center for Media literacy is an organization that collects and disseminates information about media literacy and supports educational programs aimed at teaching consumers how to become active participants in the modern media environment. The organization provides a media tool kit and a variety of online articles designed to introduce media literacy topics to a variety of consumers of different age and educational groups.

National Association for Media Literacy Education

www.namle.gov

The National Association for Media Literacy Education is a non-profit, non-partisan coalition of media experts and educators cooperating to incorporate media literacy into educational programs. The organization publishes the *Journal of Media Literacy Education*, supporting research in the field and is a primary sponsor of the national "Media Literacy Week" program held in November.

Politifact

www.politifact.com

Politifact is a fact-checking institute owned by the *Poynter Institute for Media Studies,* which publishes articles examining rumors, statements made by politicians, and interest groups. Though both liberal and conservative critics have alleged bias in reporting from the organization, the articles published through the site link to original source material and thus enable independent fact checking beyond or in addition to what is provided in official content from the organization. A sister website *punditfact.com,* fact-checks statements made by political pundits.

FactCheck

www.factcheck.org

The website *FactCheck.org,* owned and operated by the Annenberg Public Policy Center is a non-partisan website that fact-checks claims made by politicians and public figures. The website has received multiple awards for contributing to information accuracy in the public debate and is regularly used by journalists and other authors investigating complex issues.

Poynter

www.poynter.org

The Poynter Institute for Media Studies is a Florida-based, non-profit media school owned by the *Tampa Bay Times* and operating since 1975. The institute offers training to children and student journalists and provides information on media legitimacy, fact-checking, and media literacy for general readers. The institute also funds and helps to distribute research in the field.

American Press Institute (API)

www.americanpressinstitute.org

Founded in 1946, the American Press Institute is a non-profit group supporting media studies, media literacy education program, and a lobbying organization focused on issues involving the press and first amendment protections. The API provides visitors with articles on journalism and media topics and also funds and published academic studies on the industry.

Index